Early Praise for *Machine Learning in Elixir*

There is no better person to teach Machine Learning in Elixir than the person who started it all: Sean Moriarity. Regardless, if you are new to Elixir or new to Machine Learning, this book has you covered with plenty of concepts, examples, and tools.

➤ **José Valim**
Creator of Elixir, Dashbit

Machine Learning in Elixir is a superbly structured dive into the world of ML in Elixir. Sean has put tremendous care into making the learning experience as streamlined and engaging as possible. I found myself eagerly following along with practical examples in Livebook that made the information jump off the page and into my hands.

➤ **Brooklin Myers**
Elixir Instructor, DockYard

From basic concepts to building real-world applications, *Machine Learning in Elixir* guides you through the complex world of AI, with practical insights to make you a proficient developer in today's AI market.

➤ **Nicholas Franck**
Software Developer, Independent

Machine Learning in Elixir

Learning to Learn with Nx and Axon

Sean Moriarity

The Pragmatic Bookshelf

Dallas, Texas

For our complete catalog of hands-on, practical, and Pragmatic content for software developers, please visit *https://pragprog.com*.

Contact *support@pragprog.com* for sales, volume licensing, and support.

For international rights, please contact *rights@pragprog.com*.

The team that produced this book includes:

Publisher:	Dave Thomas
COO:	Janet Furlow
Executive Editor:	Susannah Davidson
Development Editor:	Tammy Coron
Copy Editor:	Corina Lebegioara
Indexing:	Potomac Indexing, LLC
Layout:	Gilson Graphics

ISBN-13: 979-8-88865-034-9
Book version: P1.0—September 2024

To Riley, Weston, and Indy.

Contents

Part I — Foundations of Machine Learning

Part III — Machine Learning in Practice

Disclaimer

The views expressed in this publication are those of the author and do not necessarily reflect the official policy or position of the Department of Defense or the U.S. government. The public release clearance of this publication by the Department of Defense does not imply Department of Defense endorsement or factual accuracy of the material.

Acknowledgments

I would first like to acknowledge José Valim for creating such a wonderful language and placing faith in me at the beginning of my open-source career. This book and the projects within would not exist without him. I would also like to acknowledge Paulo Valente, Jonatan Kłosko, and Christopher Grainger for the many design discussions and debugging sessions that helped shape the projects in this book. Finally, I would like to thank Noah DeMoes, Leo Kosta, Scott Mueller, Nick Franck, Mike Binns, Brooklin Myers, Jonatan Kłosko (again), and José Valim (again) for their valuable feedback on the contents of this book.

Preface

Machine learning, specifically deep learning, is constantly pushing the boundaries of what we thought was possible—and it's doing it in every industry.

Seemingly every day, a company or research group releases a new model that pushes the state of the art even further ahead. In recent years, ChatGPT and Stable Diffusion, among others, have taken the world by storm, bringing artificial intelligence to the forefront and redefining what types of applications are possible.

For most of their existence, Elixir and the BEAM weren't viable options for machine learning tooling. But the Nx ecosystem has changed that. Within this ecosystem, you can now write machine learning and numerical routines directly in Elixir and achieve performance that is the same as or better than an equivalent program in Python or Julia. Nx offers new capabilities to Elixir programmers. It also provides an off-ramp for existing machine learning engineers and researchers looking to explore ecosystems and build applications without Python.

My goal is for this book to serve as the definitive Nx and machine learning resource for programmers who want to explore machine learning in Elixir. While a lot of machine learning knowledge is available online, none of the existing resources are written with Elixir in mind. This book is designed to teach machine learning the Elixir way—functional, pragmatic, and fun.

You'll start with the basics of machine learning and Nx, and you'll build up to deploying powerful pre-trained models in an application with Phoenix. Throughout this book, you'll use Livebook—Elixir's interactive code notebook—to work with data and train models in an interactive and reproducible way. By the end of the book, you'll have experience working with Nx, Axon, Scholar, Bumblebee, Explorer, VegaLite, and many more libraries in the growing Elixir machine learning ecosystem.

We've finally made it to the always-promised but never-delivered golden age of artificial intelligence-enabled products. So, if you want to build powerful, intelligent applications augmented with machine learning models, Elixir is one of the best languages to use.

Why Elixir for Machine Learning?

Elixir is a dynamic, functional, general-purpose programming language that targets the BEAM virtual machine. It's proven itself as a capable language for building and maintaining scalable applications. But Elixir wasn't designed with machine learning in mind. Prior to the Nx[1] project, machine learning in Elixir was, at the very least, ill-advised. The BEAM virtual machine wasn't designed to perform the type of heavy lifting that machine learning requires. However, Nx and the ecosystem around it were built to enable Elixir programmers to perform the computationally expensive work required for machine learning applications.

Elixir and Nx are new players in the machine learning field. While the Nx ecosystem has no aim to overtake the established Python machine learning ecosystem, understanding machine learning in Elixir has numerous benefits.

First, Elixir is a *functional* programming language. While this might seem like a drawback for the heavy computation required in machine learning workloads, it's actually a benefit. In a functional world, everything is immutable. This means that when performing computations on large amounts of data, you need to return a new copy of the data after every individual operation. Fortunately, due to the rise of deep learning, computations are staged out to hardware accelerators such as GPUs before any of the actual operations are executed. These computations are staged out with just-in-time (JIT) compilers, which typically implement a functional interface for building up computation graphs. As you'll see in later chapters, you can write in Elixir's functional style and not worry about large intermediate copies.

Second, Elixir is designed for concurrency. When training machine learning algorithms, the performance bottleneck is typically in loading and preparing data for a training step on a hardware accelerator. This type of concurrent data processing is natural in Elixir because Elixir was designed with concurrency in mind. You need only to read *Concurrent Data Processing in Elixir [Gos21]* to see how good a fit Elixir is for those types of applications.

Third, Elixir and its web framework, Phoenix, are exceptional at building and scaling real-time, fault-tolerant applications. More and more machine learning systems are being deployed in scenarios where latency and uptime matter.

---

1. https://github.com/elixir-nx/nx

For example, a credit card fraud detection system should ideally work in real time, immediately alerting customers when a fraudulent transaction occurs. Additionally, with large amounts of fraudulent transactions taking place every day, those systems can't go down. Elixir and Phoenix have proven capable of building systems that are low-latency and resilient to failure. But until now, integrating machine learning in an Elixir application required leaving the safety of the BEAM to an external service.

Finally, Elixir is a lot of fun and an absolute joy to use. As you'll see throughout this book, most machine learning algorithms are naturally expressed with functional constructs that work particularly well with the beauty and thoughtfulness of the Elixir programming language.

Who This Book Is For

This book is for programmers interested in learning machine learning in Elixir and programmers with prior Elixir or machine learning experience.

Elixir programmers can pick up and read this book with no prerequisite knowledge of machine learning, mathematics, or numerical computing, as this book will teach you everything you need to know from the basics onward.

Programmers with machine learning experience but no Elixir experience will be able to follow along, but some syntactic details and functional concepts might seem unfamiliar. If you fit into this category, I recommend keeping the Elixir documentation handy to reference some language details that this book omits.

If you have no machine learning or Elixir experience, then learning both Elixir and machine learning at the same time will be a difficult task. So I recommend getting familiar with Elixir first and then returning to this book to learn machine learning in Elixir.

What's in This Book

In Chapter 1, Make Machines That Learn, on page 3, you'll answer the question, "What is machine learning?" You'll learn the fundamental concepts of machine learning and set the course for the rest of your machine learning journey. You'll create, train, and use your first machine learning model. By the end of the chapter, you'll be able to define machine learning, discuss the types of problems machine learning is good for, and solve a problem with machine learning in Elixir.

In Chapter 2, Get Comfortable with Nx, on page 21, you'll get familiar with Nx—the numerical computing library that serves as the backbone of the Elixir machine learning ecosystem. You'll learn about the fundamental data structure in numerical computing, the tensor, and a bit about what makes Nx so important for machine learning. By the end of this chapter, you'll know how to create and manipulate tensors, encode real-world data with Nx, and accelerate routines with numerical definitions.

In Chapter 3, Harness the Power of Math, on page 47, you'll channel your inner mathematician and dive into machine learning math. You'll learn the three areas of mathematics that underpin most of the concepts in this book: linear algebra, probability, and vector calculus. By the end of this chapter, you'll understand the power of mathematics and how it relates to machine learning.

In Chapter 4, Optimize Everything, on page 73, you'll start navigating an ocean of loss curves with optimization routines. You'll learn what a loss function is and how optimization and machine learning are related and different. By the end of this chapter, you'll be able to formulate machine learning problems as optimization problems. You'll also be able to implement some loss functions and optimization algorithms in Nx.

In Chapter 5, Traditional Machine Learning, on page 95, you'll graduate from machine learning's foundations to real machine learning with Scholar. You'll learn about various traditional machine learning algorithms, such as linear and logistic regression. By the end of this chapter, you'll be able to use Scholar to create and train traditional machine learning algorithms.

In Chapter 6, Go Deep with Axon, on page 117, you'll start working with Axon to create and train neural networks in Elixir. You'll learn what deep learning is and why it's so powerful. You'll create neural networks in both Nx and Axon, and you'll get a better understanding of what a neural network really is. By the end of this chapter, you'll know how to create and train basic neural networks with Axon. You'll also be able to distinguish and discuss the trade-offs between traditional and deep learning methods.

In Chapter 7, Learn to See, on page 141, you'll implement computer vision models with Axon and Elixir. You'll learn about convolutional neural networks and how they offer an improvement over traditional neural networks when working with image data. By the end of this chapter, you'll be able to create and train a convolutional neural network in Axon. You'll also be able to implement more complex machine learning training pipelines with Elixir's standard libraries.

In Chapter 8, Stop Reinventing the Wheel, on page 171, you'll make use of pre-trained models to improve performance and save time and money. You'll learn about transfer learning and fine-tuning. By the end of this chapter, you'll be able to implement transfer learning in Axon. You'll also know how to convert models from Python to Elixir to take advantage of Python's vast machine learning ecosystem.

In Chapter 9, Understand Text, on page 195, you'll teach your programs to read with recurrent neural networks, and you'll learn how to work with text in Elixir. By the end of this chapter, you'll be able to create and train recurrent neural networks in Axon, define and use various text preprocessing strategies with Elixir and Nx, and discuss why recurrent neural networks perform better than traditional models when working with sequential data-like text.

In Chapter 10, Forecast the Future, on page 219, you'll break out your crystal ball and attempt to peer into the future with recurrent neural networks. You'll learn about time-series forecasting and some of the challenges of predicting the future with machine learning. By the end of this chapter, you'll be able to create and train a recurrent neural network to perform single-step time-series predictions.

In Chapter 11, Model Everything with Transformers, on page 237, you'll unlock the power behind models like GPT-3 and Stable Diffusion with transformers. You'll learn what transformers are and why they perform so well on almost all types of data. By the end of this chapter, you'll be able to use pre-trained transformer models with Bumblebee. You'll also know how to fine-tune a pre-trained transformer with Bumblebee and Axon.

In Chapter 12, Learn Without Supervision, on page 259, you'll go off the rails and create models that learn without supervision. You'll learn about unsupervised learning and generative modeling. By the end of this chapter, you'll be able to create and train autoencoders, variational autoencoders, and generative adversarial networks.

In Chapter 13, Put Machine Learning into Practice, on page 293, you'll use everything you learned throughout this book, and you'll put a real machine learning model into a production application. You'll learn what to consider when operationalizing machine learning models, and you'll deploy a model in a Phoenix application. By the end of this chapter, you'll know how to use Nx.Serving to integrate your trained models into real applications.

In Chapter 14, That's a Wrap, on page 317, you'll conclude your journey with this book. You'll get a recipe for training models in practice, and you'll get resources for staying up to date with the latest trends in machine learning.

You'll also learn a bit about emerging trends in the field, as well as some topics this book didn't cover, such as adversarial attacks. By the end of this chapter, you'll be ready to build intelligent applications with machine learning in Elixir.

How to Use This Book

The code examples in each chapter of this book are isolated and designed to be run as standalone programs. For the best experience, read the chapters in successive order. While you can skip around, the concepts in each chapter are designed to build off one another, so you might be left confused at certain points if you skip around too much.

If you have some machine learning experience and want to dive right in, you can safely skip Chapter 1, Make Machines That Learn, on page 3, Chapter 3, Harness the Power of Math, on page 47, and Chapter 4, Optimize Everything, on page 73. I still recommend reading Chapter 2, Get Comfortable with Nx, on page 21, to get a better understanding of Nx and then reading the remaining chapters in order.

I also recommend you follow along with the examples in a Livebook as most of the chapters will assume you're running the code in a Livebook installation.

Finally, don't worry about having access to CPUs or GPUs. A modern, commercial laptop should be powerful enough to run all the examples in this book.

Part I

Foundations of Machine Learning

## CHAPTER 1

Make Machines That Learn

In 1958, Frank Rosenblatt, then a researcher at Cornell, revealed *"the first machine which [was] capable of having an original idea." [Lef19]*. At the time, Rosenblatt's primitive machine, which learned to identify markings on punch cards, was dubbed a *"Frankenstein Monster Designed by Navy That Thinks." [Met21]*. Despite the hype, it would take another 60 years of peaks and valleys for artificial intelligence and machine learning to prevail over humans in feats of intelligence.

In 2016, the artificial intelligence company, DeepMind, designed AlphaGo—a model capable of achieving superhuman performance in the game of Go. AlphaGo subsequently beat Go champions Lee Sedol and Ke Jie on a world stage, creating a resurgence in the promise of machine learning and artificial intelligence. Only a handful of years later, machine learning models, such as GPT-3 and Stable Diffusion, blur the lines between science fiction and reality, demonstrating both impressive feats of seeming intelligence and laughable shortcomings. While models such as GPT-3 and Stable Diffusion are impressive—and on the surface, they seem like feats of science outside the reach of nonacademics and researchers—the truth is these models build on the primitive foundations laid by Rosenblatt and researchers like him.

Perhaps more impressive than models like GPT-3 and Stable Diffusion are the countless models that drive billions of dollars in economic production every year. At every stage and in every industry, from startups to Forbes 500, retail to pharmaceuticals, companies are taking advantage of machine learning to accelerate products and move their industries forward.

Throughout this book, you'll learn the foundations of machine learning in Elixir by building some of the most fundamental machine learning models. You'll work through challenging problems and think critically about how to approach machine learning problems. Additionally, you'll see hands-on how to use machine learning in production. But first, let's answer the question, "What is machine learning" by working through an example.

Classifying Flowers

Imagine you've been hired by a botanist. Your job is to automate the classification of the *Iris* genus into one class from a set of species. You must also prove that your system has a minimum success rate of 85%.

The botanist has already automated the process of collecting and measuring the flowers but cannot invest time into classifying each one individually. Instead, they've given you a dataset consisting of 50 examples each of the *seneca*, *versicolor*, and *virginica* species of the *Iris* genus—150 examples total. Each example contains the sepal length (cm), sepal width (cm), petal length (cm), petal width (cm), and species.

With a clear mission and some data in hand, it's time to write your first machine learning algorithm.

Scoping the Project

Before writing the first line of code, it's always a good idea to sit down and clearly define the criteria for your project. Defining criteria for a machine learning problem is a bit different from defining criteria for a software project.

First, you need to understand *what* it means for a machine to *learn*. In his 1997 book, *Machine Learning [Mit97]*, Tom Mitchell writes, "A computer program is said to learn from experience E with respect to some class of tasks T and performance measure P, if its performance at tasks T, as measured by P improves with experiences E."

So, for a machine to learn, it requires three main components:

1. Task
2. Performance measure
3. Experience

Defining the Task

A task is what you want your model to do. A model is a predictive function. A model takes inputs and produces outputs. For example, if you want your model to differentiate between pictures of apples and oranges, the model's task is to differentiate between pictures of apples and oranges.

In machine learning, tasks are generally too complex to solve using a small set of rules. While you could probably give a model the task of sorting numbers in a list, it's not something you would generally do. You could simply write a sorting algorithm in a few minutes using a small set of rules.

The tasks you ask machine learning algorithms to solve are the ones you might consider easy but are far too complex to handle using a small number of simple rules. Consider the apples and oranges differentiator. What small set of rules would you implement to differentiate between pictures of apples and oranges? Would checking only the color be enough? What happens when you evaluate red oranges and orange apples? What rule would differentiate between those two varieties?

As you attempt to think of rules, you'll quickly find exceptions to them—and then exceptions to exceptions, and so on. A good rule of thumb to follow is that if you can't perform reasonably well with a few simple rules, machine learning *might* be a good fit for your problem.

Knowing Your Type

You can frame most machine learning tasks into one of two major categories:

1. Classification
2. Regression

While you might see some tasks thrown into their own distinct categories, such as *generative modeling*—the process of learning to generate realistic data—you can mostly formulate solutions to every machine learning problem in terms of classification and regression subtasks.

Classification problems are concerned with assigning labels to inputs. These labels are discrete, drawn from a set of categories such as "apples" and "oranges" or whole-numbers such as 0, 1, 2, 3, and so on. Your apples and oranges differentiator is an example of a classification task. Similarly, you can define fraud detection as a classification task.

Regression problems are concerned with assigning numeric values to inputs. These values are continuous and can occupy any real number value. A good example of a regression task is predicting housing prices from a set of house features or predicting a stock's future price from the current information available.

Defining your problem in terms of one of these two types of tasks will help you decide what kind of data to collect, what performance measures to use, and what models to train.

Being SMART

Machine learning tasks need to be carefully defined for a system to be successful. If you've ever read anything about setting goals, you've undoubtedly heard of the SMART acronym. SMART is a framework for goal setting. It stands for Specific, Measurable, Achievable, Relevant, and Time-bound. Although SMART is designed for goal-setting, it's a surprisingly good framework for defining machine learning tasks.

Your tasks should be *specific*. The need for specificity stems from the *no-free lunch theorem*. The no-free lunch theorem essentially states that there are no universally good machine learning algorithms. You sacrifice performance on one set of problems for performance on another set of problems. Many machine learning algorithms subscribe deeply to the Zen philosophy of "Do one thing well." If you train an algorithm to recognize cats and dogs, don't expect it to translate English to German too well. You train your algorithms to do one thing well.

Your tasks should be *measurable*. Measurability ties into the performance measure aspect of learning. It's impossible to tell if an algorithm is learning without having any measure of success. Even with a measure of success, it might not be the correct one or a good enough one. For example, if you design a machine learning system to bet on sports and measure its success in terms of profitability, it may learn to never bet at all. Is an algorithm that bets $0 on every game successful?

Your tasks should be *achievable* and *time-based*. Machine learning relies heavily on optimization. Many of the formulations in machine learning algorithms could be computed with access to perfect or infinite information. Of course, you never have access to perfect information. Instead, you need to define your task in a manner that's achievable with machine learning in a reasonable amount of time.

Finally, your tasks should be *relevant*, which may seem obvious but can be missed in subtle ways. Your task should be relevant to the problem you're trying to solve. As an example of the importance of relevance, consider autonomous driving. You might think you can solve the problem of autonomous driving on public roads by training an autonomous vehicle on closed courses. But your task wasn't to create an autonomous vehicle capable of driving on closed courses; it was to create an autonomous vehicle capable of driving on public roads.

Defining tasks correctly is critical to creating a good model. If you have a poorly or incorrectly defined task, you'll end up with a poorly or incorrectly trained model.

With a better understanding of the importance of defining a good task and some considerations when defining tasks, you need to define a task for your iris problem. Fortunately, the botanist has made your task very clear: *classify* flowers from the *Iris* genus into one of a set number of species. You can assess the viability of this task in the context of the SMART framework: your task is specific to classifying iris flowers—you weren't asked to classify other species of flowers or to create a model that makes other kinds of predictions. Your task is easily measurable as you'll find in Formulating a Performance Measure, on page 7. This task is both achievable and time-based—tasks similar to it have been solved before. Finally, you've been given data relevant to the task at hand.

Formulating a Performance Measure

With your task clearly defined, you need to choose a performance measure.

To measure a model's progress, you need some sort of measure of success. This measure of success is typically something like accuracy in classification tasks and absolute error in regression tasks. The process of learning comes from direct or indirect optimization of your performance measure, which means choosing a good performance measure is critical to the success of your model.

Choosing a good performance measure can be difficult in practice. If your problem isn't well-formulated (for example, you haven't defined a SMART task), you'll struggle to find a good performance measure. If you set out with the task of "creating artificial general intelligence," you'll probably struggle to come up with good performance measures. What is your measure of "general" intelligence?

Even for simple problems, deciding on a performance measure can be difficult. For machine translation, which can typically be formulated as a classification task, is accuracy sufficient? What is the accuracy of a translation of a sentence? Because translations aren't exactly one-to-one—and meaning changes drastically as words are changed or moved around—accuracy can be a poor measure of success in translation tasks. Another example of this is in machine learning on medical data. You could train a model that's 99% accurate in predicting whether or not a patient has cancer simply by predicting they don't every time. Is that model useful?

Because the process of creating and training models is often defined as an optimization task, you typically need to substitute actual performance measures with ones that behave better in an optimization setting. Metrics such as accuracy are discrete, not differentiable, and thus can't be optimized with gradient-based optimization. You'll learn more about differentiability and optimization in Chapter 4, Optimize Everything, on page 73. All you need to know is that you can't always optimize directly for your chosen performance measure, so instead you optimize indirectly on another.

This process of indirect optimization is akin to marathon runners indirectly tracking their progress on a marathon with times on shorter distance runs. You can't run a marathon every day, but you can track your performance in other ways. You optimize for the task of running a marathon indirectly by running shorter routes and tracking your progress over time.

The direct or indirect measure of success you use to optimize your performance measure is known as a *loss function* or *cost function*. The terminology is rooted in the mathematics of statistical learning theory, but its meaning is straightforward. A loss function is the measure of the "goodness" of a model. Machine learning often aims to minimize the loss or cost function to implicitly maximize your performance measure.

Aside from simply choosing a performance measure, you also need to define minimum thresholds for your metrics before declaring victory over a given problem. For example, 85% accuracy in flower species classification is fine, but in fraud detection is catastrophic. Success thresholds are problem-dependent and should be carefully established with input from every project stakeholder. Once again, the botanist has been very clear: your measure of success is accuracy, and your minimum objective is 85% accuracy.

Finally, you need to have a clear understanding of what your model inputs and outputs will look like. If you're in a situation where you don't have any data at all, you'll need to go out and collect data that looks like the data your model will actually experience. In this example, the botanist has told you that your model must take various flower measurements and output a label. They've also given you a dataset of features and labels already.

Given this is a classification task, it makes sense to use accuracy as a performance measure. For this example, you can define success for this problem as training a classifier that achieves 85% accuracy on an unseen test set.

Improving from Experience

Finally, to actually "learn," your model needs exposure to some sort of experience. An experience is just data. What that data looks like is dependent on the data you have and the type of learning algorithm you're trying to use. You can usually put a learning problem into one of two categories based on the type of experiences you want your model to have:

1. Supervised learning
2. Unsupervised learning

Supervised learning uses data or experiences with labels or targets. Each input to the model is associated with a correct answer, and your model learns from how close its prediction is to the target. Supervised learning problems are generally easier to work with in practice. However, if your data doesn't come with a natural label, you need to go through the time-consuming, difficult, and expensive process of annotating each input example.

Unsupervised learning uses data without labels. Rather than learning from given correct answers, unsupervised models learn properties of input data, such as how the data can be clustered into some fixed number of clusters.

You'll often see the collection of experiences your model goes through called a dataset. More accurately, the collection of experiences your model learns from is called the training set.

"Training" in machine learning refers to the process of optimizing your model on your given performance measure using experiences in your training set. Not all machine learning problems come with a fixed dataset. For example, reinforcement learning problems instead interact with nonstatic environments and learn from reward signals encoded into the environment. Rather than giving a model environment state and target action, you typically let the model explore the environment and learn from previous actions taken. Reinforcement learning isn't always considered supervised or unsupervised but is often considered its own type of machine learning.

In machine learning, you don't actually care how well your model does during training. All that matters is how well your model does on unseen data. A basketball team doesn't care about how well their players play during practice; they only care about how well they play during a live game (just ask Allen Iverson). The same goes for your models.

Typically, you train your model on a train set and evaluate your model on an unseen test set. Your concern is *generalization* (that is, how well your model generalizes to experiences it hasn't seen). In reality, evaluating your model is much more complex than throwing a static test set at it. If your models are going to be used in production, you'll need to constantly evaluate their performance as your static test set might not have accurately captured the data your model will see in production.

In this example, you've been handed experiences out of the box. The botanist has given you a large set of labeled iris flower data where each example consists of flower measurements. You can use this dataset to both train and evaluate your model.

Putting It All Together

Overall, you can define your learning problem in the following terms:

- T: Classify flowers from the *Iris* genus into one of *setosa*, *versicolor*, or *virginica* species

- P: Accuracy of classifications (minimum 85% for success)

- E: Flower measurements (sepal length, sepal width, petal length, petal width, and a species label)

Learning with Elixir

With your problem scoped, it's time to dive into the code. First, you'll need to have a working installation of Elixir. This is a book on machine learning in Elixir, so you'll need Elixir to run the code! For the examples in this book to work, you'll need at least Elixir version 1.14. The easiest way to install Elixir is through a version manager like asdf.[1] If you have asdf installed, you'll first need to install Erlang:

```
$ asdf install erlang 25.0.2
```

This installs Erlang/OTP version 25.0.2. Next, you can install Elixir:

```
$ asdf install elixir 1.14.3
```

This will install Elixir version 1.14.3. You can verify everything worked by running this:

```
$ elixir --version
```

And you'll see the following:

```
Erlang/OTP 25 [erts-13.0.2] [source] [64-bit] [smp:10:10]
  [ds:10:10:10] [async-threads:1] [jit]

Elixir 1.14.3 (compiled with Erlang/OTP 23)
```

Next, you'll want to head over to the Livebook[2] website and follow the official Livebook installation instructions. All of the code in this book is meant to run inside an Elixir Livebook. Livebooks are interactive code notebooks similar to Jupyter Notebooks. You can install Livebook locally, or run it in the cloud with Fly.[3] Once you have Livebook installed, you'll want to open it up by using the installed icon or running livebook server from your command line. After that, create a new notebook and you're ready to go.

---

1. https://asdf-vm.com/
2. https://livebook.dev
3. https://fly.io

Now, you'll need to install the libraries. For this example, you'll need Axon, Nx, Explorer, and Kino.

Axon is a library for creating and training neural networks. You can also use it to create and train more basic models as well. You'll see a lot of Axon in Part II, Deep Learning, on page 115.

Nx is the foundation of every other project in the Elixir machine learning eco-system. It's a library for creating and manipulating multidimensional arrays, or as they're called in Nx, tensors. In Chapter 2, Get Comfortable with Nx, on page 21, you'll dive deeper into Nx. But for now, all you need to know is that Nx is the common language of data spoken by every library in the Nx ecosystem. You'll represent your data as Nx tensors and your models as Nx operations.

Explorer is a library for creating and manipulating DataFrames. DataFrames are two-dimensional, tabular data structures. You'll use Explorer throughout this book to conduct data analysis, preprocessing, validation, and more.

When using Livebook, you should also install Kino. Kino is a library for interactive visualizations and smart cells in Livebook. Axon ships with some Kino integrations and visualizations that you'll use in this chapter.

To install these dependencies, run the following in a Livebook cell:

```
Mix.install([
  {:axon, "~> 0.5"},
  {:nx, "~> 0.5"},
  {:explorer, "~> 0.5"},
  {:kino, "~> 0.8"}
])
```

When working with Explorer you are encouraged to use the Explorer queries[4] API, which make use of macros for many manipulation tasks. To use these macros, you need to require them. In a new cell, run the following:

```
require Explorer.DataFrame, as: DF
```

This will include all of the query macros which you can access via the DF alias. Now you're ready to jump into the data.

Working with Data

The dataset you're using is available to download within the Explorer.Datasets module. Start by loading the dataset into a DataFrame:

```
iris = Explorer.Datasets.iris()
```

---

4.   https://hexdocs.pm/explorer/Explorer.Query.html

After running this command and downloading the dataset, you'll see the following output:

```
#Explorer.DataFrame<
  Polars[150 x 5]
  sepal_length float [5.1, 4.9, 4.7, 4.6, 5.0, "..."]
  sepal_width float [3.5, 3.0, 3.2, 3.1, 3.6, "..."]
  petal_length float [1.4, 1.4, 1.3, 1.5, 1.4, "..."]
  petal_width float [0.2, 0.2, 0.2, 0.2, 0.2, "..."]
  species string ["Iris-setosa", "Iris-setosa", "Iris-setosa",
  "Iris-setosa", "Iris-setosa", "..."]
>
```

Notice that the DataFrame has 150 rows (examples) and 5 columns (features). Each Explorer column has an associated datatype and a list of row-values within that column. The list of values, which make up an individual column, is often referred to as a Series. Most operations apply to an individual series because it only makes sense to apply them across an individual series. For example, computing the mean of the values in this DataFrame doesn't make sense. But computing the mean of sepal_length does make sense.

From here, you can do a number of interesting things with the data, such as visualizations and filtering. For now, you'll focus on getting the data into a format that's readily ingestible for model training.

Preparing the Data for Training

Machine learning isn't magic. You can't feed an algorithm any data you want and expect it to learn the relationships you want it to learn correctly. In reality, most machine learning algorithms rely on some linear algebra and probability. So, you need to get your data into a format that's conducive to learning.

One common requirement is that data should be *normalized*. In the context of machine learning, normalizing data is the process of ensuring input features operate on a common scale. Most algorithms only perform some naive mathematical operations. If you have a feature that can take on values up into the thousands or millions, that feature might get treated as significantly more important than a feature that only takes on values between 0 and 1.

There are a few ways to appropriately scale data. For instance, you can squeeze the values of a feature between 0 and 1 by subtracting every individual feature by the min value of that feature column and then dividing the result by the range between the max and min values across a feature. You can also compute a z-score for each feature. A z-score is a statistical measure that essentially represents a data point's deviation from the average data point in a feature space. Significantly positive or negative z-scores indicate that a value is significantly higher or significantly lower than the rest of the data in the distribution. You'll often see this type of scaling referred to as *standardization*.

For this example, either of those scaling strategies will work well. For now, you'll use standardization to scale your data. In a new cell, add the following standardization code:

```
cols = ~w(sepal_width sepal_length petal_length petal_width)
normalized_iris =
  DF.mutate(
    iris,
    for col <- across(^cols) do
      {col.name, (col - mean(col)) / standard_deviation(col)}
    end
  )
```

To standardize a series, all you need to do is calculate the mean and standard deviation of the series using mean and standard_deviation, respectively. You then reduce each value in the series by the mean and divide the result by the standard deviation. Notice that you didn't need to break out Enum.map or Enum.reduce for this function. Instead, you took advantage of the functions in the Explorer API. DF.mutate/2 mutates the columns in the DataFrame according to the second argument. You use across/1 to access the columns given in the list of column names, and for each column you standardize the values in the series.

You should now have a standardized DataFrame which looks like this:

```
#Explorer.DataFrame<
  [rows: 150, columns: 5]
  sepal_length float [-1.0840606189132314, -1.3757361217598396,
   -1.6674116246064494, -1.8132493760297548, -1.2298983703365356, "..."]
  sepal_width float [2.372289612531505, -0.28722789030650403,
   0.7765791108287006, 0.24467561026109824, 2.904193113099107, "..."]
  petal_length float [-0.7576391687443842, -0.7576391687443842,
   -0.7897606710936372, -0.725517666395131, -0.7576391687443842, "..."]
  petal_width float [-0.7576391687443842, -0.7576391687443842,
   -0.7897606710936372,, -0.725517666395131, -0.7576391687443842, "..."]
  species string ["Iris-setosa", "Iris-setosa", "Iris-setosa",
  "Iris-setosa", "Iris-setosa", "..."]
>
```

Notice you don't want to standardize the species. It's a *categorical* feature, so there's no notion of scale. A categorical feature is a feature that takes on one of a number of fixed values. After standardizing each series individually, you apply your changes to the DataFrame by calling DF.mutate/2.

Next, you'll want to convert your species column to a categorical feature so that it's treated properly when you convert the DataFrame into a tensor. You can do this by running the following:

```
normalized_iris = DF.mutate(normalized_iris, [
  species: Explorer.Series.cast(species, :category)
])
```

This will cast the species column to a categorical variable and thus will be handled properly when you convert your DataFrame to a tensor.

One thing you may have noticed is that your data is ordered by flower species. All of the examples of the *setosa* species are first, followed by *versicolor*, and finally by *virginica*. In a production setting, you can't expect your data to arrive ordered like that. To simulate a real-world environment, shuffle your data by running the following:

```
shuffled_normalized_iris = DF.shuffle(normalized_iris)
```

This returns the following:

```
#Explorer.DataFrame<
  [rows: 150, columns: 5]
  sepal_length float [0.08264139247320726, 1.2493434038596445,
  -0.2090341103734024, -1.3757361217598396, 0.3743168953198156, "..."]
  sepal_width float [-0.28722789030650403, 0.24467561026109824,
  3.9680001142343095, -3.4786488937121156, -0.28722789030650403, "..."]
  petal_length float [0.4308564181779819, 0.3023704087809695,
  -0.6612746616966249, -0.1473306241085746, 0.36661341347947585, "..."]
  petal_width float [0.4308564181779819, 0.3023704087809695,
  -0.6612746616966249, -0.1473306241085746, 0.36661341347947585, "..."]
  species ["Iris-versicolor", "Iris-setosa", ...]
>
```

Explorer.DataFrame.slice/2 grabs row indices from the given DataFrame in the order given. You have 150 values, so indices are 0 to 149. By shuffling the range of indices, you shuffle the order of elements in the DataFrame. Shuffling the DataFrame is important for both training and testing, as you'll soon see.

Splitting into Train and Test Sets

The botanist has asked you to prove the efficacy of your model before putting it into production. A common practice to validate a model's performance is to use a test or *holdout set*. The test or holdout set is a small percentage of an original dataset, which you don't present to the model during training. You use performance on the test set as the final evaluation of performance on your given task. It's important that your model never sees examples from the test set during training.

For this example, you can split the dataset into training and test sets with the following code:

```
train_df = DF.slice(shuffled_normalized_iris, 0..119)
test_df = DF.slice(shuffled_normalized_iris, 120..149)
```

Because you've gone through the trouble of shuffling your dataset, you can slice it into train and test sets using slice/2. Had you not shuffled your dataset, you'd have ended up with a test set filled entirely with examples of versicolor flowers. Your test set wouldn't be a good representative sample of the data, and you would have a pretty bad idea about how well your model is actually performing.

Preparing Data for Training

Now that your data is normalized and split into train and test sets, you can start thinking about training your model. But, before you create and train your model, you need to get your data into a format the model will understand.

As mentioned before, the Nx.Tensor is the common language spoken by all of the libraries in the Nx ecosystem. That means you need to convert your data into a tensor or a tensor-compatible format.

Additionally, when passing Explorer DataFrames to Nx, you need to make sure your data is in one of the specific supported Nx input types. For this example, you have a column "species" which is currently represented as a string. "species" is the categorical variable you want to train your model to predict. Typically, categorical variables are represented using integers or *one-hot encoding*. One-hot encoding produces a tensor with N columns with every value being a 0 (meaning "off") *except* the index of the class, which is a 1 (meaning "on"). As a simple example, if you consider we discretize the labels in this example into the integer values 0, 1, and 2, then the one-hot encoded representation for each class would look like this:

```
# class 0
[1, 0, 0]

# class 1
[0, 1, 0]

# class 2
[0, 0, 1]
```

For this example, you need to convert your training and testing labels to one-hot encoded tensors. Implement the one-hot encoding like this:

```
feature_columns = [
  "sepal_length",
  "sepal_width",
  "petal_length",
  "petal_width"
]

x_train = Nx.stack(train_df[feature_columns], axis: -1)

y_train =
  train_df["species"]
  |> Nx.stack(axis: -1)
  |> Nx.equal(Nx.iota({1, 3}, axis: -1))

x_test = Nx.stack(test_df[feature_columns], axis: -1)

y_test =
  test_df["species"]
  |> Nx.stack(axis: -1)
  |> Nx.equal(Nx.iota({1, 3}, axis: -1))
```

First, notice that you extract feature_columns from both the training and testing DataFrame and call the variables x_train and x_test, respectively. In machine learning, it's common to use the variable x to indicate model features. You use Nx.stack/2 to convert your features in the DataFrame into a tensor. This will stack the rows of the DataFrame into individual entries.

Next, you extract a label tensor by one-hot encoding your species column. You do this by converting the species column to a tensor, which implicitly casts each category to a unique integer, and then by making use of some Nx magic to do the one-hot encoding. Don't worry if you don't follow the Nx logic just yet. You'll get more comfortable with Nx in Chapter 2, Get Comfortable with Nx, on page 21.

Now that you have your features and targets split up for both training and testing, you're ready to create a machine learning model.

Multinomial Logistic Regression with Axon

Now that you've wrangled your data into a format conducive to training models, it's time to actually create and train a model. Training a machine learning model in Axon essentially boils down to three steps:

1. Defining the model
2. Creating an input pipeline
3. Declaring and running the training loop

Defining the Model

When you hear the term "model" in the context of machine learning, think of a function. A model is anything that takes data in and gives a value out. Axon includes a model creation API that's typically used for creating neural networks. In this example, however, you can use Axon to create a basic multinomial logistic regression model. You'll see the inner workings of logistic regression in Chapter 5, Traditional Machine Learning, on page 95. For now, simply copy and run the following code in a new Livebook cell:

```
model =
  Axon.input("iris_features", shape: {nil, 4})
  |> Axon.dense(3, activation: :softmax)
```

After declaring your model, you'll see an output that looks like this:

```
#Axon<
  inputs: %{"iris_features" => {nil, 4}}
  outputs: "softmax_0"
  nodes: 3
>
```

Every Axon model starts with an input with a specific name. You may also specify an optional :shape. The shape represents the values of each dimension in your data. Subsequent calls on the result of an Axon.input layer represent transformations of the input data. This model essentially transforms your data into three probabilities, which represent the probability that a given example belongs to one of the three classes. Remember your inputs are actually Explorer DataFrames, so you need a way to get them to work well with Axon's other functions. Axon.stack_columns/2 will process the DataFrame into a single tensor, which is a bit closer to what Axon expects.

You can visualize your model with Kino by running the following code:

```
Axon.Display.as_graph(model, Nx.template({1, 4}, :f32))
```

And you'll see the following image:

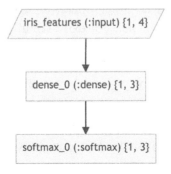

Visualizing smaller models is a useful way to debug and understand how data flows through your models.

Creating an Input Pipeline

Axon implements minibatch training with gradient descent. This means Axon's training API performs updates to the model iteratively. You'll learn about gradient descent more in-depth in Chapter 4, Optimize Everything, on page 73. The training API expects to be able to step through a dataset in "batches" or smaller groups of examples. In this example, your dataset is small, so you can update your model on the entire dataset at once. However, Axon will still expect to be able to grab data from your input pipeline for multiple steps over a given training run. You can accomplish this using Elixir's Stream module:

```
data_stream = Stream.repeatedly(fn ->
  {x_train, y_train}
end)
```

This function will repeatedly return tuples of your train features and train targets, respectively. Axon expects input data to be in pairs of {features, targets}. Here your features are the features present in x_train and the targets are y_train.

Declaring and Running the Training Loop

The Axon.Loop API is Axon's primary API for training models with gradient descent. A training loop is essentially a process consisting of the following steps:

1. Grabbing inputs from the input pipeline
2. Making predictions from inputs
3. Determining how good the predictions were
4. Updating the model based on prediction goodness
5. Repeating the steps

Axon calls the process of going through these steps one time a single iteration. You can group multiple iterations together to form a single *epoch*. For small-to medium-sized datasets, a single epoch typically means a pass through every example in the training set. For extra small and extra large datasets, a single epoch can be assigned a fixed number of steps. Because your dataset is extra small, you'll want to set a fixed number of iterations to step through to ensure Axon can update your model enough times to reach a good final model state.

An Axon training loop is actually a data structure that tells Axon things about the loop such as: how to initialize the loop, how to update the model state after every iteration, and what metrics to track during the loop. You build up the loop data structure using functions in the Axon loop API and then execute the loop with Axon.Loop.run. To implement your training loop, copy and run the following code:

```
trained_model_state =
  model
  |> Axon.Loop.trainer(:categorical_cross_entropy, :sgd)
  |> Axon.Loop.metric(:accuracy)
  |> Axon.Loop.run(data_stream, %{}, iterations: 500, epochs: 10)
```

After the loop runs, you'll see this:

```
Epoch: 0, Batch: 450, accuracy: 0.7204926 loss: 0.7272241
Epoch: 1, Batch: 450, accuracy: 0.8676836 loss: 0.5376064
Epoch: 2, Batch: 450, accuracy: 0.9028787 loss: 0.4587657
Epoch: 3, Batch: 450, accuracy: 0.9206356 loss: 0.4105419
Epoch: 4, Batch: 450, accuracy: 0.9304860 loss: 0.3763140
Epoch: 5, Batch: 450, accuracy: 0.9483036 loss: 0.3500875
Epoch: 6, Batch: 450, accuracy: 0.9500036 loss: 0.3290386
Epoch: 7, Batch: 450, accuracy: 0.9538460 loss: 0.3116082
Epoch: 8, Batch: 450, accuracy: 0.9583363 loss: 0.2968430
Epoch: 9, Batch: 450, accuracy: 0.9583363 loss: 0.2841162
```

In this example, you used one of Axon.Loop's factory functions to declare a supervised training loop with the :categorical_cross_entropy loss function optimized with :sgd or stochastic-gradient descent. The model, loss function, and optimizer correspond directly to steps 2, 3, and 4 of the previously outlined training loop process. Next, you tell the loop to keep track of accuracy during training, so you have a better idea of how training is progressing. Finally, you run your training loop for 10 epochs, with each epoch consisting of 500 iterations pulled from your input pipeline.

The output of Axon's supervised training loop is the trained model state or trained model parameters, which you can use to implement evaluation loops or make predictions on new data later on. You'll notice Axon outputs training progress at each step. You might get excited when you see the accuracy of your model on the training set approaches 90%, but remember, performance on the training set doesn't mean anything. To get a decent understanding of the model's performance, you need to evaluate it on the test set.

Evaluating the Trained Model

To prove your model's efficacy, you need to evaluate it on the test set. Fortunately, Axon also has conveniences for evaluating models. To evaluate your model, copy and run the following code:

```
data = [{x_test, y_test}]
model
|> Axon.Loop.evaluator()
|> Axon.Loop.metric(:accuracy)
|> Axon.Loop.run(data, trained_model_state)
```

This outputs the following:

```
Batch: 0, accuracy: 0.9666666
```

In this example, you create a supervised evaluation loop using Axon.Loop.evaluator/2. Next, you tell the loop to aggregate accuracy—your performance measure—as it goes through the input data. Finally, you run the loop on your test set. Notice that your final model accuracy on the test set exceeds 85%. You've successfully met the botanist's standards and trained a model to predict species of the iris flower just from a few measurements.

Wrapping Up

In this chapter, you learned what machine learning is, what kind of problems it can solve, and how to do some basic machine learning with Elixir and Nx. You have got a feel for some of the libraries in the Elixir Nx ecosystem such as Axon, Explorer, Kino, and Nx itself, and you have seen how you can integrate a machine learning model into Elixir applications. You learned about some of the important things to consider when approaching a problem with machine learning including defining problems in terms of a task, performance measure, and experience, using a SMART framework to define your tasks, differentiating between classification and regression problems, and the importance of obtaining good data.

Your implementations made use of some of the surface-level features of Axon, Nx, and Explorer. To implement more complex machine learning models, you'll need to go deeper. In the next chapter, you'll dive head first into Nx, and you'll learn more about what Nx is and the power Nx brings to Elixir. You'll see how tensors are used as the fundamental language of data, how Nx's automatic differentiation system allows you to train complex machine learning models, and how Nx enables accelerated computation on the CPU and GPU.

## CHAPTER 2

Get Comfortable with Nx

In the previous chapter, you built your first machine learning model using Nx, Axon, Explorer, and Kino. You might have noticed that most of the code helped to wrangle the data into a form your algorithm could use—the Nx.Tensor. As you read through this book, you'll see that much of your time will be spent working with data rather than writing algorithms, so you'll need to be comfortable manipulating data with Nx. In this chapter, you'll dive deeper into Nx and learn why Nx is the foundational library of the Elixir machine learning ecosystem.

Thinking in Tensors

Data is arguably the most important component in a machine learning system. Even with the most complex, cutting-edge model, you still need significant amounts of high-quality data to train a quality model. Bad data inevitably leads to bad models.

Researchers are generally divided into two schools of thought on the importance of data versus the importance of models in machine learning. Some researchers believe in a *data-centric approach*. The argument for a data-centric approach is that large amounts of high-quality data are the key to engineering quality machine learning systems. While other researchers believe in a *model-centric approach*. The model-centric approach focuses on spending more time researching new models to build quality machine learning systems.

In practice, a successful machine learning system requires balancing the two approaches, which means you need large amounts of high-quality data *and* a model with enough *capacity* to fit that data. You'll dive deeper into what model capacity means in Chapter 4, Optimize Everything, on page 73. For now, all you need to know is that capacity is a model's ability to effectively find patterns in the data.

The relationship between model and data is akin to that of an engine and fuel. In this relationship, models are the engine and data is the fuel. To build a successful machine learning system you need a balance of the right model and data.

The core abstraction for representing data in Nx is the Nx.Tensor. In Nx, a *tensor* is a multidimensional array—a potentially nested array of arrays of numbers, or for Elixir programmers, a list of lists of numbers. If you're coming from a mathematical background, this description of a tensor might confuse you. The use of the word "tensor" to describe a multidimensional array in Nx comes from the ubiquity of the word in numerical computing, not from a stance of mathematical correctness.

The Nx.Tensor is designed with two goals in mind: flexibility and performance. The abstraction needs to be flexible enough to represent real-world data and performant enough for the compute-intensive calculations involved in machine learning. Real-world data can often be easily mapped to multidimensional arrays of numbers. Additionally, multidimensional arrays are well-suited to acceleration with modern hardware.

Winning the Lottery

The multidimensional array or tensor is the most common data structure in machine learning today, which is largely driven by the popularity of deep learning. Arguably, the widespread usage of both multidimensional arrays in numerical computing and deep learning instead of other methods of machine learning is mainly because they were suited to the hardware available during the early 2010s, namely GPUs. Multidimensional arrays and deep learning won the *hardware lottery [Hoo21]* because they were well-suited for acceleration on GPUs, not because they're superior in flexibility or performance. For example, alternative abstractions, such as using *hash tables [CMFg20]*, have been proposed to train neural networks. Additionally, other algorithms might prove superior to deep learning on less data, but they're prohibitively slow on available hardware.

If you've never worked with array programming libraries or languages, such as NumPy or Matlab, programming in Nx for the first time can feel a bit strange. While Elixir emphasizes a programming paradigm based on data transformations that map well to numerical computing applications, Nx tensors are fundamentally different from other data types available in the Elixir standard library.

Getting comfortable with Nx requires some practice, so open up a Livebook and install the required dependencies:

```
Mix.install([
  {:nx, "~> 0.5"},
  {:exla, "~> 0.5"},
  {:benchee, github: "bencheeorg/benchee", override: true}
])
```

You'll be working with Nx and EXLA. EXLA is used to accelerate Nx programming; you'll see what that means in Going from def to defn, on page 40. You also need Benchee to benchmark some Nx functions.

With the required dependencies installed, you're ready to dive into some examples.

Understanding Nx Tensors

Start by running the following code in a new Livebook cell:

```
Nx.tensor([1, 2, 3])
```

This generates the following output:

```
#Nx.Tensor<
  s64[3]
  [1, 2, 3]
>
```

You've just created a tensor using one of Nx's creation methods. Nx.tensor/2 is the easiest way to create a tensor from a number, a list of numbers, or a nested list of numbers. Try creating a few more tensors using the following code:

```
a = Nx.tensor([[1, 2, 3], [4, 5, 6]])
b = Nx.tensor(1.0)
c = Nx.tensor([[[[[[1.0, 2]]]]]])
dbg(a)
dbg(b)
dbg(c)
```

This returns the following:

```
[#cell:d4okkentiv5fwvyryl47ypcqm4vkedbm:4: (file)]
a #=> #Nx.Tensor<
  s64[2][3]
  [
    [1, 2, 3],
    [4, 5, 6]
  ]
>
```

```
[#cell:d4okkentiv5fwvyryl47ypcqm4vkedbm:5: (file)]
b #=> #Nx.Tensor<
  f32
  1.0
>

[#cell:d4okkentiv5fwvyryl47ypcqm4vkedbm:6: (file)]
c #=> #Nx.Tensor<
  f32[1][1][1][1][1][2]
  [
    [
      [
        [
          [
            [1.0, 2.0]
          ]
        ]
      ]
    ]
  ]
>
```

You'll see three properties of a tensor every time you inspect its contents: type, shape, and data. All of these properties make a tensor distinctly different from a generic Elixir list.

Tensors Have a Type

Create and inspect two tensors by running the following code in a Livebook cell:

```
a = Nx.tensor([1, 2, 3])
b = Nx.tensor([1.0, 2.0, 3.0])
dbg(a)
dbg(b)
```

You'll see the following output:

```
[#cell:d4okkentiv5fwvyryl47ypcqm4vkedbm:3: (file)]
a #=> #Nx.Tensor<
  s64[3]
  [1, 2, 3]
>

[#cell:d4okkentiv5fwvyryl47ypcqm4vkedbm:4: (file)]
b #=> #Nx.Tensor<
  f32[3]
  [1.0, 2.0, 3.0]
>
```

Do you notice a difference between the two tensors, aside from the difference in data?

Notice that tensor a displays s64, whereas tensor b displays f32. Both s64 and f32 are the *numeric type* of the tensor's data. If you've worked with types in programming languages before, you're likely familiar with some of the numeric types Nx offers.

Nx types dictate how the underlying tensor data is interpreted during execution and inspection. You'll see in Tensors Have Data, on page 30, that tensor data isn't represented in an Elixir list, but instead as raw bytes. The tensor's type tells Nx how to interpret those raw bytes.

Tensor types are defined by a type class and a bit width. The type class can be a signed integer, an unsigned integer, a float, or a brain float. Signed and unsigned integers can have a bit width of 8, 16, 32, or 64. Floats can have bit widths of 16, 32, or 64. Brain floats can only have a bit width of 16. Brain floats are a special type of floating point number optimized for deep learning. You can specify types when creating tensors using a tuple of {class, bit-width}. The following table illustrates each type, their Elixir representation, and their inspected string representation:

Class	Widths	Elixir Representation	String Representation
signed integer	8, 16, 32, 64	{:s, 8}, {:s, 16}, {:s, 32}, {:s, 64}	s8, s16, s32, s64
unsigned integer	8, 16, 32, 64	{:u, 8}, {:u, 16}, {:u, 32}, {:u, 64}	u8, u16, u32, u64
float	16, 32, 64	{:f, 16}, {:f, 32}, {:f, 64}	f16, f32, f64
brain float	16	{:bf, 16}	bf16
complex	64, 128	{:c, 64}, {:c, 128}	c64, c128

Notice that you specify a type's class with an *atom*. If you're familiar with Elixir, you know an atom is a constant whose values are their own name. You then specify the type's bit width. This dictates the size each element of the tensor occupies in memory. For example, each element in a signed 64-bit tensor occupies 64 bits or 8 bytes of memory. Larger bit-width types are more *numerically precise*, which means you can represent a larger range of values and not worry as much about *underflow* or *overflow*. Underflow occurs when you try to represent a value that's too small for a computer to represent in storage. For example, create a tensor with the following code:

```
Nx.tensor(0.0000000000000000000000000000000000000000000000001)
```

You'll see the following output:

```
#Nx.Tensor<
  f32
  0.0
>
```

But you didn't want to create a tensor with a value of 0.0; you wanted a tensor with a value of 1.0e-45. The value you're trying to represent is underflowed to 0.0. A 32-bit float isn't precise enough to store your value. If you increase the bit width to 64, you'll be able to properly represent the number you want. You can tell Nx to use a specific type by passing the :type option to Nx.tensor/2:

```
Nx.tensor(1.0e-45, type: {:f, 64})
```

Running this code will return this:

```
#Nx.Tensor<
  f64
  1.0e-45
>
```

A 64-bit float occupies more memory and is thus able to store a larger range of numbers. Overflow occurs when the number you are trying to store is too large for the given type. This happens often with low-precision integer types. For example, create a tensor using the following code:

```
Nx.tensor(128, type: {:s, 8})
```

Here, you're trying to create a tensor with a value of 128 and a type of {:s, 8} or a signed 8-bit integer tensor. After running the code, you'll see the following:

```
#Nx.Tensor<
  s8
  -128
>
```

That's surprising! A signed 8-bit integer tensor occupies 1 byte of memory and can only represent values between -128 and 127. Anything outside of that range will be squeezed to some value within the supported range, which results in the behavior you see here.

Precision issues are common in machine learning because you're often working with floating-point types. Floating-point types attempt to capture a large range of real values. But it's not possible to fit an infinite range of numbers into a finite amount of storage. You'll sometimes see surprising issues due to precision issues. Throughout this book, you'll see code examples that attempt to work around the limitations of floating-point numbers.

As you may have noticed, tensors have a homogenous type. For every tensor you've created, there's always been a single type. You cannot have tensors with mixed types. Nx will choose a default type capable of representing the values you are trying to use when you create a tensor unless you explicitly state otherwise by passing a :type parameter. You can see this default typing in action by running the following code:

```
Nx.tensor([1.0, 2, 3])
```

This returns the following:

```
#Nx.Tensor<
  f32[3]
  [1.0, 2.0, 3.0]
>
```

Even though the last two values are integers, Nx cast them to floats because the highest type was a floating-point value and Nx didn't want you to unnecessarily lose precision.

Having homogenous types in an array programming library like Nx is necessary for a couple of reasons. First, it eliminates the need to store additional information about every value in the tensor. Second, it enables unique optimizations for certain algorithms. For example, imagine you want to compute the index of the maximum value in a tensor of type {:s, 8}. Because you know that every value in the tensor is a signed 8-bit integer, you also know that the maximum possible value is 127. If you ever observe 127 in the tensor, you can halt the algorithm without traversing the rest of the tensor because 127 is *guaranteed* to be maximal. Type-specific optimizations, such as this one, are common in numerical computing.

Tensors Have Shape

You've probably noticed the nested list representation of data when inspecting the contents of a tensor. However, tensor data isn't stored as a list at all. The nesting you see during inspection is actually a manifestation of the tensor's *shape*. A tensor's shape is the size of each dimension in the tensor. Consider the following tensors:

```
a = Nx.tensor([1, 2])
b = Nx.tensor([[1, 2], [3, 4]])
c = Nx.tensor([[[1, 2], [3, 4]], [[5, 6], [7, 8]]])
```

You can inspect each tensor with the following code:

```
dbg(a)
dbg(b)
dbg(c)
```

You'll see the following output:

```
[#cell:d4okkentiv5fwvyryl47ypcqm4vkedbm:1: (file)]
a #=> #Nx.Tensor<
  s64[2]
  [1, 2]
>

[#cell:d4okkentiv5fwvyryl47ypcqm4vkedbm:2: (file)]
b #=> #Nx.Tensor<
  s64[2][2]
  [
    [1, 2],
    [3, 4]
  ]
>

[#cell:d4okkentiv5fwvyryl47ypcqm4vkedbm:3: (file)]
c #=> #Nx.Tensor<
  s64[2][2][2]
  [
    [
      [1, 2],
      [3, 4]
    ],
    [
      [5, 6],
      [7, 8]
    ]
  ]
>
```

Notice the value next to each tensor's type. That value is its shape. Shapes in Nx are expressed using tuples of positive integer values. The representation you see in the previous code example is a pretty-printed version of each tensor's shape. Tensor a has a shape of {2} because it has one dimension of size 2. Tensor b has shape {2, 2} because it has two dimensions, each of size 2. Finally, tensor c has a shape of {2, 2, 2} because it has three dimensions, each of size 2. Notice that as the number of dimensions increases, so does the level of nesting in the inspected data.

The number of dimensions is typically referred to as the tensor's *rank*. Again, if you're coming from a mathematical background, this use of the word rank might confuse you. In the world of numerical computing, the rank corresponds to the number of dimensions or the level of nesting in the tensor. *Scalars* don't have any level of nesting at all because they don't have any shape. You can think of a scalar as a zero-dimensional tensor. A scalar is a single value. Run the following in a new cell:

```
Nx.tensor(10)
```

And you'll see the following output:

```
#Nx.Tensor<
  s64
  10
>
```

Notice there's no output where the shape typically is shown. That's because this is a scalar tensor, and so it has no shape.

Then why do tensors need to have a shape? Remember, the point of tensors is to have a flexible numeric representation of the outside world. If you were to try to represent an image with no semblance of shape, it would be very difficult.

Imagine you have a 28x28 RGB image. Images are typically represented with a shape {num_images, height, width, channels} where channels corresponds to the number of color channels in the image—three in this case for red, green, and blue color values. If you were asked to access the green value of the tenth pixel down and the 3rd pixel towards the center of the image, how would you do that, given only a flat representation of the image? It wouldn't be possible. You would have no idea how the image is laid out in memory. Without any information as to the shape of the image, you can't even be sure how many color channels the image has or what the height and width of the image are.

A tensor's shape helps you naturally map tensors to and from the real world. Also, a tensor's shape tells you how to perform certain operations on the tensor. For example, if tensors didn't have any shape, there would be no way to perform matrix multiplications between two tensors because you would have no understanding of the size of each dimension in your matrices.

To more naturally map a tensor's shape to the real world, Nx implements the concept of *named tensors*. Named tensors introduce dimension or axis names for more idiomatic tensor manipulation. For example, if you have an image, you might have dimension names of :height, width, and :channels. Each dimension name is an atom. You can use dimension names to perform operations on specific dimensions. You can specify the names of a tensor on creation. For example, run the following code:

```
Nx.tensor([[1, 2, 3], [4, 5, 6]], names: [:x, :y])
```

And it will return the following output:

```
#Nx.Tensor<
  s64[x: 2][y: 3]
  [
    [1, 2, 3],
    [4, 5, 6]
  ]
>
```

Notice the shape representation now tells you the size and name of each dimension. Rather than saying dimension 1, you can say dimension :y. Named dimensions give semantic meaning to otherwise meaningless dimension indices.

Tensors Have Data

As previously mentioned, tensor data is stored as a byte array or an Elixir *binary*. A binary is an array of character bytes. These bytes are interpreted as a nested list of values depending on the tensor's shape and type. Representing tensor data in this way helps simplify many Nx implementations. When you create a new tensor using Nx.tensor/2, Nx traverses the values in each list and rewrites the value in a binary representation. To view this binary representation, create a tensor with the following code:

```
a = Nx.tensor([[1, 2, 3], [4, 5, 6]])
```

Now, get the underlying binary representation using Nx.to_binary/1:

```
Nx.to_binary(a)
```

The results will be the following:

```
<<1, 0, 0, 0, 0, 0, 0, 0, 2, 0, 0, 0, 0, 0, 0, 0, 3,
  0, 0, 0, 0, 0, 0, 0, 4, 0, 0, 0, 0, 0, 0, 0, 5,
  0, 0, 0, 0, 0, 0, 0, 6, 0, 0, 0, 0, 0, 0, 0, 0>>
```

Notice the binary representation has no semblance of shape or type. It's literally a flat collection of byte values. Because Nx has to turn your data into a binary representation when you use Nx.tensor/2, it's more performant to instead create tensors using Nx.from_binary/2:

```
<<1::64-signed-native, 2::64-signed-native, 3::64-signed-native>>
|> Nx.from_binary({:s, 64})
```

The <<>> syntax creates an Elixir binary. Note you can construct binaries in the style shown using binary modifiers. The previous code creates the following tensor:

```
#Nx.Tensor<
  s64[3]
  [1, 2, 3]
>
```

Nx.from_binary/2 takes a binary and a type and creates a one-dimensional tensor from the binary data. You can change the shape of the tensor using Nx.reshape/2:

```
<<1::64-signed-native, 2::64-signed-native, 3::64-signed-native>>
|> Nx.from_binary({:s, 64})
|> Nx.reshape({1, 3})
```

This returns the following output:

```
#Nx.Tensor<
  s64[1][3]
  [
    [1, 2, 3]
  ]
>
```

Notice the usage of the native binary modifier. Because Nx operates at the byte level, *endianness* matters. Endianness is the order in which bytes are interpreted or read in the computer. The native modifier tells the virtual machine to use your system's native endianness. If you're attempting to read binary data from a computer with a different endianness than your machine's, you might run into some problems. For the most part, you shouldn't have to worry, but it's something to be conscious of if you need to work with a tensor's raw data.

Tensors Are Immutable

One notable distinction between Nx and other numerical computing libraries is that Nx tensors are immutable, which means that none of Nx's operations change the tensor's underlying properties. Every operation returns a new tensor with new data every time. In some situations, this can be expensive. Nx overcomes the limitation of immutability by introducing a programming model that enables Nx operator fusion. You'll use this programming model in Going from def to defn, on page 40.

Using Nx Operations

Now that you have a better understanding of what a tensor is, it's time to get a better understanding of how to manipulate tensors.

Nx comes with a number of operations you can use and compose into complex mathematical operations and algorithms. There are four common types of operations you should get comfortable with first: shape and type operations, element-wise unary operations, element-wise binary operations, and reductions.

Shape and Type Operations

Shape and type operations work on the shape and type properties of a tensor. Run the following code in a Livebook cell to create a new tensor with shape {3} and type {:s, 64}:

```
a = Nx.tensor([1, 2, 3])
```

Then, run the following code to cast the tensor to type {:f, 32} and change its shape to {1, 3, 1}:

```
a
|> Nx.as_type({:f, 32})
|> Nx.reshape({1, 3, 1})
```

The code returns this tensor:

```
#Nx.Tensor<
  f32[1][3][1]
  [
    [
      [1.0],
      [2.0],
      [3.0]
    ]
  ]
>
```

You'll often need to use Nx.reshape/2 and Nx.as_type/2 to get your data into the proper shape and type for your algorithms. Nx.reshape/2 is a constant-time operation. All it does is return a new tensor with an updated shape; it doesn't manipulate tensor data in any way. Changing a tensor's shape only changes how you interpret a tensor's underlying data. It doesn't change anything about the data.

Nx.as_type/2 does manipulate the tensor's underlying data. It's possible to change the underlying type in constant-time using Nx.bitcast/2. But note that a bitcast will drastically change the values you're working with and is usually not the desired behavior. You can see this by running the following code:

```
Nx.bitcast(a, {:f, 64})
```

After running the code, you'll see this outcome:

```
#Nx.Tensor<
  f64[3]
  [5.0e-324, 1.0e-323, 1.5e-323]
>
```

Notice the values are drastically different from the original ones. That's because you're trying to interpret 64-bit integer bytes as 64-bit float bytes.

Element-wise Unary Operations

Element-wise unary operations are similar to calling Enum.map/2 on a list of data with a mathematical operation. For example, imagine you wanted to calculate the absolute value of every element in a list. Most Elixir programmers would probably implement a solution that looks like this:

```
a = [-1, -2, -3, 0, 1, 2, 3]
Enum.map(a, &abs/1)
```

This would return a list:

```
[1, 2, 3, 0, 1, 2, 3]
```

The code applies &abs/1 to every element in the list. Now, imagine you were given a nested list of lists. Calculating the absolute value of every value in the list would require a nested Enum.map/2. As the degree of nesting increases, so does the difficulty of the problem.

If you were asked to do the same thing with a tensor, you might be tempted to use a solution that resembled your usage of Enum.map/2. But Nx implements a number of operations that work element-wise on the tensor's data, regardless of the degree of nesting present. These operations work on the flattened representation of tensor data while still preserving the tensor's shape. To see this in action, create the following tensor:

```
a = Nx.tensor([[[-1, -2, -3], [-4, -5, -6]], [[1, 2, 3], [4, 5, 6]]])
```

To calculate the absolute value of every value in the tensor, use this:

```
Nx.abs(a)
```

You'll get the following output:

```
#Nx.Tensor<
  s64[2][2][3]
  [
    [
      [1, 2, 3],
      [4, 5, 6]
    ],
    [
      [1, 2, 3],
      [4, 5, 6]
    ]
  ]
>
```

You didn't need any nested maps, loops, or recursion. The solution is a single call to an Nx library function. Nx has a number of functions that work in exactly the same way for computing element-wise square roots, exponentials, logarithms, and so on. If you need to apply a function to every element in a tensor, you should be composing already existing unary operations and not attempting to manually iterate over every value in the tensor. That's because Nx's backends and compilers likely already have efficient routines for Nx operations, which are significantly more efficient than any manual loops or maps you can write by hand.

Element-wise Binary Operations

Inevitably you'll want to add, subtract, multiply, and divide your data. In Elixir, you would probably try to accomplish this task with Enum.zip_with/3. For example, if you wanted to add corresponding elements in each list of data, you would probably do something like this:

```
a = [1, 2, 3]
b = [4, 5, 6]
Enum.zip_with(a, b, fn x, y -> x + y end)
```

It would return this list:

```
[5, 7, 9]
```

Once again, as the level of nesting increases, so does the complexity of the problem. Fortunately, Nx has library functions that take care of this zip-map operation for you. Start by creating the following two tensors:

```
a = Nx.tensor([[1, 2, 3], [4, 5, 6]])
b = Nx.tensor([[6, 7, 8], [9, 10, 11]])
```

Now, add the tensors together with the following code:

```
Nx.add(a, b)
```

This returns the following result:

```
#Nx.Tensor<
  s64[2][3]
  [
    [7, 9, 11],
    [13, 15, 17]
  ]
>
```

You can try a number of other binary operations, such as multiplication:

```
Nx.multiply(a, b)
```

This returns the following output:

```
#Nx.Tensor<
  s64[2][3]
  [
    [6, 14, 24],
    [36, 50, 66]
  ]
>
```

Binary operations work on corresponding elements in two tensors. But what if the tensors aren't the same shape?

If you have tensors with different shapes and you attempt to perform a binary operation on them, Nx will attempt to *broadcast* your tensors together. Broadcasting is the process of repeating an operation over the dimensions of two tensors to make their shapes compatible. For example, what if you wanted to add a scalar tensor and a tensor with shape {3}? You can add the tensors together by broadcasting the scalar over the entire tensor of shape {3}. You would add the scalar to every value in the shape {3} tensor. Two shapes can be broadcast together only when either of the following conditions are met:

1. One of the shapes is a scalar.
2. Corresponding dimensions have the same size OR one of the dimensions is size 1.

For example, the {1, 3, 3, 2} and {4, 1, 3, 2} can be broadcast together because every dimension either matches or nonmatching dimensions are size 1. On the other hand, the shapes {1, 3, 3, 2} and {4, 2, 3, 2} cannot be broadcast together because the second dimension has a mismatch. You can't broadcast 3 to 2, and thus these shapes cannot be broadcast together.

If the ranks of shapes don't match, Nx will try to prepend dimensions of size 1 to the lower rank shape to perform broadcasting. For example, if you try to broadcast the shapes {3} and {2, 3}, it will work because Nx can prepend 1 into the first shape such that you get shape {1, 3}. The shapes {1, 3} and {2, 3} can be broadcast together according to our broadcasting rules.

Try running the following to get a feel for how broadcasting works:

```
Nx.add(5, Nx.tensor([1, 2, 3]))
```

You'll see the following output:

```
#Nx.Tensor<
  s64[3]
  [6, 7, 8]
>
```

Notice the 5 was added to each element in the tensor. You can further see the impact of broadcasting by running this:

```
Nx.add(Nx.tensor([1, 2, 3]), Nx.tensor([[4, 5, 6], [7, 8, 9]]))
```

You'll see the following output:

```
#Nx.Tensor<
  s64[2][3]
  [
    [5, 7, 9],
    [8, 10, 12]
  ]
>
```

Notice how the values in the first tensor are applied to each row of the second tensor.

Reductions

The final type of operation you should get comfortable with in Nx is a reduction operation. Imagine you had a tensor that represented revenues over the last 12 months:

```
revs = Nx.tensor([85, 76, 42, 34, 46, 23, 52, 99, 22, 32, 85, 51])
```

How would you calculate the total revenue across all 12 months? If your data was in a list, you would probably want to use Enum.reduce/3. Nx offers a number of out-of-the-box reductions that allow you to compute aggregates over entire tensors or specific axes. To compute the total revenue, you can use Nx.sum/2:

```
Nx.sum(revs)
```

It returns this:

```
#Nx.Tensor<
  s64
  647
>
```

Nx reductions can work on single axes as well. Imagine you have revenues from the last four years:

```
revs = Nx.tensor(
  [
    [21, 64, 86, 26, 74, 81, 38, 79, 70, 48, 85, 33],
    [64, 82, 48, 39, 70, 71, 81, 53, 50, 67, 36, 50],
    [68, 74, 39, 78, 95, 62, 53, 21, 43, 59, 51, 88],
    [47, 74, 97, 51, 98, 47, 61, 36, 83, 55, 74, 43]
  ], names: [:year, :month])
```

You can compute the total revenue per year or per month by specifying an axis to sum over. If you wanted to know the total revenue for each month over the last four years, you could sum over the :year dimension:

```
Nx.sum(revs, axes: [:year])
```

This returns the following result:

```
#Nx.Tensor<
  s64[month: 12]
  [200, 294, 270, 194, 337, 261, 233, 189, 246, 229, 246, 214]
>
```

Alternatively, you could get the total revenue for each year by summing over :month:

```
Nx.sum(revs, axes: [:month])
```

And it returns this result:

```
#Nx.Tensor<
  s64[year: 4]
  [705, 711, 731, 766]
>
```

The Nx library has a number of reduction functions for computing aggregates over axes or entire tensors. You can compute averages, sums, mins, maxes, and so on.

Representing the World

The purpose of the Nx tensor abstraction is to give you a flexible data structure for representing the real world. Machine learning is applicable to nearly every field. To use machine learning for your applications, you need to choose an appropriate numerical representation for your data. Depending on the type of data you have, there's likely already a common or natural way to represent the data as a tensor.

Tabular Data

Tabular data or structured data is data with a structure similar to what you would find in a relational database or CSV file. Each column represents a feature of the data, such as petal length in the iris example from Chapter 1, Make Machines That Learn, on page 3. You'll often see tabular data represented in a two-dimensional tensor with the shape {num_examples, num_features}.

num_examples corresponds to the total number of examples in your dataset. num_features corresponds to the total number of features in the tabular data.

Encoding information in this way loses some semantic information about what the values in the tensor represent, which needs to be considered when using structured data in a machine learning algorithm. For example, if you have a field that represents home price and another field that represents interest rate, you'd end up with a tensor that contains values with drastically different orders of magnitudes.

Images

If you consider an image as just a collection of pixels, it maps naturally to a tensor. In reality, images are represented as a four-dimensional tensor with the shape {num_examples, height, width, channels}, where num_examples is the number of examples in your dataset, height is the pixel height of the image, width is the pixel width of the image, and channels is the number of color channels in the image. For an RGB image, channels is equal to 3 because for each pixel, there are three color values: red, green, and blue.

You might also see images with the following shape: {num_examples, channels, height, width}. This is a *channels first* representation of an image, whereas the {num_examples, height, width, channels} is a *channels last* representation. The position of the channels dimension differs from framework to framework. Historically, PyTorch—a Python machine learning framework—used channels first configurations for images while TensorFlow used channels last. From a performance perspective, representing an image with the channels last format is a bit faster when performing operations such as convolutions. You'll learn more about working with images in Chapter 7, Learn to See, on page 141.

Video

If you consider a video as a collection of images, then you can easily extend your image representation to represent a video as well. A video is simply a sequence of images where each frame of the video is a tensor representation of an image.

It's common to represent videos with a tensor shape of {num_examples, frames, height, width, channels} where num_examples is the number of examples in your dataset, frames is the number of frames per video example, height is the pixel height of each frame, width is the pixel width of each frame, and channels is the number of color channels in the video. For example, one video filmed at 15 frames per second for four seconds at a resolution of 224x224 with three color channels would have a shape of {1, 60, 224, 224, 3}.

Audio

Audio is represented as a sequence of samples where each sample represents an amplitude or strength of the audio signal at a specific time. The number of samples depends on the audio sampling rate and the total length of a recording. You can also have multiple audio channels. For example, in a stereo audio file, you have samples for left and right speakers. You can represent audio with a shape of {num_examples, samples, channels} where num_examples is the number of examples in the dataset, samples is the number of audio samples in each example, and channels is the number of audio channels in each example.

Text

There are many ways to extract numerical representations of text. You'll use a few common ways to model text throughout this book. In models that make use of deep learning, text is usually *tokenized* in some way.

Tokenization is the process of splitting text into smaller units of representation. For example, you can tokenize text at the character level and then assign a numeric value to each character. You can represent each token with a one-hot encoding or with a numeric value. Remember from Preparing Data for Training, on page 15, one-hot encoding is essentially a binary representation where each index represents the presence of a value. If you have a one-hot encoded representation of the value 0 for a variable with three possible values, the one-hot representation will look like this:

```
#Nx.Tensor<
  u8[3]
  [1, 0, 0]
>
```

After tokenization, you're left with a sequence of numeric values, which means the shape of a numeric representation of text would be {num_examples, sequence_length, token_features} where num_examples is the number of examples in your dataset, sequence_length is the length of each text sequence, and token_features is the size of the feature space for each token. For example, imagine you had 32 text examples, each 255 characters long and tokenized at the character level, and one-hot encoded with 100 possible characters. The shape of your dataset would be {32, 255, 100}.

You can also tokenize text into a sequence of integers such that the shape will end up being {num_examples, sequence_length}. For example, imagine you have these sentences: ["My name is Sean", "I love Elixir"]. Assuming each word in those sentences represents a unique token, your tensor might look something like this:

```
#Nx.Tensor<
  s64[2][4]
  [
    [32, 49, 27, 5],
    [68, 34, 55, 0]
  ]
>
```

Note that the sequence "I love Elixir" has an additional token at the end called a *padding token* such that its sequence length matches the length of all the sequences in the dataset. You'll learn about padding more in Chapter 9, Understand Text, on page 195.

Going from def to defn

So far in this chapter, you've learned about what a tensor is, how to create and manipulate tensors in Nx, and how to model the real world with tensors. This is all great, but you still haven't learned how to unlock the true power of Nx just yet.

If you've been working with Elixir for a while, you've probably heard the argument Elixir and the Erlang Virtual Machine aren't designed for the type of computations required in machine learning and scientific computing. All the examples you've seen in this chapter run in pure Elixir without any acceleration. The lack of acceleration is fine for the examples in this chapter, but for the computations required in machine learning, you'll need acceleration. Enter the magic of defn.

Typical function definitions in Elixir look something like this:

```
defmodule MyModule do

  def adds_one(x) do
    Nx.add(x, 1)
  end

end
```

The code you just saw creates a module named MyModule with a function adds_one, which uses Nx.add/2 to add 1 to the parameter x. When you execute MyModule.adds_one/1, your code will run in pure Elixir without any acceleration. Now, tweak your module to look like this:

```
defmodule MyModule do

  import Nx.Defn

  defn adds_one(x) do
    Nx.add(x, 1)
  end
end
```

You've made two small but significant changes here. First, you added import Nx.Defn, which imports the definition for Nx *numerical definitions*. A numerical definition is an Elixir function that will be *just-in-time (JIT) compiled* using a valid Nx compiler. Just-in-time compilation means that a special version of your function will be compiled when the function is invoked. The function compiled is dependent on the type and shape of the inputs to your function. Second, you should notice the change from def adds_one to defn adds_one. This change actually creates a numerical definition that can be JIT-compiled to the CPU or GPU.

Numerical definitions make use of a multistage programming model. On function invocation, rather than executing the function, Nx computes an expression representation of your program and then gives that expression to an Nx compiler such as EXLA. EXLA traverses the expression and compiles an optimized program from the given expression, which can then be executed on the CPU or GPU. To see this in action, tweak the adds_one/1 function:

```
defn adds_one(x) do
  Nx.add(x, 1) |> print_expr()
end
```

The additional print_expr/1 will output the Nx expression representation of your function. Now, run your function:

```
MyModule.adds_one(Nx.tensor([1, 2, 3]))
```

And you'll see the following:

```
#Nx.Tensor<
  s64[3]

  Nx.Defn.Expr
  parameter a:0    s64[3]
  b = add 1, a     s64[3]
>
```

You can think of an Nx expression as a sort of numerical assembly for your Nx functions. Compilers such as EXLA know how to interpret and work with this assembly to create optimized numerical programs.

Nx compilers and numerical definitions are how Nx gets around the limitation of immutability. Rather than eagerly execute a program with a lot of intermediate data copies, Nx stages computation out to an external compiler such as EXLA, which generates an optimized program that appears to run as a single function call. To see the performance boost offered by Nx compilers first hand, create the following module:

```
defmodule Softmax do
  import Nx.Defn

  defn softmax(n), do: Nx.exp(n) / Nx.sum(Nx.exp(n))
end
```

This code creates a module with a single numerical definition of the *softmax* function. The softmax function is common in machine learning algorithms. You'll see it throughout this book.

Softmax computes a normalized probability distribution based on input weights. That simply means it assigns each input weight a probability between 0 and 1, and the value of all weights sums to 1. One thing to note is that this is actually an unstable implementation of the softmax function—it overflows for large values of n. For simplicity's sake, you don't need to be concerned with that for now. Next, execute the following code:

```
key = Nx.Random.key(42)
{tensor, _key} = Nx.Random.uniform(key, shape: {1_000_000})

Benchee.run(
  %{
    "JIT with EXLA" => fn ->
      apply(EXLA.jit(&Softmax.softmax/1), [tensor])
    end,
    "Regular Elixir" => fn ->
      Softmax.softmax(tensor)
    end
  },
  time: 10
)
```

This code creates a random tensor with one million elements and then runs two benchmarks. The first benchmark uses JIT compilation to execute the softmax function. The second uses regular Elixir to execute the softmax function. You'll see the following output:

```
Operating System: Linux
CPU Information: AMD Ryzen 5 3600 6-Core Processor
Number of Available Cores: 12
Available memory: 31.35 GB
Elixir 1.13.0
Erlang 24.2

Benchmark suite executing with the following configuration:
warmup: 2 s
time: 10 s
memory time: 0 ns
parallel: 1
inputs: none specified
Estimated total run time: 24 s
```

```
Benchmarking JIT with EXLA...
Benchmarking Regular Elixir...

Name                  ips        average  deviation        median
JIT with EXLA      180.60        5.54 ms    ±9.26%        5.51 ms
Regular Elixir       2.33      428.55 ms    ±2.95%      431.50 ms

Comparison:
JIT with EXLA      180.60
Regular Elixir       2.33 - 77.40x slower +423.01 ms
```

This is a 78x speedup just from using JIT compilation. You would probably see even better speedups using a GPU. Rather than explicitly calling EXLA.jit/2, you can tell Nx to always JIT-compile numerical definitions with a given compiler by setting defn options like this:

```
Nx.Defn.global_default_options(compiler: EXLA)
```

Now, run the benchmark again, and you'll see this:

```
Operating System: Linux
CPU Information: AMD Ryzen 5 3600 6-Core Processor
Number of Available Cores: 12
Available memory: 31.35 GB
Elixir 1.13.0
Erlang 24.2

Benchmark suite executing with the following configuration:
warmup: 2 s
time: 10 s
memory time: 0 ns
parallel: 1
inputs: none specified
Estimated total run time: 24 s

Benchmarking JIT with EXLA...
Benchmarking Regular Elixir...

Name                  ips        average  deviation        median
Regular Elixir     192.45        5.20 ms   ±10.15%        5.20 ms
JIT with EXLA      176.71        5.66 ms   ±10.74%        5.62 ms

Comparison:
Regular Elixir     192.45
JIT with EXLA      176.71 - 1.09x slower +0.46 ms
```

Notice the benchmark results are essentially the same. Setting the default compiler tells Nx to always JIT-compile all defn invocations with the given compiler. With a single additional character and some configurations, Nx can give you 75x speedups for numerical applications.

Backend or Compiler?

When working with Nx, you'll encounter two fundamental ways of speeding up your code: backends and compilers. The relationship between backends and compilers is kind of like the relationship between interpreted programming languages and compiled programming languages.

Nx backends are implementations of the Nx library that eagerly evaluate Nx functions. The default Nx backend is Nx.BinaryBackend, which uses pure Elixir to manipulate tensors. Backends evaluate Nx functions and yield the result every time. There's no possibility for fusion or other compiler optimizations. Backends are slower, but you can more rapidly prototype as you don't have to structure your code into modules and numerical definitions. Working with a backend is also more flexible as you don't need to adhere to a numerical definition's strict programming model. You can set a default backend using Nx.default_backend/1:

```
Nx.default_backend(EXLA.Backend)
```

Or, you can use it in your application's configuration:

```
config :nx, default_backend: EXLA.Backend
```

This will tell Nx to use the EXLA backend for every call to Nx in your application.

Compilers implement the multistage programming model mentioned in Going from def to defn, on page 40. Compilers are often more performant, but they require a stricter programming model. You've already seen how you can set the default compiler using Nx.Defn.global_default_options/1:

```
Nx.Defn.global_default_options(compiler: EXLA)
```

You can also set the default compiler in your application's configuration:

```
config :nx, :default_options, [compiler: EXLA]
```

There are some pitfalls when setting a default compiler for your application. To avoid these pitfalls, it's often recommended to only set a default backend, and then explicitly JIT-compile functions when you deem it necessary. You'll see this pattern followed throughout the examples in this book.

Wrapping Up

In this chapter, you learned what a tensor is and how to do some common operations on tensors. You also learned how to use tensors to represent the real world and how to accelerate your Nx code using numerical definitions and JIT compilation. With a better understanding of the principles of Nx, you're ready to start unlocking the power of machine learning. In the next chapter, you'll use your newfound Nx abilities to better understand the math that underlies the machine learning algorithms in this book.

## CHAPTER 3

Harness the Power of Math

In the previous chapter, you learned about the core Nx data structure, the tensor, and the array programming paradigm that Nx encourages. You also used JIT compilation and saw how Nx defn enables acceleration via pluggable backends and compilers, which make machine learning workloads practical in Elixir. Before you start writing some machine learning algorithms, you need to dig a little deeper into the mathematics, which backs modern machine learning.

In this chapter, you'll get a baseline understanding of machine learning math and what it looks like in practice with Nx. This chapter isn't meant to be a comprehensive study of mathematics. Rather, it's meant to give you a better idea about the inner workings of your machine learning algorithms. If you're interested in diving deeper into this topic, check out *Mathematics for Machine Learning [DFO20]*.

Now, fire up a new Livebook and get ready to learn some math.

Understanding Machine Learning Math

Mathematics is the foundation of every scientific field. Machine learning is no different. The earliest machine learning research was born from theoretical mathematical analysis. Researchers working in machine learning lacked sufficient computing power and data to test their ideas. As a result, machine learning was often overlooked in favor of *expert systems* and more logical approaches to artificial intelligence.

Expert systems and logic-based approaches generally centered around the idea that it should be possible to "create" intelligence from a finite set of rules and logical primitives. Programming languages like Prolog stemmed from this belief. Today, with an abundance of computing power and data, machine learning reigns supreme, though it's not necessarily well-grounded in theory—it's much easier to test machine learning ideas than it is to develop the theory to support those ideas.

Many researchers argue that machine learning—especially deep learning— lacks a rigorous mathematical foundation, ultimately inhibiting its progress. Other researchers take a more relaxed stance, feeling that some approaches empirically *just work*, and putting them on a rigorous mathematical foundation is unnecessary. It's probably best to be somewhere in the middle of the "mathematical deference" spectrum. You should understand enough math to know why your algorithms work (or don't work), but it's okay if you don't write proofs for every model you put into practice.

While many areas of mathematics lay at the foundation of machine learning, the biggest are linear algebra, probability, and vector calculus. If you have a STEM background, you likely have experience with some or all of these. If you don't—or you cringe at the thought of computing another *singular-value decomposition* or *derivative* by hand—don't worry. You don't need to go that deep into any of these fields. Having a high-level understanding is attainable with a bit of work. To get you started, the rest of this chapter will provide a surface-level introduction to each of these mathematical fields in the context of machine learning and Nx.

Speaking the Language of Data

You'll often hear linear algebra referred to as the *language of data*. Recall from Chapter 2, Get Comfortable with Nx, on page 21, that Nx tensors give you a powerful and flexible abstraction for modeling and manipulating data. The power of Nx tensors and Nx operations comes from the fact that they build on existing theory and operations in linear algebra. Many of the algorithms you'll see in this book rely heavily on established principles in linear algebra. Deep learning especially leans heavily on the power of linear algebra. In this section, you'll get a quick feel for what linear algebra is all about, and you'll see some linear algebra in action with Nx. This conversation is meant to serve only as an introduction to an in-depth topic. If you'd like to explore deeper, I strongly recommend *Linear Algebra by Gilbert Strang [Str16]* and the 3Blue1Brown YouTube series on Linear Algebra.

Before diving in, open up a new Livebook and install the following dependencies:

```
Mix.install([
  {:nx, "~> 0.5"},
  {:exla, "~> 0.5"},
  {:kino, "~> 0.8"},
```

```
  {:stb_image, "~> 0.6"},
  {:vega_lite, "~> 0.1"},
  {:kino_vega_lite, "~> 0.1"}
])
```

You will be using Nx and EXLA for manipulating tensors to illustrate some mathematical concepts. You should already be familiar with Kino. You will use some of the conveniences Kino provides for working with Livebook. StbImage is a library for loading and manipulating images, as well as for converting images to and from Nx tensors. Finally, you need to install VegaLite[1] and its Kino counterpart. VegaLite is an Elixir library for building graphics. You'll be working with VegaLite quite a bit throughout this book.

Finally, you'll also want to set EXLA to be the default backend by running:

```
Nx.default_backend(EXLA.Backend)
```

Now you're ready to dive in.

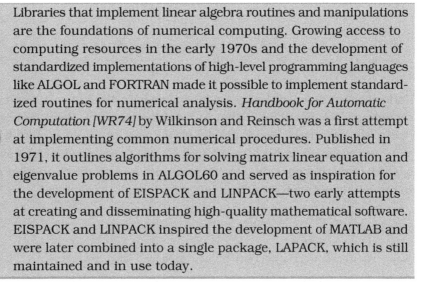

Linear Algebra Routines

Libraries that implement linear algebra routines and manipulations are the foundations of numerical computing. Growing access to computing resources in the early 1970s and the development of standardized implementations of high-level programming languages like ALGOL and FORTRAN made it possible to implement standardized routines for numerical analysis. *Handbook for Automatic Computation [WR74]* by Wilkinson and Reinsch was a first attempt at implementing common numerical procedures. Published in 1971, it outlines algorithms for solving matrix linear equation and eigenvalue problems in ALGOL60 and served as inspiration for the development of EISPACK and LINPACK—two early attempts at creating and disseminating high-quality mathematical software. EISPACK and LINPACK inspired the development of MATLAB and were later combined into a single package, LAPACK, which is still maintained and in use today.

The Building Blocks of Linear Algebra

The fundamental object in linear algebra is the *vector*. You can think of a vector as a collection of numbers that map to some real-world properties. There are different, but somewhat complementary meanings for vectors in computer science, physics, and math. Nx doesn't explicitly differentiate between scalars,

1. https://hexdocs.pm/vega_lite/VegaLite.html

vectors, and matrices. Everything in Nx is a tensor. Vectors are represented as Nx tensors with a rank of 1, or a single-dimensional tensor. In this book, when something is referred to as a vector, it means it's a rank-1 tensor. To help visualize this concept, run the following cell to create a vector with Nx:

```
a = Nx.tensor([1, 2, 3])
b = Nx.tensor([4.0, 5.0, 6.0])
c = Nx.tensor([1, 0, 1], type: {:u, 8})
IO.inspect a, label: :a
IO.inspect b, label: :b
IO.inspect c, label: :c
```

This returns the following tensors:

```
a: #Nx.Tensor<
  s64[3]
  [1, 2, 3]
>
b: #Nx.Tensor<
  f32[3]
  [4.0, 5.0, 6.0]
>
c: #Nx.Tensor<
  u8[3]
  [1, 0, 1]
>
```

Notice how each tensor has a single dimension with a size of 3 and is represented as a list of values. Often in machine learning, these values map to real-world properties. For example, if you were trying to predict whether a stock will move up or down, you might choose to represent stocks as a *vector of stock properties* such as current price, price-to-earnings, market cap, and so on. You could then represent individual stocks as vectors:

```
goog_current_price = 2677.32
goog_pe = 23.86
goog_mkt_cap = 1760
goog = Nx.tensor([goog_current_price, goog_pe, goog_mkt_cap])
```

Another object in linear algebra is the *scalar*. Scalars are just numbers.

In the previous chapter, you learned that scalars are represented as zero-dimensional tensors, for example, tensors with no shape. Most of the time in machine learning and linear algebra, you're concerned with a collection of numbers, rather than individual numbers. But understanding scalars and how to create them is important.

With Nx, you can either represent scalars as tensors or leave them as regular numbers:

```
i_am_a_scalar = Nx.tensor(5)
i_am_also_a_scalar = 5
```

Nx will interpret both variables as scalars when performing operations. For readability, it's typically best not to wrap scalars in the tensor constructor. Scalars are useful for encoding things such as discount rates or factors.

When modeling multiple real-world objects as vectors, you'll probably find a need to represent the objects as a collection in two dimensions. A two-dimensional array of numbers, or a package of vectors, is known as a *matrix*. For example, if you have information regarding multiple stocks, you can encode the entire collection of data as a matrix. In Nx, you can think of a matrix as a tensor with rank-2, for example, a tensor with two dimensions. Run the following code to see what a matrix looks like in Nx:

```
goog_current_price = 2677.32
goog_pe = 23.86
goog_mkt_cap = 1760

meta_current_price = 133.93
meta_pe = 11.10
meta_mkt_cap = 360

stocks_matrix = Nx.tensor([
  [goog_current_price, goog_pe, goog_mkt_cap],
  [meta_current_price, meta_pe, meta_mkt_cap]
])

IO.inspect stocks_matrix
```

The snippet returns the following output:

```
#Nx.Tensor<
  f32[2][3]
  [
    [2677.320068359375, 23.860000610351562, 1760.0],
    [133.92999267578125, 11.100000381469727, 360.0]
  ]
>
```

Notice that a matrix is represented as a two-dimensional grid of numbers. The concept of matrices arises often in linear algebra as they can be conveniently used to represent *linear transformations*. You'll learn more about linear transformations in Linear Transformations, on page 55.

Important Operations in Linear Algebra

Now that you understand the basic building blocks of linear algebra and how they map to Nx data structures, your next task is to learn about some of the most common operations in linear algebra and how they map to Nx. This discussion isn't meant to be a comprehensive introduction to linear algebra and the mechanics of linear algebra operations, but it'll get you started. If you want to know more, read *The Matrix Cookbook [PP08]*.

Vector Addition

Maintaining the property of vector addition is a fundamental characteristic of a vector. For Nx vectors, vector addition computes an *element-wise sum* that adds individual components of vectors to obtain a new vector. An element-wise sum adds individual elements along a tensor. Vector addition is an element-wise sum of rank-1 tensors. For example, imagine you have two vectors encoded as Nx tensors which represent sales of multiple different products in a catalog across two different days:

```
sales_day_1 = Nx.tensor([32, 10, 14])
sales_day_2 = Nx.tensor([10, 24, 21])
```

If you wanted to draw conclusions about sales in the aggregate, you could simply sum the two vectors together using vector addition:

```
total_sales = Nx.add(sales_day_1, sales_day_2)
```

This returns the following:

```
#Nx.Tensor<
  s64[3]
  [42, 34, 35]
>
```

Vector addition adds the individual components of a vector to obtain a new vector. Intuitively, total sales represent the sales per-product across both days. This definition of addition also extends to matrices and other higher-dimensional tensors in Nx. Recall from the previous chapter that Nx tensors also obey specific broadcasting rules. With broadcasting, you can conveniently add vectors to scalars, vectors to matrices, scalars to matrices, and so on.

Scalar Multiplication

The other fundamental property of a vector is scalar multiplication. In Nx, scalar multiplication is a broadcasted multiplication of a scalar and a vector. Imagine you're trying to draw more conclusions about the sales data discussed in Vector Addition, on page 52. For example, you want to determine how your given sales volume will translate to revenue. You assume about 10% of sales will result in an item being returned, which means that only about 90% of each product's sales will count toward revenue. You can represent this discounting with scalar multiplication:

```
sales_day_1 = Nx.tensor([32, 10, 14])
sales_day_2 = Nx.tensor([10, 24, 21])
total_sales = Nx.add(sales_day_1, sales_day_2)

keep_rate = 0.9
unreturned_sales = Nx.multiply(keep_rate, total_sales)
```

This returns the following:

```
#Nx.Tensor<
  f32[3]
  [37.79999923706055, 30.599998474121094, 31.5]
>
```

Of course, you can't sell a percentage of an item. But scalar multiplication is still useful for making a projection into the future. Element-wise multiplication also generalizes out to higher-dimensional tensors in Nx. But it wouldn't be correct to call the element-wise multiplication of two N-dimensional tensors a scalar multiplication. Instead, you'll commonly see element-wise multiplication referred to as a *Hadamard product*—a binary operation that multiplies matrices of the same size, element-wise.

The Hadamard Product

 The Hadamard product is named after mathematician Jacques Hadamard, who is recognized as one of the mathematicians who originally described the properties of the operation.

You can use element-wise multiplication to convert sales totals to revenue. Imagine you have another vector that represents the price of each product. You can multiply price by unreturned sales to get revenue per product:

```
price_per_product = Nx.tensor([9.95, 10.95, 5.99])
revenue_per_product = Nx.multiply(unreturned_sales, price_per_product)
```

This returns the following:

```
#Nx.Tensor<
  f32[3]
  [376.1099853515625, 335.0699768066406, 188.68499755859375]
>
```

Transpose

The *transpose* of a matrix is accomplished by flipping it along its diagonal, where the rows and columns of the matrix are swapped. In Nx, you can take the transpose of a matrix using Nx.transpose/2.

Imagine you've decided to encode your sales data into a matrix. Each row of the matrix represents a day of sales while each column represents the sales data for a given product. You might want to flip this relationship, such that each column represents a day of sales and each row represents a product:

```
sales_matrix = Nx.tensor([
  [32, 10, 14],
  [10, 24, 21]
])
Nx.transpose(sales_matrix)
```

This returns the following:

```
#Nx.Tensor<
  s64[3][2]
  [
    [32, 10],
    [10, 24],
    [14, 21]
  ]
>
```

Notice the rows and columns switch places. The transpose operation also generalizes to higher dimensions. Rather than simply fixing rows and columns, you can permute the dimensions of a tensor. For vectors or one-dimensional tensors in Nx, the transpose operation is an identity operation, returning the tensor identical to the input tensor because Nx doesn't differentiate between row vectors and column vectors. You can see the difference by running the following code:

```
vector = Nx.tensor([1, 2, 3])
Nx.transpose(vector)
```

This code returns the following output:

```
#Nx.Tensor<
  s64[3]
  [1, 2, 3]
>
```

Row Vectors and Column Vectors

In linear algebra, it's common to represent vectors as a column of scalar entries. You can distinguish between vectors with a single column and vectors with a single row by referring to them as row vectors and column vectors respectively. Nx doesn't truly distinguish between row vectors and column vectors. However, languages such as MatLab do. If the distinction is important in your calculations, you can create a rank-2 tensor where one of the dimensions is 1.

Linear Transformations

In machine learning, you'll often see mentions of *linear transformations*. A linear transformation, also known as a linear map, is a function that maps inputs to outputs. Linear transformations are special because they preserve linearity. What this means is that they produce a different representation of an input, while still preserving its fundamental properties. This type of function is useful, for example, when you need to get a different or more convenient representation of the input.

Imagine you have the following image of a cat, and you want to invert the colors.

You can achieve this task using a linear transformation:

```
invert_color_channels = Nx.tensor([
  [-1, 0, 0],
  [0, -1, 0],
  [0, 0, -1]
])

"Cat.jpg"
|> StbImage.read_file!()
|> StbImage.resize(256, 256)
|> StbImage.to_nx()
|> Nx.dot(invert_color_channels)
|> Nx.as_type({:u, 8})
|> Kino.Image.new()
```

After doing so, you'll have a newly color-inverted image:

Most visual transformations map directly to linear transformations. You can use linear transformations to reverse images, rotate images, shear images, and more. Every linear transformation is associated with a matrix and can be thought of as applying matrix multiplication between the input matrix and the transformation matrix.

In Nx, matrix multiplications are done via the Nx.dot/2 operator. Dot products between vectors are treated as normal dot products would be—taking an element-wise product between each vector and then computing the sum. Vector-matrix and matrix-matrix dot products are computed according to the rules of matrix multiplication, meaning that the last dimension of the left-hand side of the operation contracts along the first dimension of the right-hand side of the operation. You can see the semantics of the Nx dot product in action in the following code snippet:

```
vector = Nx.dot(Nx.tensor([1, 2, 3]), Nx.tensor([1, 2, 3]))
vector_matrix = Nx.dot(Nx.tensor([1, 2]), Nx.tensor([[1], [2]]))
matrix_matrix = Nx.dot(Nx.tensor([[1, 2]]), Nx.tensor([[3], [4]]))

vector |> IO.inspect(label: :vector)
vector_matrix |> IO.inspect(label: :vector_matrix)
matrix_matrix |> IO.inspect(label: :matrix_matrix)
```

This code returns the following output:

```
vector: #Nx.Tensor<
  s64
  14
>
```

```
vector_matrix: #Nx.Tensor<
  s64[1]
  [5]
>
matrix_matrix: #Nx.Tensor<
  s64[1][1]
  [
    [11]
  ]
>
```

Don't worry too much if the semantics of the dot product doesn't make much sense. You'll get plenty of practice working with them throughout this book.

Thinking Probabilistically

Now that you understand how linear algebra helps you model data, you're ready to learn how probability helps you think about data and make predictions from it.

A crucial aspect of modern approaches to artificial intelligence is the acceptance of probabilistic methods over logic-based approaches. Earlier generations of researchers believed the secret to creating artificial intelligence was finding enough good formal rules to capture patterns in language, speech, and other areas. Unfortunately, logic-based systems grow exponentially with the difficulty of the problem, and they don't adapt well to chaotic systems. Modern approaches succeed because they embrace uncertainty as a rule.

There are three primary tools used in machine learning to reason about data and make predictions: *probability theory*, *decision theory*, and *information theory*. In this section, you'll learn about all three and how they lay the foundation for modern machine learning algorithms. Once again, this isn't a comprehensive discussion. If you want to dive deeper into the topic, read *Pattern Recognition and Machine Learning [Bis06]* or *Probabilistic Machine Learning [Mur22]*.

Reasoning About Uncertainty

Probability theory is a framework for understanding uncertainty. Recall that earlier approaches to artificial intelligence relied on enumerating formal logic-based rules to come to conclusions about data. With perfect information and infinite computing power, logic-based approaches would yield perfect results. In this context, "perfect information" means you have access to every scenario your algorithm will be exposed to in practice.

Imagine you were given the task of designing a machine that sorts coins. You were guaranteed your machine will only ever be given US denominations—specifically quarters, dimes, nickels, and pennies. You have access to "perfect information," and you can design a system that handles all four cases correctly. For example, because you know the specifications of each case ahead of time, you can design a machine that sorts coins based on their size. Unfortunately, this "perfect information" scenario requires strong assumptions that break down in real-world contexts:

1. You assume your machine will only ever encounter four coins in US denominations. What if somebody accidentally gives your machine a half-dollar or a gold-dollar? What happens if somebody gives your machine a non-US coin?

2. You assume all of the coins fed to your machine will perfectly match the specs of one of the four scenarios you expect. What if some of the coins are damaged? What if some of the coins are stuck together? What if the US mint incorrectly mints a quarter the size of a dime?

3. Is sorting by size a perfect method? Is it possible you've built the machine imperfectly and occasionally a dime might slip in with the pennies?

You'll see that uncertainty is a fact of life, and while in some applications it makes sense to ignore uncertainty, in others it's best to fully embrace it. For example, if you wanted to design an algorithm that detects images that contain birds, you couldn't possibly enumerate every species of bird, their possible orientations in the images, the environments the images were taken in, and so on. Machine learning shines in uncertain situations because uncertainty is a built-in assumption.

Very few applications are absolutely certain. In the *Deep Learning Book* *[GBC16]*, the authors identify three sources of uncertainty that will pop up in every problem:

1. Inherent stochasticity. Some problems are inherently *stochastic*. That means a source of uncertainty or randomness is built in. No matter what, the outcome isn't deterministic.

2. Incomplete observability. If you don't know all of the variables dictating the behavior of a system, the system will always have an element of uncertainty. In machine learning, you'll never have access to every variable that dictates an outcome.

3. Incomplete modeling. Some models discard information intentionally. For example, it's common to downsample images for faster processing. Downsampling intentionally discards some information, and thus you cannot fully model the problem at hand.

Given you'll inevitably encounter sources of uncertainty when creating models, you need to understand how to quantify uncertainty, interpret uncertain quantities, and use uncertainty to your advantage.

In mathematics and machine learning, *probability* is a measure or quantification of uncertainty. You're probably familiar with probability in the traditional sense. No doubt, you were introduced to probability as the likelihood of an event occurring in the long run. Your understanding of probability equips you to answer questions such as, if you have two red balls and three blue balls in a hat, what is the probability you'll draw a red ball? Probability from the *frequentist perspective* as it's presented in the previous question represents the long-run frequencies of events. The frequentist interpretation of probability places an emphasis on repeated trials. As an example, in a Livebook cell, run the following code:

```
simulation = fn key ->
  {value, key} = Nx.Random.uniform(key)
  if Nx.to_number(value) < 0.5, do: {0, key}, else: {1, key}
end
```

This function creates a scalar random variable using the Nx.Random module and converts it to a regular Elixir number. Note that Nx makes use of stateless pseudo-random number generators (PRNGs), which means you need to explicitly pass a key every time you want a random number. Nx.Random.uniform/1 and similar functions return an updated key that you can pass to a subsequent random function to get a different result. Passing the same key to one of Nx's random functions with the same parameters will result in deterministic behavior.

After creating a random number, the simulation checks the variable. If the variable is less than 0.5, it returns 0, and if the variable is greater than or equal to 0.5, it returns 1. The simulation also returns the updated key for use in subsequent runs of the simulation.

Assuming the random number generator is perfectly random, how many times do you think this function will return 1 if you run it 10 times? 100 times? 1,000 times? 10,000 times? Run the following code to see the results:

```
key = Nx.Random.key(42)

for n <- [10, 100, 1000, 10000] do
  Enum.map_reduce(1..n, key, fn _, key -> simulation.(key) end)
  |> elem(0)
  |> Enum.sum()
  |> IO.inspect()
end
```

And, after about two minutes, you'll see this result:

```
6
49
501
5025
```

Notice how the frequency of a 1 occurring starts to converge to about half the time as you increase the number of trials. This means that if you were to run this simulation *forever*, one out of every two events would be a 1.

In this example, you can say the probability of the simulation returning a 1 is 0.5. From the frequentist perspective, a probability of 0.5 means that for an infinite number of trials, an event would occur exactly one time out of every two trials. The probability of the event occurring in an infinite time frame gives you a framework for discussing the expected results of a single simulation. The result of a single simulation has uncertainty built in. You can't come up with a logic-based rule to assess the result of individual runs. Instead, you can quantify the results of a single simulation with a probability that helps you express the uncertainty of the event.

Not So Random

 In reality, random number generators on the computer don't produce truly random numbers, so the true probability of drawing a 1 is likely slightly skewed in one direction or another—albeit likely within a small level of precision. Random number generators on computers are often pseudo-random number generators with a very large period. That means they start repeating the same sequence after a finite number of draws. On an infinite scale, the probability of a PRNG drawing a 1 is equal to the observed probability of it drawing a 1 during one full period.

All About Bayes

The frequentist interpretation of probability is useful and easy to understand in scenarios that are easily repeatable, but some applications aren't concerned with easily repeatable trials. For example, if a doctor predicts there's a 60% chance a patient has some disease, what do they really mean? The doctor isn't really making a statement about the patient having a disease over an infinite number of trials (unless they believe in an infinite number of universes). Instead, the doctor is presenting a quantification of uncertainty that the patient has the disease given the information available to them. The bayesian perspective is fundamentally tied to available information, and probabilities are updated as more information becomes available.

One famous example of the bayesian interpretation in action is the *Monty Hall problem*. The Monty Hall problem is named after the host of "Let's Make a Deal." In the show, contestants are presented with a choice between three doors. One door has a prize behind it, such as a sports car, while the other doors have "Zonks," or prizes that you didn't want. After a contestant picks a door, the host, Monty Hall, opens one of the unpicked doors that contains a Zonk. Then Monty gives the contestant an opportunity to switch between the original door and the other remaining unopened door.

The problem is concerned with the optimal strategy when you're presented with the option to switch or keep the original door after being shown a Zonk behind one of the doors. Mathematically speaking, you should *always* switch because the probability the prize is behind the unopened door is 2/3—much higher than the probability that the prize is behind your originally picked door. At first, this might not make much sense. The probability of each door containing the prize started at 1/3. But remember, you need to update your assessment based on the available information. The probability the prize is behind the door the contestant picks is 1/3, and the probability the prize isn't behind the door the contestant picks is 2/3. After Monty Hall opens one of the doors and reveals a Zonk, the probability the prize isn't behind your door "concentrates" on the remaining unpicked door.

The Monty Hall problem is a classic illustration of *Bayes' Theorem* in action. Bayes' Theorem describes the *conditional probability* of an event based on available information or the occurrence of another event. Bayes' Theorem is a rule describing how probabilities should be updated in the face of new evidence.

You can see this outcome visually in the table on page 62.

Notice how in six of the nine scenarios where you choose to switch, you win a car.

Door with car	I chose	If stay	If switch
A	A	Win car	Win goat
A	B	Win goat	Win car
A	C	Win goat	Win car
B	A	Win goat	Win car
B	B	Win car	Win goat
B	C	Win goat	Win car
C	A	Win goat	Win car
C	B	Win goat	Win car
C	C	Win car	Win goat

As you read this book, you'll get a stronger feel for the mechanics of manipulating probabilities. Additionally, you'll see why the bayesian perspective on probability fits in nicely with machine learning. Humans are natural practitioners of bayesian probability. As you go through life gaining new information, you update your estimates. You are making *inferences* or predictions about your surroundings. Machine learning models do the same thing. But what do you do after making predictions? You make decisions.

Making Decisions

Imagine that you've been told that your favorite sports team has a 60% chance of winning their next game. You're then asked to make a bet on that game. How do you decide? You use *decision theory*. Decision theory provides a framework for acting optimally in the presence of uncertainty.

When making decisions in the presence of uncertainty, you first need to consider your goals. In the betting example, your goal is to make money, so it might not make sense to bet on the team with a 60% chance of winning their next game because the potential reward may be too low. This same logic applies to machine learning models as well. You need to consider the objective of your model to make decisions after inference.

Typically, making decisions after inference is easier. For example, if you have a model that predicts the probability that an image is an apple versus an orange, and your goal is to maximize accuracy, you'd want to classify the object as an apple if the probability that it's an apple is greater than 0.5. If it's not, classify the image as an orange. This rule, based on inference probabilities, represents a *decision boundary*. Imagine a line in space: if your prediction falls on one side, you take one action, and if it falls on the other, you take the other action.

Of course, there are also more complex scenarios to consider in machine learning. For example, rather than only maximizing accuracy, you might want to also maximize reward or minimize cost. Again, if you imagine the betting example, choosing to bet on the given sports team might not be the best choice even though you're more certain your team will win than lose. This is because the action has an associated cost or risk.

A final scenario to consider when making decisions from probabilities involves making no decision at all. Depending on the application, it might make sense to take no action based on a given probability. For example, imagine your apples and oranges classifier is given a picture of a banana, and it spits out a probability that makes you think it's unsure about which class the image belongs to. In this instance, it would be correct to not classify the image as an apple or an orange.

Learning from Observations

The final tool you should be aware of in probabilistic machine learning is information theory. Information theory provides a framework for reasoning about information in systems. Information theory was pioneered by mathematician Claude Shannon in his *Mathematical Theory of Communication [Sha48]*.

Information theory is the mathematical study of coding information in sequences and symbols and the study of how much information can be stored and transmitted in these mediums. Typically, information theory is thought of in the context of communications and signals; however, information theory provides a strong foundation for the development of machine learning algorithms.

To understand how information theory fits in, let's consider an example. Say you always see your neighbor walking by your house every day at the same time. Without fail, day after day, your neighbor walks by at the same time. What new information do you glean from seeing your neighbor walk by every day? Outside of what you immediately observe, you can't gather much else. Your neighbor's walks are essentially a certainty. But what if one day you don't see your neighbor walk by? What do you learn? Has something happened? How surprised are you? In information theory, we are concerned with the degree of surprise of a particular observation. Observing your neighbor on their daily walk isn't surprising. Not observing your neighbor on their daily walk is surprising.

Tracking Change

If you've dabbled a little in machine learning, you more than likely have heard of words like *derivative, gradient,* and *automatic differentiation.* All of these terms come from vector calculus.

Vector calculus is concerned with the *differentiation* and *integration* of *vector fields* or functions. If you're not a math person, all of this probably sounds a bit overwhelming. Fortunately, you don't need to have an intimate understanding of these concepts; you only need to be familiar with them. If you don't get confused when somebody says "differentiable function," you probably know enough calculus for machine learning. In this section, you'll go through a bit of vocabulary and see how vector calculus relates to machine learning. Then you'll see how Nx does most of the heavy lifting for you.

Understanding Differentiation

The most important concept from calculus to understand in machine learning (and to even understand in calculus) is the *derivative.* A derivative is a measure of the instantaneous rate of change of a function. A classic example of a derivative is position and velocity. Let's say you have a function that plots your position on a fixed axis over time. The derivative of your position function gives you your velocity, or how fast your position is changing at a given point in time. For example, if you were plotting the height of a rocket over time, its position would correspond to its height, and the velocity would correspond to how fast the rocket is moving (for example, how fast the position is changing).

You can visualize the derivative of a function at a given point as the line that runs tangent to that point or *just touches* it:

But why should you care so much about derivatives? If you have taken a calculus class, you might remember using derivatives to find local (and global) maxima and minima by hand. Visually, you can see that the derivative at the maximum and minimum of this function shown on the following interval is 0:

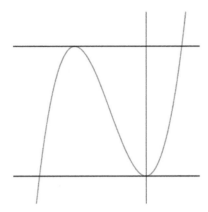

Given a function, you can compute its derivative by hand to determine which input maximizes or minimizes the function. For example, imagine you ran a berry farm and had access to an analytic which projected profits based on the number of berry trees planted for a given year. To maximize profits for the year, you could compute the derivative of your profit function to determine the quantity of berry trees that maximizes profit. Nx makes the process of finding derivatives easy. For example, consider you have this function which models the profit of your berry farm given an input variable x for the number of berry trees planted in a year:

```
defmodule BerryFarm do
  import Nx.Defn

  defn profits(trees) do
    trees
    |> Nx.subtract(1)
    |> Nx.pow(4)
    |> Nx.negate()
    |> Nx.add(Nx.pow(trees, 3))
    |> Nx.add(Nx.pow(trees, 2))
  end
end
```

You can visualize this function with VegaLite, Elixir's bindings to the Vega plotting library, by running this code:

```
trees = Nx.linspace(0, 4, n: 100)
profits = BerryFarm.profits(trees)

alias VegaLite, as: Vl

Vl.new(title: "Berry Profits", width: 1440, height: 1080)
|> Vl.data_from_values(%{
  trees: Nx.to_flat_list(trees),
  profits: Nx.to_flat_list(profits)
})
|> Vl.mark(:line, interpolate: :basis)
|> Vl.encode_field(:x, "trees", type: :quantitative)
|> Vl.encode_field(:y, "profits", type: :quantitative)
```

After running it, you'll see the following plot:

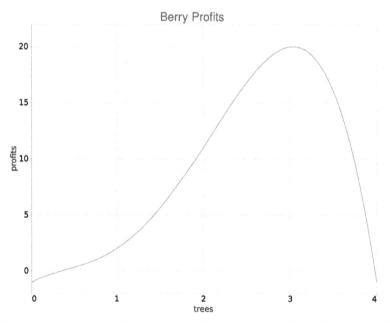

Using Nx, you can compute and visualize the derivative of your profits, or
how your profits change with respect to the number of trees by adding the
following function to your BerryFarm module:

```
defmodule BerryFarm do
  import Nx.Defn

  defn profits(trees) do
    -((trees - 1) ** 4) + (trees ** 3) + trees ** 2
  end

  defn profits_derivative(trees) do
    grad(trees, &profits/1)
  end
end
```

Now you can plot the profits function and its derivative overlayed by running this:

```
trees = Nx.linspace(0, 3, n: 100)
profits = BerryFarm.profits(trees)
profits_derivative = BerryFarm.profits_derivative(trees)

alias VegaLite, as: Vl

title = "Berry Profits and Profits Rate of Change"
Vl.new(title: title, width: 1440, height: 1080)
|> Vl.data_from_values(%{
  trees: Nx.to_flat_list(trees),
  profits: Nx.to_flat_list(profits),
  profits_derivative: Nx.to_flat_list(profits_derivative)
})
|> Vl.layers([
  Vl.new()
  |> Vl.mark(:line, interpolate: :basis)
  |> Vl.encode_field(:x, "trees", type: :quantitative)
  |> Vl.encode_field(:y, "profits", type: :quantitative),

  Vl.new()
  |> Vl.mark(:line, interpolate: :basis)
  |> Vl.encode_field(:x, "trees", type: :quantitative)
  |> Vl.encode_field(:y, "profits_derivative", type: :quantitative)
  |> Vl.encode(:color, value: "#ff0000")
])
```

Then, you'll see the following plot:

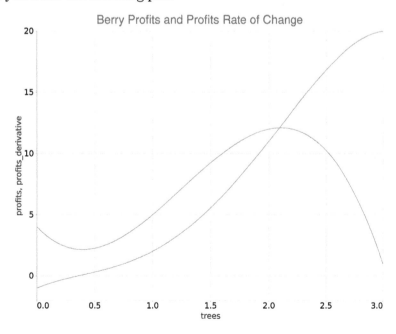

One thing you should notice is that the derivative of your profit function is 0 at exactly the same time your profit function maxes out. By tracing the derivative until it reaches 0, you can find the maximums and minimums of the original function.

In this berry farm example, you used the grad/2 function inside a numerical definition. But why is this function called grad/2 and not derivative or something else? grad/2 is an Nx function that's capable of taking the *gradient* of a function.

The gradient is the direction of greatest change of a scalar function. You can think of a scalar function as an Nx function which takes a rank-N tensor as input and returns a scalar tensor as output. The gradient is like a heat-seeking missile attracted to change. For high-dimensional inputs, you can compute the gradient to find the maximums and minimums. Consider an example. Say you are on a boat in a lake. You've been asked to find the location of the deepest point in the lake as quickly as possible, using just a depth finder. You're dropped off in the middle of the lake and don't have time to map out the depth at each point in the lake. How do you solve this problem? One method is to compute the depth change in every direction and always travel in the direction of steepest descent. That way you can guarantee you're always following a path toward a deeper point in the lake. If the bottom of the lake resembles a valley, you're guaranteed to find the steepest point.

Finding the deepest point in the lake using the direction of steepest descent is the same process used in gradient descent to optimize objective functions in machine learning. Gradient descent is useful because you don't often have access to the complete gradient of your objective function—just like you don't have access to depth changes in the lake. Instead, you need to look at a few samples at a time and move accordingly.

Throughout this book, you'll use gradients to optimize the parameters of models in order to maximize performance on some machine learning tasks. In many of the examples you'll implement in this book, the usage of grad/2 will be abstracted away; but you'll still need to break it out a few times. So, what is grad/2 and how does it work?

Automatic Differentiation with defn

One of the key features of Nx is its ability to perform automatic differentiation. Automatic differentiation is the process of computing derivatives from programs. It's far more accurate than numerically approximating gradients, and it's far more efficient than symbolic differentiation. Automatic differentiation is a rich field of research.

In this section, you'll see how you can use Nx to calculate the gradient of a simple function so you can use the power of Nx to optimize more complex models later on. For a more in-depth treatment of automatic differentiation, check out *Evaluating Derivatives [GW08]*.

Nx defn allows you to calculate the derivative of a scalar function using the grad function. Start by creating the following scalar function in a new module:

```
defmodule GradFun do
  import Nx.Defn

  defn my_function(x) do
    x
    |> Nx.cos()
    |> Nx.exp()
    |> Nx.sum()
    |> print_expr()
  end
end
```

This function takes the *element-wise cosine*, followed by the *element-wise exponential* of an input tensor, before taking the sum of the entire tensor. Both the element-wise cosine and element-wise exponential apply mathematical functions to each element in the input. The element-wise cosine applies the cosine function, while the element-wise exponential applies the exponential function. Remember, gradients are the direction of steepest change for scalar functions, so your function must return a scalar tensor. Additionally, gradients are only valid for continuous value functions, so your function must return a floating-point type.

Next, add the following function to your module:

```
defn grad_my_function(x) do
  grad(x, &my_function/1) |> print_expr()
end
```

Here, you take the gradient of my_function and return its value. You also inspect the gradient expression for my_function. The complete module looks like this:

```
defmodule GradFun do
  import Nx.Defn

  defn my_function(x) do
    x
    |> Nx.cos()
    |> Nx.exp()
    |> Nx.sum()
    |> print_expr()
  end
```

```
  defn grad_my_function(x) do
    grad(x, &my_function/1) |> print_expr()
  end
end
```

Now, run the following cell to obtain the gradient of a given input tensor:

```
GradFun.grad_my_function(Nx.tensor([1.0, 2.0, 3.0]))
```

You'll see these outputs:

```
#Nx.Tensor<
  f32

  Nx.Defn.Expr
  parameter a:0                             f32[3]
  b = cos a                                 f32[3]
  c = exp b                                 f32[3]
  d = sum c, axes: nil, keep_axes: false    f32
>
#Nx.Tensor<
  f32[3]

  Nx.Defn.Expr
  parameter a:0       f32[3]
  b = cos a           f32[3]
  c = exp b           f32[3]
  d = sin a           f32[3]
  e = negate d        f32[3]
  f = multiply c, e   f32[3]
>
#Nx.Tensor<
  f32[3]
  [-1.444406509399414, -0.5997574925422668, -0.05243729427456856]
>
```

First, take note of the two expression outputs. The first expression is the original function, but you never invoked the original function. So how is this possible? Under the hood, Nx is actually executing a *forward pass* or *evaluation trace* of the original function given your inputs. Nx computes the forward expression, and then recursively applies the *chain-rule* backwards through the forward trace to obtain the gradient of the original function. This backwards evaluation of the chain-rule is called *backpropagation* or *reverse-mode automatic differentiation*. If you're familiar with the differentiation rules for the functions used in my_function/1, the connection between the first and second expressions should be obvious. The derivative of cos(x) is negate(sin(x)), and the derivative of exp(x) is exp(x). You can see Nx computed both of those derivatives for you, and correctly applied the chain-rule by composing the derivatives of the decomposed function. You can more easily visualize it here, where d indicates the derivative of an expression:

```
paramater a:0    ->   da = a
b = cos a        ->   db = negate(sin(a))
c = exp b        ->   dc = multiply(exp(b), db)
```

Notice that computing the derivative of the original function is essentially as easy as recursively computing derivatives of intermediate functions. You transform your original function into a new one by transforming the intermediate expressions with established gradient rules. If you're interested in a deeper dive, the Nx source code is a great place to look and understand what's going on under the hood.

Forward or Backward?

 Nx strictly uses reverse-mode automatic differentiation, which is common in most automatic differentiation libraries. An alternative mode of differentiation is forward-mode, in which you evaluate the derivative at the same time as you evaluate the actual expression itself. There are compute and memory trade-offs to both modes of differentiation. Some libraries, such as JAX, can compute both forward- and reverse-mode gradients and even combine modes for more efficient gradient computations.

The output tensor represents the vector with the maximum rate of change with respect to your original input. So why does this matter? *Gradient-based optimization* is a powerful form of optimization and is widely used in machine learning, especially deep learning. With automatic differentiation, all you need is an objective function and you can optimize it with respect to some model parameters.

Nx's automatic differentiation can backpropagate through complex expressions and with wide operator coverage. In the spirit of the original *Autograd paper [Mac16]*, Nx allows you to focus on writing objective functions for your models and to let Nx take care of the differentiation for you. There are a number of other unique applications of automatic differentiation in simulations, graphics rendering, and more.

Wrapping Up

In this chapter, you learned about the high-level mathematical concepts used in machine learning algorithms. You now have a better understanding of the foundations your future models will build on and the resources and tools you'll need to study the math further. In the next chapter, you'll see some of this math tie together, and you'll see how to frame machine learning problems as optimization problems.

## CHAPTER 4

Optimize Everything

In the previous chapter, you read about the three pillars of machine learning math: linear algebra, probability, and vector calculus. Even so, you may not understand how they fit together to form the foundations of machine learning because you haven't seen anything concrete. In this chapter, you'll discover how these topics help to frame machine learning as an optimization problem, and more importantly, you'll implement real techniques for solving that optimization problem.

Learning with Optimization

Optimization is the search for the best. But how does this have anything to do with learning? Recall from Chapter 1, Make Machines That Learn, on page 3, that you can define a machine learning system as any computing system that's capable of improving from experience with a specific task according to some arbitrary performance measure. The end goal is to have a system capable of providing predictions about unseen examples. Fundamentally, you want an interface that looks something like this:

```
def predict(input) do
  label = do_something(input)
  label
end
```

At its core, a trained machine learning system transforms inputs into labels. But what do these transformations look like? Is a machine learning algorithm synthesizing some sort of decision-making program under the hood that assigns labels based on some ever-changing rules to each input? For some algorithms, you could justifiably argue that's what's happening. However, it makes more sense to think about these transformations visually as shown in the scatterplot on page 74.

In this scatterplot, notice the relationship between inputs X and outputs Y. How would you draw a line to minimize the total distance between the line and every example in that scatterplot? Then, using the line you just drew, how would you make predictions about the Y value of the new X inputs? Take a step back, and you'll start to see that the line you drew is a visual representation of the do_something function in predict.

When given an unseen input X, you can predict its expected output Y by following the line. If you can recall your primary school math lessons, you'll remember that lines are nothing more than visualizations of two parameters: m, or the slope of the line, and b, or the intercept of the line. When you consider the line you drew is a visual representation of the transformation occurring in the predict function, you can understand the function looks more like this:

```
def predict(input, m, b) do
  label = m * input + b
  label
end
```

Here, input is equivalent to X; label is equivalent to Y; and m and b are the parameters of the line you drew.

All of this is to say that machine learning, in practice, revolves around finding input parameters that best transform inputs into labels. But the form these parameters assume won't always look like m and b. This demonstration is a simplified example of *linear regression* in two dimensions—more about linear regression in Chapter 5, Traditional Machine Learning, on page 95.

In practice, the forms of the transformations and parameters in your machine learning algorithm will vary from problem to problem and will typically have much higher *dimensionality*. So, rather than fixating on m and b, it's more practical and generalized to say that predict looks something more like this:

```
def predict(input) do
  label = f(input, params)
  label
end
```

Here, f represents the transformation performed by your machine learning algorithm of choice, and params represent the learned parameters for your algorithm. The goal is to find the parameters that best map inputs to labels with the function. Ideally, you want params for f that yield the best performance on the task at hand. You want to *optimize* params to achieve the best performance on your task.

Minimizing Risk to Maximize Performance

Machine learning boils down to finding the best parameters for a model. Recall from Chapter 1, Make Machines That Learn, on page 3, that a machine learning system's performance is measured on an unseen test set. You also saw this in the previous section of this chapter.

If the goal is to end up with a predict function whose parameters are optimized to correctly assign labels to unseen inputs, you might be wondering: how do you optimize something you can't observe?

Rather than optimize for performance on an unobserved test set, you optimize for performance on an available training set. In doing this, you hope that the training set will capture enough of the features of the unseen test set that your model's parameters are able to optimally assign labels to unseen inputs.

During training, you define a *loss function*, or *cost function*, that you then attempt to optimize according to your model's parameters. The parameterized loss function is your overall objective function. The relationship between the model, parameters, loss function, and objective function in a machine learning problem looks something like the following Elixir code:

```
def model(params, inputs) do
  labels = f(params, inputs)
  labels
end

def loss(actual_labels, predicted_labels) do
  loss_value = measure_difference(actual_labels, predicted_labels)
  loss_value
end

def objective(params, actual_inputs, actual_labels) do
  predicted_labels = model(params, actual_inputs)
  loss(actual_labels, predicted_labels)
end
```

model is a function that uses params to transform inputs into labels. loss is a function that measures the difference between an actual label and a predicted label. Loss functions are supposed to give some indication or measure of correctness.

Suppose you wanted to train a model to predict the number of total points that both teams will score in an NBA game. You could measure loss as the squared difference, or *squared error*, between the actual score of a given game and the model's predicted score. If the model predicts a combined score will be 242, and the actual combined score is 245, the loss for this game is 9. You'll see many different types of loss functions in Defining Objectives, on page 77.

Also, notice that the objective function is the loss function parameterized with your model and parameters. The objective function measures the loss of your model with respect to true training examples. The process of *learning* in machine learning boils down to optimizing an objective function.

You can optimize objective functions with any of a number of known optimization techniques or solvers. Some objective functions can be solved analytically, while others require numerical optimization to find approximate solutions to the optimization problem.

As you now know, machine learning relies heavily on optimization—so much that it might be difficult to see how machine learning differs from pure optimization or curve fitting. Consider this: machine learning is concerned with performance on unseen inputs. More specifically, it's concerned with reducing *generalization errors* on unseen inputs.

In statistical learning theory, generalization error is also known as *risk*, and your goal is to minimize risk. However, you can't optimize for risk when you don't have access to the entire distribution of possible inputs to your model.

So instead, you optimize *empirical risk*, which is the performance of your model on the *empirical distribution* or training set.

Theoretically, the empirical distribution has some equivalence to the true distribution of inputs, so minimizing empirical risk is equivalent to minimizing true risk. In practice, there are always sources of errors when trying to capture infinite distributions with finite data and computing power.

The process of minimizing empirical risk is known as *empirical risk minimization (ERM)* and is a key distinction between pure optimization and machine learning. When you have access to an entire distribution, you can minimize risk directly with optimization. When you don't, you can minimize risk indirectly by minimizing empirical risk. The first case is an optimization problem; the second case is a machine learning problem.

Defining Objectives

The definition of *best parameters* for a model is subject to the constraints and objectives put forth by you when defining your machine learning task. Remember from Chapter 1, Make Machines That Learn, on page 3, that you need to define SMART tasks when designing machine learning systems. This need becomes evident during the training process of machine learning.

Additionally, machine learning algorithms almost never directly optimize for the performance measures you actually care about. For example, you'll not find a machine learning algorithm that directly optimizes for the accuracy or classification error of a model. Instead, machine learning algorithms use *surrogate loss functions*.

Surrogate loss functions serve as proxies for true objectives. These loss functions are typically much easier to optimize, and optimizing them also indirectly optimizes the performance objectives you care about. For example, it's much more common to use squared error as a surrogate for absolute error because the squared error function has properties that make optimization easier. The choice of surrogate loss function often depends on the machine learning task and the type of model.

For the rest of this section, you'll do the following:

- Study two of the most common loss functions used in machine learning.
- Learn about why and when they're used.
- See how they relate to some of the probability lessons you read about in the previous chapter.

Likelihood Estimation

At this point, you might be wondering what loss functions actually measure. To answer that question, you first need to understand *likelihood*.

In statistics, the *likelihood function* (or simply "likelihood") describes the probability of observed data as a function of its parameters. Think of likelihood as a sort of truth meter. Statistical learning theory assumes there exists some true function that generates data, maybe something like this:

```
def datagen(true_params) do
  true_f(true_params)
end
```

In this example, datagen is a data-generating function with a true model true_f and true parameters true_params. The datagen/1 function can represent any distribution of data.

Let's assume datagen/1 is the data-generating function for a series of winning lottery numbers. You have a series of lottery numbers and want to know the likelihood that those are winning numbers. If you have access to true_params and true_f, you can measure the likelihood by measuring the difference between your lottery numbers and multiple samples of winning numbers generated by datagen/1.

This scenario is a bit unrealistic because you rarely have access to perfect information about data-generating functions and their parameters. A more likely scenario is that you have a number of winning lottery tickets and want to recover the true function that generates winning lottery numbers. You start by creating an estimate of the original true_f and true_params:

```
def estimate_datagen(estimate_params) do
  estimate_f(estimate_params)
end
```

Now, you can measure the likelihood of estimate_params generating your winning lottery tickets, which essentially amounts to measuring the similarity or distance between your estimate of the data-generating function and the true data-generating function.

After measuring the similarity between your estimated data-generator and the true data generator, you update estimate_params with some optimization routine and try again. You optimize estimate_params to maximize the likelihood that estimate_params are the same parameters that generated your winning lottery tickets. In statistical learning theory, this optimization process is known as *maximum likelihood estimation (MLE)*. When using the maximum likelihood estimator, your loss function is a measure of similarity between functions.

Cross-Entropy

In machine learning, you'll commonly see the term *cross-entropy* used in the context of classification tasks. The meaning of cross-entropy in these contexts is given by the following function (assuming a binary classification task):

```
defn binary_cross_entropy(y_true, y_pred) do
  y_true * Nx.log(y_pred) - (1 - y_true) * Nx.log(1 - y_pred)
end
```

This function assumes y_true is a label of 0 or 1, representing a binary class; and y_pred is a probability between 0 and 1, predicting the true label y_true.

Cross-entropy as a loss function can also be used for categorical classification tasks, where the number of possible classes extends out indefinitely. The definition of cross-entropy as a loss function only for classification tasks isn't necessarily true in an academic sense. However, its usage in the context of classification problems is a convention in machine learning frameworks.

Numerical Stability

 The given implementation of binary cross-entropy may not be numerically stable in all cases. You should use the implementations from around the Nx ecosystem in Axon and Scholar.

Mean Squared Error

Mean squared error measures per-example loss as the average squared difference between true labels and predicted labels. You can implement mean squared error in Nx using the following code:

```
defn mean_squared_error(y_true, y_pred) do
  y_true
  |> Nx.subtract(y_pred)
  |> Nx.pow(2)
  |> Nx.mean(axes: [-1])
end
```

Mean squared error is often used in place of *absolute error* when optimizing objectives for regression tasks. Absolute error is the absolute difference between true labels and predicted labels. It's computed as Nx.abs(Nx.subtract(y_true, y_pred)). Mean squared error is always a nonnegative value (assuming you're only dealing with real values) because the difference between y_true and y_pred is squared.

Converging to a Solution

One thing to be aware of as you continue your machine learning journey is the concept of *convergence* in the context of optimization and machine learning. Most of the optimization algorithms used in machine learning don't have any guarantees of optimality. This means they don't guarantee they'll find the best set of model parameters.

The best set of model parameters is the *global optima* of the entire parameter space. With infinite parameter spaces and functions that cannot be optimized analytically, finding the global optima is impossible. Instead, optimization routines are mechanical and designed to loop until some desired performance threshold.

While it's nearly impossible to find the global optima in high-parameter spaces, it's possible for your models to converge on the *local optima*. Local optima are localized regions of a parameter space that are better than neighboring points.

Consider your model's parameter space as the ocean: the global optima is the Mariana trench, and the local optima are the small trenches and valleys in the ocean. Fortunately, you do not need to be concerned about not having your model converge on a global optima. Remember, when training a machine learning system, the goal is performance on a real-world task. Your models will still perform well on the task without needing to converge on global optima— or possibly any optima at all.

Regularizing to Generalize

As you learned in the previous section, the difference between machine learning and optimization is that machine learning is concerned with performance on *unseen data*. In Chapter 1, Make Machines That Learn, on page 3, you learned that this concept is known as generalization. Your objective is to train models that generalize—performance on training data isn't necessarily important.

Imagine you have two models. Model A performs noticeably worse on the training set than model B but noticeably better on the test set than model B. In this scenario, which model would you prefer?

Given your primary objective is performance on unseen data, for example, the test set, you'd likely prefer model B from a model performance perspective. But how can you have a model that performs noticeably worse on the training set and noticeably better on the test set?

The answer is *regularization*. Before diving into regularization, it's important to understand a few things about model *capacity* and the concepts of *overfitting* and *underfitting*.

Overfitting, Underfitting, and Capacity

In this chapter, you discovered two learning frameworks for solving learning problems as optimization problems: empirical risk minimization (ERM) and maximum likelihood estimation (MLE). Both ERM and MLE optimize model parameters with respect to errors on a training set, which means they are explicitly fitting functions to match training data. Both techniques are prone to *overfitting*.

Overfitting is a scenario in which a trained model has low training error but high generalization error. If you were to visually represent overfitting, it would look something like the following graph:

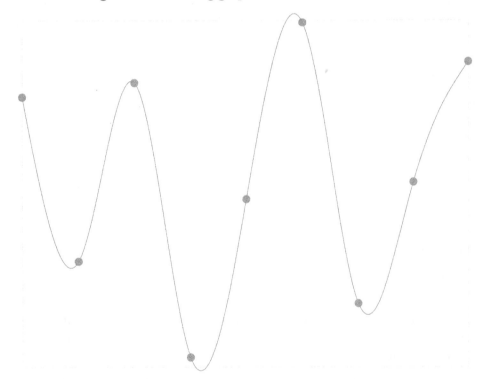

Notice how the line traces perfectly through every point in the original dataset. The traced function perfectly matches what's available in the current dataset but likely won't generalize to new data too well.

It's also possible for models to be prone to *underfitting*. Underfitting is a scenario in which a model doesn't even have low training error. You can see how overfitting and underfitting compare in the following image:

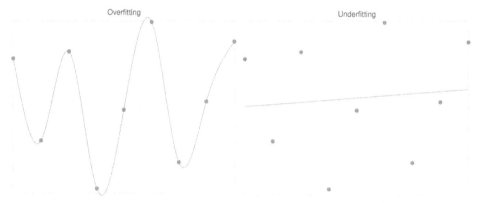

Both overfitting and underfitting are typically functions of a model's *capacity*. A model's capacity is its ability to fit many different functions. When designing machine learning models, you have to choose a *hypothesis space* of functions. For example, linear regression assumes the true model you want to fit is a linear model with respect to observation data. That means that linear regression has a hypothesis space that's restricted to linear functions. Consider you assume a model that has the form of the equation of a line:

```
def model(x, params) do
  {m, b} = params
  m * x + b
end
```

This model only has enough capacity to fit lines. You can increase its capacity to include quadratic functions by adding another term:

```
def model(x, params) do
  {w0, w1, w2} = params
  w0 + w1 * x + w2 * x ** 2
end
```

Notice this process can go on forever—you can keep adding additional polynomial terms and parameters to increase the capacity of the model to fit nth-degree polynomials.

Models with higher capacity are more prone to overfitting than models with lower capacity because models with high capacity can fit a wider range of complex functions. For example, you can model all quadratic functions with a cubic function, but you cannot model all cubic functions with a quadratic function. Designing good models means finding the balance between scenarios of overfitting and underfitting.

Defining Regularization

In machine learning, regularization is any technique used to combat *overfitting*, or more generally, any technique used to reduce generalization error, for example, error on the test set without necessarily reducing training error.

ERM and MLE are both prone to overfitting. So regularization is a necessary step for many machine learning algorithms. There are many forms of regularization you'll use throughout this book. This section will cover two that are more or less universal to all machine learning algorithms.

Complexity Penalties

Complexity penalties are a commonly used regularizer for training machine learning models that generalize. Complexity penalties impose a cost at model evaluation time by adding a penalty term with some penalty weight. The penalty term is typically a function of the model's parameters. For example, *weight decay* is a common regularization penalty that introduces a penalty term equal to the *L2-Norm* of the model's parameters.

The L2-Norm is a term you can interpret as meaning "distance from the origin." For example, in two-dimensional space, the L2-Norm of the point {3, 4} is 5, given by the distance formula:

```
defn distance(x, y) do
  x
  |> Nx.pow(2)
  |> Nx.add(Nx.pow(y, 2))
  |> Nx.sqrt()
end
```

Assuming you're using the mean squared error loss and weight decay, your complete objective function might look something like the following:

```
def objective(params, actual_inputs, actual_labels) do
  lambda = 0.5
  predicted_labels = model(params, actual_inputs)
  loss = mean_squared_error(actual_labels, actual_inputs)
  penalty = l2_norm(params)

  loss + lambda * penalty
end
```

lambda controls the strength of the weight-decay penalty, with higher lambda having a higher impact on model training. Weight decay expresses the preference for smaller model weights. Mathematically, it constrains the feasible parameter space of a given model to those that lie closer to the origin. Intuitively, you can think of weight decay as penalizing a model that gets too confident in particular weights.

Early-Stopping

Early-stopping is another commonly used regularizer for training machine learning models in which model training is stopped if overfitting is detected. It's not possible to perfectly detect overfitting, so the typical approach for monitoring overfitting is with a *validation set*.

Validation sets or holdout sets are portions of the original training data that aren't used to train but to periodically monitor model performance. Typically, if training errors continue to decrease and validation errors start to increase, the model is starting to overfit. Early stopping halts the training process *before* the model has a chance to overfit to the training set. You'll see several examples of early stopping in practice in the deep learning section of this book.

Descending Gradients

Now that you know a little more about optimization and how it applies to machine learning, it's time to see how optimization for machine learning is implemented in the context of a real problem. In this section, you'll implement *stochastic gradient descent* to estimate the true parameters, which were used to generate some training data.

Gradient descent is an iterative optimization routine using the gradients of a function evaluated at a particular point to minimize that particular function. As you learned in the previous chapter, the gradients of a scalar function are indicative of the direction of steepest descent, so they can be useful in determining how to navigate a function in order to find the minimum. Thanks to Nx's automatic differentiation capabilities, implementing stochastic gradient descent is a breeze. Start by opening up a Livebook and installing Nx:

```
Mix.install([
  {:nx, "~> 0.5"}
])
```

Now, you need to initialize some train data and test data. (For this example, you have access to the true data-generating function and parameters, so you can check your work afterward to make sure the gradient descent went smoothly.)

The true_params of the data-generating function is a random vector with length 32. This means each individual component of the vector is a random value between 0 and 1—you should notice that simply guessing or brute-forcing through all possible values for each parameter component is impossible. The data-generating function is a linear combination of the inputs and model parameters. If you remember from the previous chapter, you can compute this using Nx.dot to compute the dot-product of the true parameters and input values. Copy the following code to generate 10,000 examples of train and test data:

```
key = Nx.Random.key(42)

{true_params, new_key} = Nx.Random.uniform(key, shape: {32, 1})
true_function = fn params, x ->
  Nx.dot(x, params)
end

{train_x, new_key} = Nx.Random.uniform(new_key, shape: {10000, 32})
train_y = true_function.(true_params, train_x)
train_data = Enum.zip(Nx.to_batched(train_x, 1), Nx.to_batched(train_y, 1))

{test_x, _new_key} = Nx.Random.uniform(new_key, shape: {10000, 32})
test_y = true_function.(true_params, test_x)
test_data = Enum.zip(Nx.to_batched(test_x, 1), Nx.to_batched(test_y, 1))
```

Each example is a tuple of {input, label}, where input is a uniform random vector and label is obtained by evaluating the true data-generating function, true_function.

Next, create a new module named SGD in a new cell. As you saw in the previous chapter, you'll need to use defn to get access to Nx's automatic differentiation capabilities, so you'll need to import Nx.Defn as well:

```
defmodule SGD do

  import Nx.Defn

end
```

Getting a Good Initialization

Stochastic gradient descent typically starts from a random set of parameters. Remember, the goal of optimization in machine learning is to find the best parameterization for a particular function.

Unfortunately, when you don't know anything about what the best parameters *should* be, then you can't intelligently choose a starting point. For certain learning algorithms, such as in deep learning, there is some research to support various initializers converging better than others. But for now, you can initialize your parameters with a random uniform vector of size 32. To do so, add the following function to your SGD module:

```
defn init_random_params(key) do
  Nx.Random.uniform(key, shape: {32, 1})
end
```

Next, you need to implement your model, which is an attempt to model true_function. Add the following function to your SGD module to represent your model:

```
defn model(params, inputs) do
  labels = Nx.dot(inputs, params)
  labels
end
```

In this example, you know the original form of true_function, so you can use the same form to implement model. In a real machine learning problem, you wouldn't have access to the same information as you do here, so the form of model would depend on your own intuition about the data. Here, you know the original function transforms the input with a dot product between it and the true parameters—you only need to find out what the true parameters are.

Defining an Objective

You now need to implement your loss function. Remember, the stated objective is to minimize mean squared error on an evaluation set, so you can optimize for that directly by using mean squared error as your loss. You already saw how to implement mean squared error earlier in this chapter, so you can use the same implementation here:

```
defn mean_squared_error(y_true, y_pred) do
  y_true
  |> Nx.subtract(y_pred)
  |> Nx.pow(2)
  |> Nx.mean(axes: [-1])
end

defn loss(actual_label, predicted_label) do
  loss_value = mean_squared_error(actual_label, predicted_label)
  loss_value
end
```

Your loss function gives you a measure of how close your predicted distribution is to the actual distribution you're trying to replicate. Intuitively, you can think of gradient descent as if you're on a mission to find the deepest point in a body of water.

Your random initialization, init_random_params, drops you off at a random position in the body of water. You measure depth, loss, at your given parameterization and figure out how rapidly the depth is changing in all directions. You then update your position in the direction of steepest descent. To figure out loss at your current parameterization, you need to define an objective function. To do so, add the following code to your SGD module:

```
defn objective(params, actual_inputs, actual_labels) do
  predicted_labels = model(params, actual_inputs)
  loss(actual_labels, predicted_labels)
end
```

objective/3 makes predictions on actual_inputs and returns loss/2 with respect to predicted_labels and actual_labels. It's the indication of depth with respect to your current position in the boat example described previously.

At this point, your module should look familiar. Notice that the code is nearly identical to the original description of a machine learning problem described in Minimizing Risk to Maximize Performance, on page 75. It's slightly more specific to this problem, but the key points are all the same. Almost every machine learning algorithm follows a pattern similar to this one.

Stepping in the Right Direction

The final piece to your stochastic gradient descent algorithm is a step function that moves your parameters in the right direction—you find the direction of steepest descent and move your boat in that direction.

Recall from Chapter 3, Harness the Power of Math, on page 47, that you can find the direction of steepest descent of a function with respect to some parameter by computing its gradient. You can do that with ease using Nx's automatic differentiation capabilities. Add the following code to your SGD module to implement the step function:

```
defn step(params, actual_inputs, actual_labels) do
  {loss, params_grad} = value_and_grad(params, fn params ->
    objective(params, actual_inputs, actual_labels)
  end)
  new_params = params - 1.0e-2 * params_grad
  {loss, new_params}
end
```

This function makes use of a special Nx kernel function value_and_grad, which returns both the value and gradient of a function with respect to some parameter. Using value_and_grad is more desirable than just grad alone when you want access to the value of the function and its gradient at the same time. You take the gradient of objective/3 with respect to params, which measures the gradient of the loss function with respect to your model's parameters.

Next, you assign new_params to be the difference between params and a scaled version of params_grad.

In a machine learning context, you'll see the scaling factor shown here, 1.0e-2, referred to as the *learning rate*. It essentially controls the size of jumps or changes between parameters for each example. The learning rate is generally a value smaller than 1 because you only measure the gradient of the loss function with respect to a small number of points. You can't be overly confident in the gradient of a small sample. The fact that you are only using a sample of the whole dataset is what makes stochastic gradient descent actually *stochastic*. If you had access to the "true gradient" or the gradient over the entire dataset, you wouldn't necessarily need to scale params_grad, however, it's often intractable to compute the true gradient.

Putting It All Together

Finally, you need something that glues all of the pieces of your SGD implementation together. You also need to add an evaluation function for evaluating the final performance of your optimization routine. Add the following code to your module to implement both train and evaluate:

```
def evaluate(trained_params, test_data) do
  test_data
  |> Enum.map(fn {x, y} ->
    prediction = model(trained_params, x)
    loss(y, prediction)
  end)
  |> Enum.reduce(0, &Nx.add/2)
end

def train(data, iterations, key) do
  {params, _key} = init_random_params(key)
  loss = Nx.tensor(0.0)

  {_, trained_params} =
    for i <- 1..iterations, reduce: {loss, params} do
      {loss, params} ->
        for {{x, y}, j} <- Enum.with_index(data), reduce: {loss, params} do
          {loss, params} ->
            {batch_loss, new_params} = step(params, x, y)
            avg_loss = Nx.add(Nx.mean(batch_loss), loss) |> Nx.divide(j + 1)
            IO.write("\rEpoch: #{i}, Loss: #{Nx.to_number(avg_loss)}")
            {avg_loss, new_params}
        end
    end

  trained_params
end
```

evaluate/2 takes your trained model parameters and test_data, computes the loss for every example in test_data, and then sums the losses for every example. train/2 takes training data and an iterations parameter which controls the number of iterations to step through data.

What Is an Epoch?

 You'll often see one iteration through a dataset referred to as an *epoch*. There's not a good academic definition of an epoch, and the abstraction is meaningless in the context of gradient descent. However, it's so common in machine learning literature that you ought to know it. A single epoch in this context means one iteration of the outer for-loop.

---

train/2 makes use of Elixir's for-reduce syntax, which iterates over some Enumerable, reducing some initial value with a reduction function. In this case, you're reducing your initial parameters. The inner for-loop performs the real work of gradient-descent by calling step on each example in data and returning the updated parameters. The IO.write/1 will log training progress after each iteration—so you can monitor what's going on with your algorithm while you wait for it to finish.

Evaluating the Algorithm

Your SGD model is complete and ready to test. First, run the following code to get a baseline of performance from a random set of parameters:

```
key = Nx.Random.key(100)
{random_params, _} = SGD.init_random_params(key)
SGD.evaluate(random_params, test_data)
```

After running the code, you'll see this:

```
#Nx.Tensor<
  f32[1]
  [4059.184814453125]
>
```

Next, run a single iteration of SGD and assign the output to a variable trained_params:

```
key = Nx.Random.key(0)
trained_params = SGD.train(train_data, 1, key)
```

After some time, you'll see the returned parameters:

```
#Nx.Tensor<
  f32[32][1]
  [
    [0.32836729288101196],
    [0.09456641972064972],
    [0.3363123834133148],
    [0.4877675473690033],
    [0.6099048852920532],
    [0.7853176593780518],
    [0.40266865491867065],
    [0.22026798129081726],
    [0.1402876228094101],
    [0.13440364599227905],
    [0.7953506708145142],
    [0.3691302239894867],
    [0.47869911789894104],
    [0.14079436659812927],
    [0.6659020185470581],
    ...
  ]
>
```

Now, run evaluate/2 to see how well your model matches the true data-generating function:

```
SGD.evaluate(trained_params, test_data)
```

You'll see something like this:

```
#Nx.Tensor<
  f32[1]
  [168.16705322265625]
>
```

Your loss over the entire test set is only around 168.

Notice how a trained version does significantly better than an untrained version. Gradient descent was able to optimize your parameters such that they're significantly closer to the true parameters.

Making It Fail

This example is a bit impractical because, in the real world, you won't have access to information about the true data-generating function. You can see how challenging it might be without this information by slightly changing the form of true_function without changing the form of your model. Adjust true_function and generate new train and test data with the following code:

```
key = Nx.Random.key(42)

{true_params, new_key} = Nx.Random.uniform(key, shape: {32, 1})
true_function = fn params, x ->
  Nx.dot(x, params) |> Nx.cos()
end

{train_x, new_key} = Nx.Random.uniform(new_key, shape: {10000, 32})
train_y = true_function.(true_params, train_x)
train_data = Enum.zip(Nx.to_batched(train_x, 1), Nx.to_batched(train_y, 1))

{test_x, _new_key} = Nx.Random.uniform(new_key, shape: {10000, 32})
test_y = true_function.(true_params, test_x)
test_data = Enum.zip(Nx.to_batched(test_x, 1), Nx.to_batched(test_y, 1))
```

true_function now combines parameters with x using a dot-product, and then it applies the cosine function to the output. Rerun your training and evaluation to see what happens:

```
key = Nx.Random.key(0)
trained_params = SGD.train(train_data, 10, key)
SGD.evaluate(trained_params, test_data)
```

You'll see something like this:

```
#Nx.Tensor<
  f32[1]
  [2591.621337890625]
>
```

Overall you'll notice that your performance on this problem is much worse than the previous run. By adding a nonlinearity to the true function, your linear model couldn't completely recover the original parameters. Adding Nx.cos is a relatively minor change—real-world data-generating processes are likely much more complex. That's not to say your model doesn't perform decently well. A total error of around 2,000 for 10,000 examples is pretty good and might even be good enough to use in production if this were a real-world example. As you'll see in the Learning Linearly, on page 95, linear models work well, even though most processes aren't linear.

Peering into the Black Box

Before moving on in your machine learning journey, it's important to know about one more type of optimization problem you'll encounter in machine learning: *hyperparameter search*.

Hyperparameters are the details about an algorithm that aren't directly learnable but affect the structure and outcome of the model training process. For example, the learning rate 1.0e-2 used in the previous section is a hyperparameter.

Hyperparameter search is concerned with finding hyperparameters that lead to the optimal performance of a model on an evaluation set. Hyperparameters can have a big impact on the evaluation of a model, so finding better hyperparameters can drastically improve model performance. Unfortunately, it's difficult to describe hyperparameter search in terms of a differentiable objective function.

The goal in hyperparameter search is typically to maximize validation metrics. But this cannot be readily quantified in a simple function similar to the objective function you wrote in the previous section. Because of the lack of a well-defined, differentiable objective function, hyperparameter search often relies on *black-box optimization* and *exhaustive search*. Black-box optimization optimizes solutions based on objective observations without needing access to an explicit objective function. An exhaustive search is a brute-force search.

There are many approaches to black-box optimization. Additionally, you'll often see different forms of optimization used in contexts outside of hyperparameter search. In fact, some of these approaches, such as evolutionary algorithms, can pose as viable alternatives to machine learning. This section will briefly introduce you to two approaches used in the context of hyperparameter search: evolutionary algorithms and grid search.

Evolutionary Algorithms

Evolutionary algorithms are a class of optimization algorithms based on the principles of artificial selection. In an evolutionary algorithm, you generate a population of solutions to a problem (for example, a set of hyperparameters), evaluate each solution in the population, and then combine the best solutions to form better solutions. Evolutionary algorithms can even be used in tandem with neural networks in a process called neuroevolution, in which the parameters and structure of a neural network are evolved through several generations to yield better networks. Evolutionary algorithms are also popular outside of machine learning and have been used in the intelligent design of radio antennas[1] and *scenario generation for game design [SFF19]*.

Evolutionary algorithms are easily parallelizable and benefit from the parallelization and acceleration Nx offers with its JIT compilation to CPU/GPU. Unfortunately, a detailed description of genetic algorithms is outside of the scope of this book. If you'd like to learn more, check out *Genetic Algorithms in Elixir [Mor21]*, as well as the MEOW library.[2]

---

1. https://www.jpl.nasa.gov/nmp/st5/TECHNOLOGY/antenna.html
2. https://github.com/jonathanklosko/meow

Grid Search

Grid search differs from black-box optimization in that it's actually an exhaustive search over a discrete grid of parameters. Grid search is the most common approach to hyperparameter optimization used in machine learning. In a grid search, you define which parameters you want to optimize for and what values you want to test for each parameter. For example, you might specify 1.0e-4, 1.0e-3, and 1.0e-2 as values to try for the learning rate. Grid search will try combinations of your hyperparameters and return the combination that yields the best model.

Wrapping Up

In this chapter, you framed machine learning as an optimization problem to understand how machine learning and optimization are related. Additionally, you learned about regularization and how the key difference between optimization and machine learning is machine learning's emphasis on generalization. You applied optimization to a machine learning problem by implementing your own version of stochastic gradient descent. Finally, you learned a bit about black-box optimization and hyperparameter optimization in the context of machine learning.

With the foundations of machine learning and Nx covered, you're ready to start solving real-world machine learning problems with Elixir and the Nx ecosystem. In the next chapter, you'll jump straight into traditional machine learning algorithms, such as linear and logistic regression, nearest neighbors learning, and decision trees.

## CHAPTER 5

Traditional Machine Learning

In the previous chapters, you've become more grounded in the foundations of machine learning. At this point, you should feel more comfortable working with Nx, and it's okay if you don't grasp everything. Part of the beauty of the tooling in the Nx ecosystem is that it greatly reduces the complexity of common machine learning tasks. You don't need to be a math expert to train a machine learning model in Elixir. You need only to understand a bit of Elixir, and a bit of Nx.

In Chapter 4, Optimize Everything, on page 73, you wrote a linear regression model from scratch using Nx. While following along, you might have noticed the task was a bit verbose to write from scratch. Nx offers a lot of flexibility, but you don't want to have to write every algorithm from scratch. Thankfully, Elixir has a library for performing common machine learning tasks in a few lines of code. Scholar[1] is a set of machine learning tools built on top of Elixir and Nx. In this chapter, you'll implement some traditional machine learning algorithms using Scholar, and you'll start to unlock the potential of the Elixir Nx ecosystem.

Learning Linearly

Recent advances in machine learning have largely been attributed to deep learning. The popularity of deep learning—thanks to impressive feats in natural language processing, computer vision, and generative modeling—has made it almost synonymous with machine learning. However, the field of machine learning is vast. Deep learning refers to a subset of machine learning that uses neural networks. You'll learn more about deep learning in Chapter 6, Go Deep with Axon, on page 117. But first, you'll focus on *shallow machine learning* algorithms.

---

1. https://github.com/elixir-nx/scholar

Shallow machine learning refers to non-deep-learning-based algorithms. But the term is a bit of a misnomer. In a deep-learning-centric world, it's easy to classify algorithms into one of two classes: deep learning and everything else. In reality, the "everything else" covers a vast amount of algorithms. Many of these algorithms find significant use in the real world today.

When tackling a problem using machine learning, it's easy to immediately reach for a complex solution such as deep learning. However, many times you can do just as well with a much simpler and more interpretable machine learning algorithm. You can get a lot of value out of a simple linear regression model.

Perhaps the simplest class of traditional machine learning algorithms is *linear models*. They assume linearity in the underlying relationship between inputs and outputs. To think about it simply, linear models assume that input data can be modeled with a line. While this might seem like an overly simplistic assumption, it turns out that you can create pretty accurate models in this way. Remember, there's no such thing as a perfect model. A lot of times all we care about is having a model that's *good enough* for the task at hand. Reality is almost never linear, but linear models are still powerful at modeling the real world.

Linear Regression with Scholar

You're already familiar with one type of linear model—linear regression—from Descending Gradients, on page 84. Linear regression is an approach for modeling the relationship between some scalar target variable and one or more input variables. If you dust off your primary school mathematics lessons, you might remember the infamous equation for a line:

y = mx + b

This equation represents a linear relationship between the target variable y and the input variable x. m and b represent the slope and intercept of the line, respectively. Given an m and a b, you can predict any y from any x. For example, if you know m is 3.0 and b is 2.0, you can create a function such as the following:

```
def model(x) do
  3.0 * x + 2.0
end
```

You can then use your model to get the correct value of y at different values of x:

```
IO.inspect model(2) # prints 8
IO.inspect model(3) # prints 11
IO.inspect model(4) # prints 14
```

In the real world, you often don't have access to the parameters m and b, which drive the relationship between your target and input variables. Instead, you need to infer or learn these parameters using machine learning. For example, consider this scatterplot from Learning with Optimization, on page 73:

You'll notice the points on the plot loosely follow a line. Your goal with linear regression is to draw a line on that graph, such that it minimizes the total distance between the line and every point in your dataset. The line you end up drawing is often called the *best-fit line* and can be used as a predictive model for the relationship between inputs and outputs. In Descending Gradients, on page 84, you took the long way to find the best-fit line by implementing stochastic gradient descent by hand. Now, you'll use Scholar to do the same thing.

Start by installing the following dependencies in a new Livebook:

```
Mix.install([
  {:scholar, "~> 0.2"},
  {:nx, "~> 0.5"},
  {:exla, "~> 0.5"},
  {:vega_lite, "~> 0.1.6"},
  {:kino_vega_lite, "~> 0.1.6"},
  {:scidata, "~> 0.1"}
])
```

You'll use Scholar to access a number of traditional machine learning algorithms and tools: Nx for manipulating tensors, EXLA for JIT-compilation and acceleration, and VegaLite/KinoVegaLite for creating visualizations of your data. You'll also need SciData for downloading datasets later on.

Now, set the default backend to EXLA and the default defn compiler to EXLA by running the following code in a new cell:

```
Nx.default_backend(EXLA.Backend)
Nx.Defn.default_options(compiler: EXLA)
```

Next, you'll need to create some data. Run the following code to generate training data:

```
m = :rand.uniform() * 10
b = :random.uniform() * 10

key = Nx.Random.key(42)
size = 100
{x, new_key} = Nx.Random.normal(key, 0.0, 1.0, shape: {size, 1})
{noise_x, new_key} = Nx.Random.normal(new_key, 0.0, 1.0, shape: {size, 1})

y =
  m
  |> Nx.multiply(Nx.add(x, noise_x))
  |> Nx.add(b)
```

In this snippet, you start by declaring the target parameters m and b as random scalars. You then create a new random PRNG key using Nx's random module. Remember, Nx's random number generation modules are stateless, so you always need to pass a key for generating random numbers. Next, you create two random normal tensors: x and noise_x. x is a random distribution of input variables. noise_x is gaussian noise added to x. This is necessary to simulate what data looks like in the real world— imperfect.

Now, you can run the following code to create a scatterplot of your data:

```
alias VegaLite, as: Vl

Vl.new(title: "Scatterplot", width: 720, height: 480)
|> Vl.data_from_values(%{
  x: Nx.to_flat_list(x),
  y: Nx.to_flat_list(y)
})
|> Vl.mark(:point)
|> Vl.encode_field(:x, "x", type: :quantitative)
|> Vl.encode_field(:y, "y", type: :quantitative)
```

You'll see the plot as shown on page 99.

Scatterplot

Notice the data generally follows a line. But the line isn't perfect thanks to your gaussian noise.

Next, you want to fit a linear regression model on input variables x and output variables y. Using Scholar, you can do this with a single line:

```
model = Scholar.Linear.LinearRegression.fit(x, y)
```

After running this code, you'll notice you get the following output:

```
%Scholar.Linear.LinearRegression{
  coefficients: #Nx.Tensor<
    f32[1][1]
    [
      [3.4556338787078857]
    ]
  >,
  intercept: #Nx.Tensor<
    f32[1]
    [9.695785522460938]
  >
}
```

Scholar.Linear.LinearRegression.fit/3 returns a %LinearRegression{} struct with attributes coefficients and intercept. These variables represent the values m and b.

If you inspect m and b, you'll notice they're close to the predicted coefficients and intercept. Note that your m and b will be different than what's presented here due to randomization.

Under the hood, Scholar's Scholar.Linear.LinearRegression.fit/3 finds a best-fit using *ordinary least-squares regression*. Fortunately, you don't need to know what that means because Scholar abstracts away the complexities into an easy-to-use API. You can now use the returned model to make predictions on new data. For example, after running the following:

```
Scholar.Linear.LinearRegression.predict(model, Nx.iota({3, 1}))
```

You'll see this:

```
#Nx.Tensor<
  f32[3][1]
  [
    [9.695785522460938],
    [13.151419639587402],
    [16.607053756713867]
  ]
>
```

You can further validate your model by visualizing the relationship it predicts overlayed with your original scatterplot. To do this, start by running the following code to generate predictions over the same interval as your training data:

```
pred_xs = Nx.linspace(-3.0, 3.0, n: 100) |> Nx.new_axis(-1)
pred_ys = Scholar.Linear.LinearRegression.predict(model, pred_xs)
```

The first line of code creates a vector with 100 entries, where values linearly increase from -3.0 up to 3.0. In the next line of code, you make predictions over your entire interval using Scholar.Linear.LinearRegression.predict/2.

You can now plot the predictions overlayed with your original data using the following code:

```
title = "Scatterplot Distribution and Fit Curve"
Vl.new(title: title, width: 720, height: 480)
|> Vl.data_from_values(%{
  x: Nx.to_flat_list(x),
  y: Nx.to_flat_list(y),
  pred_x: Nx.to_flat_list(pred_xs),
  pred_y: Nx.to_flat_list(pred_ys)
})
```

```
|> Vl.layers([
  Vl.new()
  |> Vl.mark(:point)
  |> Vl.encode_field(:x, "x", type: :quantitative)
  |> Vl.encode_field(:y, "y", type: :quantitative),
  Vl.new()
  |> Vl.mark(:line)
  |> Vl.encode_field(:x, "pred_x", type: :quantitative)
  |> Vl.encode_field(:y, "pred_y", type: :quantitative)
])
```

After running this cell, you'll see the following output:

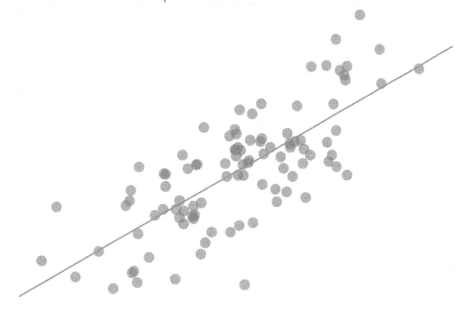

Scatterplot Distribution and Fit Curve

You'll probably notice the line doesn't even intersect any of the points in the original training data. Remember, this line is meant to be a best-fit line that represents a generalization of the patterns seen in the training data. It's more or less an average of the patterns in the training data.

In this example, you performed a linear regression of a single variable. But you can extend linear regression to as many features as you'd like. For example, if you were predicting how many points a team is going to score in an NBA game, you can use a number of different features to predict this: average three-point shots made per game, average points per game, whether or not Tim Donaghy is refereeing, and so on. As long as the relationship between input variables and target variables can be reasonably represented with a line, you can use linear regression to solve it.

Logistic Regression with Scholar

A close relative of linear regression that's often used for classification problems is *logistic regression*. Logistic regression is almost identical to linear regression. However, after applying the linear transformation on the input variables, you also apply a *logistic function*, which squeezes the output between 0 and 1. Often, the output represents a probability for a binary classification problem. But it can also be extended to work for multi-class classification problems. For example, imagine you're a sommelier trying to develop a model to predict the type of wine from a chemical analysis of each wine. You have a dataset of measurements, along with a label representing one of three types of wine. This problem is a perfect candidate for applying logistic regression.

Start by downloading the wine dataset using SciData:

```
{inputs, targets} = Scidata.Wine.download()
```

Next, split the dataset into training and test sets, so you can validate the performance of your model:

```
{train, test} =
  inputs
  |> Enum.zip(targets)
  |> Enum.shuffle()
  |> Enum.split(floor(length(inputs) * 0.8))

{train_inputs, train_targets} = Enum.unzip(train)
train_inputs = Nx.tensor(train_inputs)
train_targets = Nx.tensor(train_targets)

{test_inputs, test_targets} = Enum.unzip(test)
test_inputs = Nx.tensor(test_inputs)
test_targets = Nx.tensor(test_targets)
```

The first part of this code shuffles the original input dataset, such that the classes are uniformly distributed between the training and test set. It then splits the dataset into an 80/20 training and testing split. Finally, it transforms the training and test sets into tensors.

Now, you'll want to do a little bit of preprocessing before continuing. Most of the time, you want your input features normalized on some scale. This often makes it easier for models to learn patterns from input data. For example, it's common to squeeze input features between 0 and 1. You can use Scholar's preprocessing methods to do this:

```
train_inputs = Scholar.Preprocessing.min_max_scale(train_inputs)
test_inputs = Scholar.Preprocessing.min_max_scale(test_inputs)
```

This code scales both train and test inputs between 0 and 1 by normalizing according to the min and max of the input data.

Next, you can train a logistic regression model using Scholar.Linear.LogisticRegression.fit/3:

```
model = Scholar.Linear.LogisticRegression.fit(
  train_inputs,
  train_targets,
  num_classes: 3
)
```

Notice that you must specify num_classes: 3 because the original dataset has three classes. This code will treat the original problem as a multi-class classification problem. After some time running, you'll see the following output:

```
%Scholar.Linear.LogisticRegression{
  coefficients: #Nx.Tensor<
    f32[13][3]
    [
      [57.30550765991211, 40.04463577270508, 21.67230796813965],
      [9.130376815795898, 6.3609209060668945, 5.055447101593018],
      [9.905561447143555, 7.361076831817627, 3.8778562545776367],
      [70.83293914794922, 67.13773345947266, 35.777008056640625],
      [457.4987487792969, 298.3395080566406, 170.00132751464844],
      [11.34200668334961, 6.753108978271484, 2.0085954666137695],
      [11.833603858947754, 6.091976165771484, 0.4948000907897949],
      [1.158339500427246, 1.3611177206039429, 0.7777756452560425],
      [7.858388900756836, 4.755614280700684, 1.6751126050949097],
      [21.37252426147461, 9.511534690856934, 12.442154884338379],
      [4.333345890045166, 3.347238063812256, 1.008358359336853],
      [13.530704498291016, 8.850102424621582, 2.6361520290374756],
      [4223.81689453125, 1395.7369384765625, 934.896240234375]
    ]
  >,
  bias: #Nx.Tensor<
    f32
    0.0
  >,
  mode: :multinomial
}
```

Similar to your linear regression model, Scholar produces a struct specific to logistic regression, which can be used for making predictions later on. You'll notice the shape of the coefficients tensor is {13, 3}. That maps to thirteen features per class. In a multi-class logistic regression model, you actually train a model to predict multiple binary probabilities. For each class, you predict a probability between 0 and 1 of whether or not the input is a member of that class, and then you normalize across all classes.

You can now use this model to make predictions on your test set:

```
test_preds = Scholar.Linear.LogisticRegression.predict(model, test_inputs)
```

In addition to implementing a number of machine learning algorithms, Scholar also implements routines for evaluating models. For example, you can compute the accuracy of your model:

```
Scholar.Metrics.Classification.accuracy(test_targets, test_preds)
```

After running that cell, you'll see the following output:

```
#Nx.Tensor<
  f32
  0.75
>
```

Another common metric for classification problems is a *confusion matrix*. A confusion matrix is a table that lays out the performance of a model with respect to each class in a classification problem. The table is two-dimensional, where the columns represent the predicted class, and the rows represent the actual class. You can think of each cell in the table being represented by a tuple, such as {0, 0}, {0, 1}, and so on. The value at {0, 0} represents the number of times the model correctly predicted an input belonged to class 0 when it actually belonged to class 0. The value at {0, 1} represents the number of times the model predicted the input belonged to class 0 when it actually belonged to class 1. This pattern repeats for every class in your dataset. You can compute the confusion matrix for this problem using the following:

```
Scholar.Metrics.Classification.confusion_matrix(
  test_targets,
  test_preds,
  num_classes: 3
)
```

After running this code, you'll see this:

```
#Nx.Tensor<
  s64[3][3]
  [
    [9, 0, 0],
    [19, 0, 0],
    [8, 0, 0]
  ]
>
```

You can also turn this confusion matrix into a plot by running the following code:

```
Vl.new(title: "Confusion Matrix", width: 1440, height: 1080)
|> Vl.data_from_values(%{
  predicted: Nx.to_flat_list(test_preds),
  actual: Nx.to_flat_list(test_targets),
})
|> Vl.mark(:rect)
|> Vl.encode_field(:x, "predicted")
|> Vl.encode_field(:y, "actual")
|> Vl.encode(:color, aggregate: :count)
```

After running that code, you'll see this:

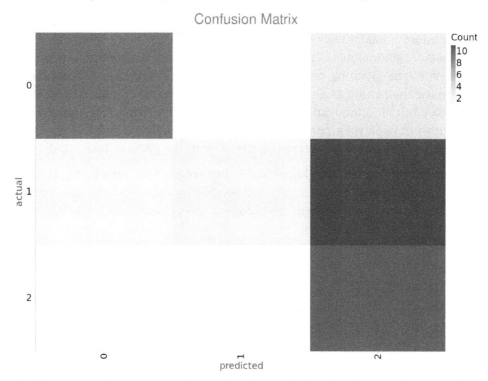

Confusion matrices are good visualizations of classification performance for your models.

Dealing with Nonlinear Data

A lot of real-world data is not linear. That means linear models often don't have sufficient capacity or modeling power to represent real-world relationships. There are a few ways around this problem.

First, you can simply deal with it. In reality, no model is perfect. If you have a linear model such as a linear regression model that does a decent job at predicting values from your data, then there's no reason to mess with it. You know what they say, "If it's not broken, don't fix it." Linear models are simple, fast, and interpretable, which makes them excellent candidates for business applications. A lot of times, you can deploy a linear regression model that's much simpler and faster than an alternative model and get 90% of the value of using a more expensive or complex model.

Another way to deal with nonlinear data is to perform transformations on your data until a linear relationship arises. This is, in a sense, *feature engineering*.

Feature engineering is the process of manipulating features by hand to provide better information for your model. If you're a sports fan, you might be familiar with advanced analytics. For example, in basketball, it's common to look at a player's true shooting percentage over only their field goal percentage to determine their value as a shooter. Over time, teams have realized advanced analytics, which often combine many surface-level metrics, are much more indicative of a player's performance. Advanced analytics are features that have been engineered from expert knowledge of the game of basketball.

With linear models, such as linear and logistic regression models, if you know your input data is more accurately represented by a *power model* or *logarithm model*, then you can transform the inputs to reflect that. Look at the following graph:

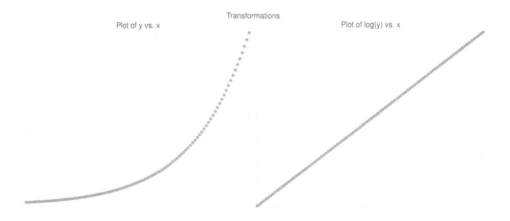

Notice that data, which previously couldn't be represented linearly, now can be with a simple transformation applied. For example, rather than looking at y vs. x in the first graph, you look at log(y) vs. x. These types of transformations are a bit of an oversimplification of a famous technique in machine learning known as the *kernel trick*.

The kernel trick is usually mentioned in reference to *support vector machines*, which are a type of linear model outside the scope of this book. With the kernel trick, you apply high-dimensional transformations to the original data, such that it becomes linearly separable. The kernel trick allows you to model nonlinear data with linear models.

As it turns out, not all data can be transformed in such a way that it's *linearly separable*. Linear separability is literally the ability for a dataset to be partitioned or separated by a line. In some cases, linear models simply won't cut it, and you need to find other ways to solve a problem. In the rest of this chapter, you'll briefly look at a few of these approaches before moving away from traditional machine learning methods and into deep learning.

Learning from Your Surroundings

Linear models are one of many traditional machine learning models implemented in Scholar. Another common model you'll come across in the wild is the *K-Nearest Neighbors (KNN)* model. The idea behind KNN models is relatively simple: you are likely very similar to the things nearest to you. Intuitively this makes sense. If you were to pluck a random person off the streets of Philadelphia and ask them their favorite football team, they'd likely say the Eagles. That's because the Eagles are the hometown team, and they're close in proximity to where the Eagles play. As you drift away from Philadelphia, the distribution of favorite NFL teams changes.

KNN works simply by classifying new points as belonging to the most common class of its K-closest neighbors. You can use KNN for both regression and classification. In both cases, the K-Nearest Neighbors determine the class or final value of new data points. KNN is simple and powerful. You can quickly train and evaluate a KNN model in Scholar and compare it against your Logistic Regression model on the wine dataset.

Run the following code to fit a new KNN classifier:

```
model = Scholar.Neighbors.KNearestNeighbors.fit(
  train_inputs, train_targets, num_classes: 3
)
```

After running the code, you'll see the following output:

```
%Scholar.Neighbors.KNearestNeighbors{
  data: #Nx.Tensor<
    f32[142][13]
```

```
    [
      [0.00769107136875391, 9.762659901753068e-4, ...]
      ...
    ]
  >,
  labels: #Nx.Tensor<
    s64[142]
    [0, 0, 2, 2, 2, 2, 1, ...]
  >,
  default_num_neighbors: 5,
  weights: :uniform,
  num_classes: 3,
  p: nil,
  task: :classification,
  metric: {:minkowski, 2}
}
```

Note that running the KNN fit method doesn't *actually* fit anything. KNN doesn't require any training because you only sample from existing data during inference time. The model simply keeps track of points in the training set to make predictions about the test set.

Let's start making predictions on test data and evaluating your model. Start by predicting classes for the test inputs:

```
test_preds = Scholar.Neighbors.KNearestNeighbors.predict(model, test_inputs)
```

You can now predict the accuracy of your model:

```
Scholar.Metrics.accuracy(test_targets, test_preds)
```

After running the code, you'll see the following output:

```
#Nx.Tensor<
  f32
  0.75
>
```

You can also compute a confusion matrix, like so:

```
Scholar.Metrics.confusion_matrix(test_targets, test_preds, num_classes: 3)
```

Run the code, and you'll see the following:

```
#Nx.Tensor<
  s64[3][3]
  [
    [9, 0, 0],
    [2, 11, 6],
    [0, 1, 7]
  ]
>
```

Note that your nearest neighbor model was pretty much identical in performance to your logistic regression model. You could continue fiddling with hyperparameters or choose to deploy one model over another. You'll find that Scholar makes it easy to prototype a broad range of classifiers and then evaluate each to determine which one is best for deployment in production.

You can see that Scholar is an excellent tool for creating supervised learning methods, but it's not limited to just that. Scholar also provides a number of tools for performing unsupervised learning and data analysis.

Using Clustering

In addition to supervised methods, Scholar offers a number of tools for unsupervised learning and analysis. Recall from Chapter 1, Make Machines That Learn, on page 3, that unsupervised learning is a type of machine learning where you learn only from inputs without access to any target information. Perhaps the most common type of unsupervised learning is *clustering*. Clustering is the process of identifying clusters or groups of similar data points in a dataset. There are many approaches to clustering, such as *K-Means clustering*, *hierarchical clustering*, *spectral clustering*, and more.

The most common type of clustering you'll likely see in practice is K-Means clustering, which randomly assigns K centroids to random points in the dataset and iteratively updates each centroid until an optimal configuration is reached.

Clustering can be useful for identifying general patterns from groups in your dataset. For example, if you have a dataset derived from shopper behavior on your online store, you can cluster shopper behavior and get an idea of the general types of shoppers that visit your store. One cluster might represent heavy spenders, while another might represent noncommittal browsers.

One of the central challenges in clustering is determining an appropriate number of clusters to use. Typically, you need to visualize your dataset and do some sort of high-level analysis to determine an appropriate number of clusters. Real-world data doesn't always cluster nicely. Real-world data is messy.

You can also use K-Means as an unsupervised approach to classification. For example, you can apply K-Means clustering to your wine problem by running the following code:

```
model = Scholar.Cluster.KMeans.fit(train_inputs, num_clusters: 3)
```

Note that, here, you only need to pass the train inputs because K-Means is an unsupervised approach. It relies only on input data without access to targets. After running the code, you'll see an output like the following:

```
%Scholar.Cluster.KMeans{
  num_iterations: #Nx.Tensor<
    s64
    4
  >,
  clusters: #Nx.Tensor<
    f32[3][13]
    [
      [0.008120134472846985, 0.001020378083921969, ...]
      ...
    ]
  >,
  inertia: #Nx.Tensor<
    f32
    0.6914953589439392
  >,
  labels: #Nx.Tensor<
    s64[142]
    [2, 2, 2, 1, 1, 1, 1, 0, 2, 2, 1, 1, 2, 2, ...]
  >
}
```

This struct contains metadata about the algorithm, as well as the cluster
centroids and cluster assignments for each member in the training dataset.
K-Means finds centroids for each cluster and assigns data points to their
closest centroid. You can visualize the centroids against features in your
dataset. The wine dataset has thirteen dimensions, so we'll need to reduce
that down to two or three dimensions for easier visualization. You can run
the following code to produce a visual of the centroids relative to each point:

```
wine_features = %{
  "feature_1" => train_inputs[[.., 1]] |> Nx.to_flat_list(),
  "feature_2" => train_inputs[[.., 2]] |> Nx.to_flat_list(),
  "class" => train_targets |> Nx.to_flat_list()
}

coords = [
  cluster_feature_1: model.clusters[[.., 1]] |> Nx.to_flat_list(),
  cluster_feature_2: model.clusters[[.., 2]] |> Nx.to_flat_list()
]

title =
  "Scatterplot of data samples pojected on plane wine"
    <> " feature 1 x wine feature 2"

Vl.new(
  width: 1440,
  height: 1080,
```

```
    title: [
      text: title,
      offset: 25
    ]
)
|> Vl.layers([
  Vl.new()
  |> Vl.data_from_values(wine_features)
  |> Vl.mark(:circle)
  |> Vl.encode_field(:x, "feature_1", type: :quantitative)
  |> Vl.encode_field(:y, "feature_2", type: :quantitative)
  |> Vl.encode_field(:color, "class"),
  Vl.new()
  |> Vl.data_from_values(coords)
  |> Vl.mark(:circle, color: :green, size: 100)
  |> Vl.encode_field(:x, "cluster_feature_1", type: :quantitative)
  |> Vl.encode_field(:y, "cluster_feature_2", type: :quantitative)
])
```

This will create a scatterplot of wine features 1 and 2 with a green dot representing where the centroid falls with respect to both of those features. After running this code, you'll see the following plot:

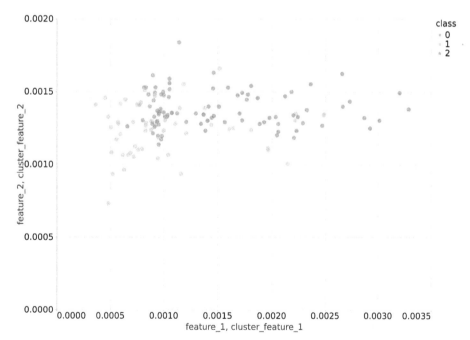

Note that this isn't very pretty, and the clusters aren't easily discernible. That's because your clusters were made against thirteen features—so while the data isn't clearly separable with respect to these two features, it may be separable with respect to all thirteen features.

Now you can assign test inputs to clusters by running the following:

```
test_preds = Scholar.Cluster.KMeans.predict(model, test_inputs)
```

This code assigns test inputs to one of the clusters created in the previous step. After running the code, you can evaluate the accuracy of your clusters using the following code:

```
Scholar.Metrics.accuracy(test_targets, test_preds)
```

After running this code, you'll see the following output:

```
#Nx.Tensor<
  f32
  0.8333333134651184
>
```

Surprisingly, your unsupervised approach performed better than both supervised approaches.

Making Decisions

Perhaps the most popular non-deep-learning algorithms in use today are *decision trees* and their ensemble variants, such as *gradient boosting*.

Decision trees behave exactly as they sound: they construct nested trees based on input features. Decision trees construct a hierarchical decision flow that partitions input features into one of a desired number of classes. For example, imagine you were trying to create a model to predict whether or not a patient was at risk of heart disease. A decision tree would construct a tree that analyzes data in an interpretable way. Does the patient smoke? Does the patient have high blood pressure? Is the patient physically active?

Decision trees are incredibly popular because they are interpretable, and they perform very well on certain classes of data. Decision trees are one of the few classes of algorithms that outperform deep learning models, specifically on *tabular data* and time-series data. As tabular data contains a majority of business intelligence data, decision trees have a wide use in business applications.

Gradient boosting is a type of *ensemble method* that constructs many weak classifiers iteratively by building classifiers to cover the weaknesses of previous classifiers. Ensemble methods are a class of machine learning methods that construct a model, which is an aggregate of many models. You can construct ensembles in many ways. You can think of ensembling as getting multiple diverse opinions on the same topic. Each model brings its own strengths and weaknesses to the table, so generally, the final decision is more sound. Gradient boosting is an ensemble technique that commonly uses decision trees as the underlying classifier.

Elixir has a new decision tree library in EXGBoost.[2] EXGBoost integrates directly with Nx tensors and is relatively simple. Decision trees are outside the scope of this book, but they are important to be aware of and explore as a blooming machine learning engineer.

Wrapping Up

In this chapter, you implemented a few types of traditional machine learning algorithms—supervised and unsupervised—using Scholar. You modeled linear data with linear regression. You predicted wine type in three ways with logistic regression, KNN, and K-Means.

You also learned a little about decision trees and boosting. This chapter is a short introduction to the functionality available in Scholar and the power of traditional machine learning algorithms. As you continue your machine learning journey, try some of the other algorithms available in Scholar, and compare them to the models you'll create in the rest of this book.

At this point, you've completed your introduction to the foundations of machine learning, and you're ready to go deeper with Axon. In the next chapter, you'll start to unveil the mystery behind the techniques that power the likes of ChatGPT, DALL-E 2, and Stable Diffusion: deep learning.

---

2. https://hex.pm/packages/exgboost

Part II

Deep Learning

## CHAPTER 6

Go Deep with Axon

In the previous chapter, your focus was primarily on understanding "traditional" or "shallow" machine learning approaches. The approaches you used, such as linear and logistic regression, ensemble methods, and decision trees, are well-suited for creating valuable, performant solutions to many machine learning problems you will encounter in production. However, the rise of deep learning over the past decade has led to significant progress in the field of artificial intelligence and machine learning.

Today, variants of deep learning models boast state-of-the-art results on countless tasks in computer vision, natural language processing, reinforcement learning, and more. The rapid adoption of deep learning and the progress it has brought to machine learning mean that being familiar with how to create, train, and deploy neural networks is an absolute must for any aspiring machine learning practitioner. In this chapter, you'll dive head-first into deep learning in Elixir and set the stage for the coming chapters where you'll learn to apply deep learning to different data modalities. You'll start by breaking down neural networks in Nx and then move on to Axon and learn more about what Axon is and what conveniences it supplies.

Understanding the Need for Deep Learning

Imagine you've been asked to create an algorithm that automatically scrapes handwritten phone numbers from a field on a paper form. Your team has already automated the process of extracting individual digits from the form into a 28x28 grayscale image. How would you go about solving this problem using the approaches you've used in the previous chapters of this book?

Your initial thoughts might be that it's easy enough to throw this problem at a logistic regression model or a decision tree. But what would you use for the feature space of your model? Would you treat each individual pixel value as a feature?

You could potentially divide the image into a grid, as shown in the following image.

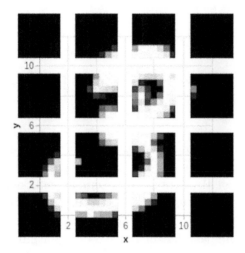

From there, you could then reduce each cell into a scalar metric and use the vector of the scalar metrics as your feature space. However, this approach has the potential to lose critical information about the image.

The algorithms you worked with in the previous chapter rely on in-depth feature engineering on the part of the programmer. Traditional machine learning algorithms require heavy investment in discovering rich-enough representations of the data *prior* to the learning process—but discovering representations by hand can be challenging.

Domains that are rich in information and those that have seemingly complex, unstructured relationships are often the ones that pose the most challenges. For data types such as images, text, and audio it's difficult to extract features by hand. While you could spend hours developing code to extract information about your images, such as corners and contours, the process would still be imperfect, sensitive to distribution changes, and lossy in nature.

A better way to extract meaningful representations of your data is to delegate that task to your machine learning algorithm. By doing so, your algorithm learns not only how to make predictions from features but also how to extract features from information-dense inputs. The ability to extract representations from high-dimensional inputs—and learn to make predictions from those representations—is the draw of deep learning.

Deep Learning's Kodak Moment

Deep learning has been around for a long time. But, until the last decade, deep learning was an afterthought of the machine learning community. Deep learning researchers and practitioners made up a fraction of a fraction of the machine learning community. Collectively, the machine learning community believed deep learning was a ridiculous idea and could never be used to solve anything of merit. This all changed in 2012 when graduate students Alex Krizhevsky and Ilya Sutskever, along with their advisor Geoffrey E. Hinton, won the "ImageNet" competition with their model dubbed *AlexNet [KSH12]*. Their model outperformed competitors by such a large margin that both industry and academics started opening their eyes to the power of deep learning.

The Curse of Dimensionality

Complex inputs, such as images, audio, and text, are often represented in high-dimensional space. Recall from Chapter 2, Get Comfortable with Nx, on page 21, how each of these inputs is often encoded as tensors. Images, for example, are represented as rank-3 tensors of {height, width, channels}. When flattened to a vector for input into a model, an image has the following dimensions: height * width * height. With the 28x28 grayscale images, a single image has 784 pixels, or 784 features given by 28 * 28 * 1.

The complexity of a machine learning problem increases significantly as the *dimensionality* of the inputs increases. Consider for inputs with a single feature, you only need a model to capture how the variations in that single feature map to the variations in the output. As you increase the number of features, your model needs to capture how the variations in many features, which may or may not be related, map to the variations in the output.

In machine learning, as the number of dimensions of the input space increases, the quality of the model increases too. However, at a certain point, the dimensionality becomes too high, and the quality of the model diminishes. This phenomenon is known as the *curse of dimensionality*.

To better understand this concept, think of your model as a conductor in an orchestra. The conductor's job is relatively easy when only one instrument is in the band. Adding more instruments may improve the sound quality and music, but the conductor's job becomes more challenging with each addition. At a certain point, adding instruments leads to diminishing returns, which means the conductor's job becomes too difficult, and the sound quality diminishes. This relationship between instruments and conductors illustrates the curse of dimensionality in machine learning.

The differentiator between deep learning and the algorithms you learned about in the previous chapters is that deep learning is able to overcome the curse of dimensionality. But how?

Cascading Representations

Understanding why deep learning works so well is still an active area of research. One theory on how deep learning is able to overcome the curse of dimensionality lies in how a neural network transforms input data. Neural networks transform inputs into hierarchical representations via composing linear and nonlinear transformations. A neural network has a series of *layers*—each of which takes the previous layer's representation as input and transforms it into its own representation before finally outputting a prediction. You'll break down the anatomy of a layer in Breaking Down a Neural Network, on page 121. For now, you need only to understand that a layer is just a function.

Going back to the conductor/orchestra analogy, deep learning overcomes the problem of "too many instruments" by adding additional conductors. One conductor is responsible for the violins, another for the trumpets, and another for the flutes. Each conductor only needs to pay attention to their section, and as a whole, the orchestra sounds significantly better than if a single conductor was responsible for getting everybody on the same sheet of music.

More concretely, the theory of why deep learning works so well is deep models are able to learn successive, hierarchical representations of input data. For example, if you train a model to identify images of cats from input data, the first layer might learn to extract colors, the second might learn to extract corners and edges, and so on. The first few layers extract simple relationships from the input data, while later layers start to extract more complex relationships from those simple relationships. Later layers might learn to identify ears or paws. By composing simple representations, a neural network is able to learn more complex representations and, consequently, make predictions on complex inputs.

In a sense, neural networks eliminate the need for methodical feature engineering by making feature extraction a part of the learning process. That's not to say that training a neural network does not require quality data—and time spent discovering new features isn't necessary to train better neural networks. It's just that neural networks perform well with complex, high-dimensional inputs and eliminate the need to perform complex dimensionality reduction or feature extraction on those inputs.

Representing Any Function

Theoretically, neural networks are said to be *universal function approximators*. A universal approximator is a model that can approximate any complex function when given the correct parameters. At first, this idea seems a bit silly. You're not interested in approximating functions; you're interested in making models that make predictions. But, if you consider the idea that the data you want to make predictions on comes from some black-box function, the universal approximation becomes much more appealing. In theory, a neural network—when given the right configuration—can approximate any of the functions you want to learn.

In reality, it's left to be said whether or not universal approximation is all that useful. The theory behind deep learning is still well behind the empirical results of the field, and therefore, theoretical assertions aren't backed by much mathematical rigor.

Another way to think of neural networks is they're learned computer programs. Imagine each layer in a neural network as an instruction, and the input to each layer as the state of the program at the time of instruction execution. You may be familiar with the sarcastic quip that artificial intelligence in production is nothing more than a bunch of if-else statements. Viewing a neural network as a learned program might support this assertion—the neural network may just learn the right configuration of if-else statements to be an effective model.

Breaking Down a Neural Network

With an understanding of why neural networks are necessary and why they're so powerful, it's time to dive into the question of what is a neural network. In this section, you'll break down the vocabulary surrounding deep learning, the anatomy of neural networks, and what a neural network actually looks like in Elixir. Understanding the building blocks of neural networks will help build your intuition as you start to use Axon.

Getting the Terminology Right

Deep models, neural networks, artificial neural networks (ANNs), multi-layer perceptrons (MLPs)—if you've spent some time reading about deep learning, you likely have encountered all of these terms used almost interchangeably.

The terminology of deep learning can be more daunting than implementing the models themselves.

Deep learning refers to a subset of machine learning algorithms that make use of deep models, or artificial neural networks. These models are considered "deep" as opposed to other models with respect to their layers of successive computation. If you roll out the computation graph of operations that take place in a deep model, the computation graph would appear deep (for example, lots of operations). You can also consider models deep with respect to the number of intermediate layers—with each successive layer increasing the depth of the model.

Artificial neural networks (ANNs) are one term for deep models. The term artificial neural network probably invokes the thought of images similar to this:

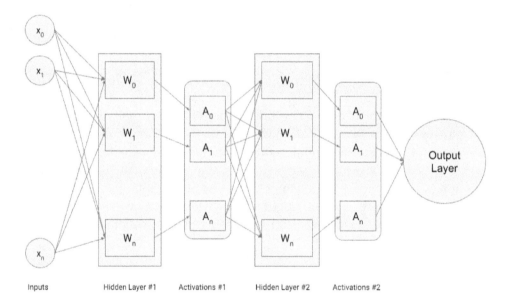

ANNs are named for their brain-inspired design. The transformation of inputs in an ANN is meant to simulate the firing of neurons passing information around the brain. The usage of the term ANN is probably a bit of a misnomer, as there's little evidence to suggest the brain works in the same way that neural networks do.

Multi-layer perceptrons (MLPs) are a class of deep learning models that make use of *fully connected layers* or *densely connected layers*. You will see what this means in The Anatomy of a Neural Network, on page 123. All you need to know is that MLPs are a specific class or *architecture* of neural networks. You might also see them referred to as *feed-forward networks* because information flows from previous layers forward toward output layers. You will implement many other architecture types in this book, including Convolutional Neural Networks (CNNs) in Chapter 7, Learn to See, on page 141, Recurrent Neural Networks (RNNs) in Chapter 9, Understand Text, on page 195, and Generative Adversarial Networks (GANs) in Chapter 12, Learn Without Supervision, on page 259.

The Rebranding

 Before deep learning had its watershed moment in 2012, the field was led by a relatively small number of researchers. Most top machine learning conferences would accept only one or two deep learning papers per year—if they accepted any. At the time, researchers working on deep learning were referred to as "connectionists" because of the connections between layers when visualizing deep models. Deep learning came about as a strategic rebranding by connectionists in an attempt to overcome the bias against neural networks at the time.

The Anatomy of a Neural Network

Most neural networks can be simplified down to a few key components. The most common abstraction for a unit of computation or work in a neural network is a layer. Typically, a layer represents a transformation of the input which is to be forwarded to the next layer. The number of layers in the model is typically referred to as the *depth* of the model. Generally, increasing the depth of the model also increases the capacity of the model. However, at a certain point, making a model too deep can hinder the learning process.

You'll use many different types of layers throughout the rest of this book. In a neural network, you'll generally have three classes of layers: *input layers*, *hidden layers*, and *output layers*.

Input Layers

Input layers are placeholders for model inputs. Certain operations on a neural network require a known input shape. You can refer back to Chapter 2, Get Comfortable with Nx, on page 21, to get a better idea of how certain real-world data maps to tensor inputs.

Hidden Layers

Hidden layers are where the magic happens in a neural network. They are intermediate layers of computation that transform the input into a useful representation for the output layer. They are the additional conductors in a large orchestra that make high-dimensional inputs manageable for the output layer.

The most common hidden layer is the densely connected, *fully connected*, or simply *dense layer*. The dense layer is named for the dense connections it creates between two layers—in other words, every input to a dense layer maps to an output in the dense layer. Dense layers have a number of output *units*, which represent the dimensionality of the dense layer. If you like the analogy of neural networks to the brain, you can think of an individual unit as a *neuron*. A dense layer with 128 units has 128 neurons.

The number of units in a dense layer is referred to as the *width* of the layer. Wider dense layers have more representational capacity. However, there's also a point of diminishing returns. It's common to use hidden widths that are multiples of two. This is because of how memory layouts work on modern accelerators.

Mathematically, dense layers are matrix multiplications or linear transformations. Dense layers learn to project inputs in such a way that extracts a useful representation for successive layers.

Activations

Hidden layers often have an *activation* function that applies a nonlinear function to the output. The introduction of nonlinearities into the neural network is what makes it a universal approximator. It's common to use activation functions that scale or squeeze inputs into some useful output range. For example, the sigmoid function is often used as an activation because it squeezes outputs between 0 and 1. Because neural networks are trained with gradient descent, it's important that activation functions be differentiable.

You can think of activation functions as a means of signaling certain input features. For example, your neural network might learn to only have certain neurons firing on certain input features. A neuron's activation can be interpreted as its importance to the final output. Some neurons that aren't important will be entirely "turned off."

You can use a number of activation functions in a neural network. Finding better activation functions is a popular area of research. The activation functions you should be familiar with are ReLU, sigmoid, and softmax.

ReLU

The Rectified Linear Unit (ReLU) activation function is a popular intermediate activation that computes the function:

```
defn relu(x) do
  Nx.max(0, x)
end
```

ReLU takes all negative inputs to 0 and maps positive inputs to the same value.

Sigmoid

The sigmoid activation function is a popular output activation because it squeezes outputs to the range 0-1. It computes the logistic sigmoid function:

```
defn sigmoid(x) do
  1 / (1 + Nx.exp(-x))
end
```

The sigmoid function is especially useful when you're trying to compute an output probability between 0 and 1.

Softmax

The softmax function is a popular output activation for multi-class classification problems. It outputs a categorical probability distribution.

Output Layers

From an implementation perspective, output layers are no different than input layers. Output layers are the final result of your neural network. After transforming your inputs into useful representations with hidden layers, output layers transform those representations into something you can meaningfully use or interpret, such as a probability.

For classification problems, it's common to use a dense layer with a sigmoid or softmax activation as the final output layer. For binary classification problems, the final layer will usually be a dense layer with one output unit and sigmoid activation. For multi-class classification problems, the final layer will usually be a dense layer with N output units and softmax activation, where N is the number of possible classes.

For scalar regression problems, it's common to use a dense layer with one output unit and no activation—so the output neuron just maps to a scalar.

The form of an output layer is problem-dependent. You'll see lots of different output layers throughout the rest of this book.

Using Nx to Create a Simple Neural Network

While neural networks might seem conceptually challenging to understand, they're actually surprisingly easy to implement. To illustrate this point, you'll implement a simple neural network using Nx. Open a Livebook and add the following dependencies:

```
Mix.install([
  {:nx, "~> 0.5"}
])
```

Remember from the previous section that a neural network consists only of inputs, hidden layers, intermediate activations, and output layers. Start by creating a new module named NeuralNetwork:

```
defmodule NeuralNetwork do
  import Nx.Defn
end
```

Next, you need to implement a hidden layer. Your hidden layer will be a densely connected or a dense layer that performs a matrix multiplication of two dense matrices followed by a bias add. A bias add is just a shift in the original input. The dense layer takes two parameters—weight and bias—and transforms the input using both weight and bias. Implement the dense layer like so:

```
defn dense(input, weight, bias) do
  input
  |> Nx.dot(weight)
  |> Nx.add(bias)
end
```

Hidden layers are followed by intermediate activation functions. To keep things simple, you'll implement only the sigmoid activation function using Nx. Implement your activation function like this:

```
defn activation(input) do
  Nx.sigmoid(input)
end
```

You can combine both dense and activation into a single hidden layer like this:

```
defn hidden(input, weight, bias) do
  input
  |> dense(weight, bias)
  |> activation()
end
```

Finally, you need an output layer. Your output layer will simply be another dense layer, followed by your activation function. The implementation is identical to hidden, but you should be explicit here to get an idea of what's going on:

```
defn output(input, weight, bias) do
  input
  |> dense(weight, bias)
  |> activation()
end
```

Now, add a predict function to your NeuralNetwork module:

```
defn predict(input, w1, b1, w2, b2) do
  input
  |> hidden(w1, b1)
  |> output(w2, b2)
end
```

The predict function shown here actually implements a simple neural network. It takes an input and some trainable parameters and produces a transformed output. Notice that the neural network is simply a composition of functions. You can add additional hidden layers by adding some additional parameters and additional calls to the hidden function.

Your final NeuralNetwork module will look like this:

```
defmodule NeuralNetwork do
  import Nx.Defn

  defn dense(input, weight, bias) do
    input
    |> Nx.dot(weight)
    |> Nx.add(bias)
  end

  defn activation(input) do
    Nx.sigmoid(input)
  end

  defn hidden(input, weight, bias) do
    input
    |> dense(weight, bias)
    |> activation()
  end

  defn output(input, weight, bias) do
    input
    |> dense(weight, bias)
    |> activation()
  end

  defn predict(input, w1, b1, w2, b2) do
    input
    |> hidden(w1, b1)
    |> output(w2, b2)
  end
end
```

Your next step is to generate the intermediate parameters w1, b1, w2, and b2 for your hidden and output layers. To keep things simple, you'll only input scalar shapes to your neural network, so your parameters can all be scalars as well:

```
key = Nx.Random.key(42)
{w1, new_key} = Nx.Random.uniform(key)
{b1, new_key} = Nx.Random.uniform(new_key)
{w2, new_key} = Nx.Random.uniform(new_key)
{b2, new_key} = Nx.Random.uniform(new_key)
```

Finally, you can start generating predictions for random inputs:

```
Nx.Random.uniform_split(new_key, shape: {})
|> NeuralNetwork.predict(w1, b1, w2, b2)
```

You'll see outputs similar to the following:

```
#Nx.Tensor<
  f32
  0.6635995507240295
>
```

One thing you'll notice is that it's trivial to implement neural networks without any additional dependencies other than Nx. Combined with Nx's automatic differentiation capabilities—and some of the optimization concepts you learned about in Chapter 4, Optimize Everything, on page 73—you can add training functionality and train complicated neural networks on real training data.

Another thing you'll notice is that there's a lot of boilerplate code that goes into creating neural networks in Nx. While you could theoretically write complicated neural networks without anything other than Nx, it would be a bit of a cumbersome process. Fortunately, you can use Axon.[1]

Creating Neural Networks with Axon

Axon is a library for creating and training neural networks in Elixir and is the primary tool for deep learning in the Elixir ecosystem. For the remainder of this book, you'll spend time diving deep into the Axon API and using Axon to create and train neural networks on complex problems. As you saw in the previous section, there's a lot of boilerplate code associated with creating neural networks in Nx. Axon abstracts all of the boilerplate code and offers a simplified API for building and training neural networks.

---

1. https://github.com/elixir-nx/axon

As an introduction to deep learning in Elixir, you'll train an algorithm that solves the problem of classifying handwritten digits, as described earlier in Understanding the Need for Deep Learning, on page 117. The best way to follow along is to fire up another Livebook and install the following dependencies:

```
Mix.install([
  {:axon, "~> 0.5"},
  {:nx, "~> 0.5"},
  {:exla, "~> 0.5"},
  {:scidata, "~> 0.1"},
  {:kino, "~> 0.8"},
  {:table_rex, "~> 3.1.1"}
])
```

Most of these dependencies should look familiar because you've already used Nx, EXLA, and Scidata extensively throughout this book. Nx acts as the core library for working with numerical data, and EXLA accelerates your code. Scidata contains the dataset you'll need for training, and Axon is what you'll use to create and train your model. Both Kino and TableRex are useful for visualizing Axon models in Livebooks and consoles directly.

Before moving on, you'll need to set some notebook options:

```
Nx.default_backend(EXLA.Backend)
```

This ensures that all of your defn-compiled code makes use of the EXLA backend. A decent CPU is all you need for this problem, but GPU acceleration never hurts.

Working with Data

With all of the administrative work done, it's time to prepare your data for training. This problem uses the MNIST[2] dataset, which consists of 60,000 28x28 grayscale images of handwritten digits from 0 to 9. MNIST is an incredibly popular dataset in the field of machine learning and often serves as the "Hello world" example of deep learning.

Scidata has built-in functionality for downloading MNIST. You can get both MNIST images and labels like this:

```
{images, labels} = Scidata.MNIST.download()
```

Remember that Scidata isn't designed to be Nx-aware. Both images and labels consist of tuples of the form {data, type, shape}, which can be used with Nx functions to convert raw data into Nx functions. If you inspect image_type, you'll

---

2. http://yann.lecun.com/exdb/mnist/

notice it's {:u, 8}, which is an unsigned 8-bit integer. The MNIST images are grayscale, with each pixel having a value between 0 and 255. You've learned throughout this book that it's important to normalize data before passing it through a model. The same concept holds true for deep learning, so you'll need to rescale pixel values to be between 0 and 1. You can do that by dividing the entire images tensor by 255.

Additionally, image_shape is a tuple of {60_000, 1, 28, 28}. You can design neural networks to work with this image representation, but for this example, you'll flatten each image into a vector.

Finally, you might notice that labels consists of 60,000 labels from 0 to 9. That's not necessarily a bad thing, but in Axon, it's easier to work with labels that are one-hot encoded, so you'll turn them into one-hot labels.

With all of these requirements in mind, you can transform the raw data Sci-data returned into Nx tensors like so:

```
{image_data, image_type, image_shape} = images
{label_data, label_type, label_shape} = labels

images =
  image_data
  |> Nx.from_binary(image_type)
  |> Nx.divide(255)
  |> Nx.reshape({60000, :auto})
labels =
  label_data
  |> Nx.from_binary(label_type)
  |> Nx.reshape(label_shape)
  |> Nx.new_axis(-1)
  |> Nx.equal(Nx.iota({1, 10}))
```

Notice that you use Nx.from_binary on the raw data and type for both images and labels to transform them into an Nx tensor. You divide image data by 255 to rescale pixel values between 0 and 1 before reshaping the entire images tensor into a collection of 60,000 image vector representations. You one-hot encode the labels by taking advantage of Nx's broadcasting and comparing each label to a vector of numbers from 0 to 9.

With preprocessed data in hand, you'll need to divide your data into training and test sets. To do this, you'll take the first 50,000 images in the dataset as your training set and the last 10,000 images in the dataset as your test set. You can slice the dataset using Nx's slice notation to accomplish this:

```
train_range = 0..49_999//1
test_range = 50_000..-1//1
```

```
train_images = images[train_range]
train_labels = labels[train_range]

test_images = images[test_range]
test_labels = labels[test_range]
```

As you'll see later on in this section, Axon offers a training API that performs minibatch stochastic gradient descent. Remember from Chapter 4, Optimize Everything, on page 73, that machine learning algorithms often iteratively update models on the training set using optimization techniques, such as gradient descent. To perform gradient descent on minibatches, you need to turn your data into minibatches as well:

```
batch_size = 64

train_data =
  train_images
  |> Nx.to_batched(batch_size)
  |> Stream.zip(Nx.to_batched(train_labels, batch_size))

test_data =
  test_images
  |> Nx.to_batched(batch_size)
  |> Stream.zip(Nx.to_batched(test_labels, batch_size))
```

This code creates both train and test datasets that consist of minibatches of tuples {input, target}—which is the format expected by Axon.

Now that you've preprocessed train and test sets, it's time to create the model.

Building the Model

Axon's key feature is its model-creation API. The API allows you to build complex models by composing Axon layers. All models start with an input layer that specifies the shape Axon should expect inputs to be. You then pass input layers through successive transformations until you have your desired output. Start by implementing a basic Axon model, like this:

```
model =
  Axon.input("images", shape: {nil, 784})
  |> Axon.dense(128, activation: :relu)
  |> Axon.dense(10, activation: :softmax)
```

After executing this cell, you'll see some summary information about your model:

```
#Axon<
  inputs: %{"images" => {nil, 784}}
  outputs: "softmax_0"
  nodes: 5
>
```

Designing Models

You specify a model that takes an input shape of {nil, 784}. Axon allows you to use nil as a placeholder for values that will be filled at inference time. The input layer is passed through a hidden dense layer with 128 units and a :relu activation before going through another dense layer with 10 units and :softmax activation.

Creating models with Axon is relatively straightforward—the difficult part is developing an understanding of what combination of layers to use to create the best model.

For this example, the input layer with shape {nil, 784} maps directly to input images that are batches of vectors of dimensionality 784. Axon needs to know input shapes ahead of time because it affects how successive layers are built. If you pass an input with a shape that doesn't match what Axon expects, it will raise an error.

The intermediate dense layer with 128 units and :relu activation is an arbitrary choice. You can freely change the input units and activation function and even add extra hidden layers. Hypothetically, more hidden units and more hidden layers increase the representational capacity of the model. However, there's a point where your neural network becomes too wide or too deep for your training data, and the model will struggle to learn. You'll often want to experiment with multiple configurations to find one that produces the best result on your data.

The output layer has ten units and :softmax activation. Remember that your goal is to map input images to a label between 0 and 9. This layer will output a probability at each index that represents the probability that the input digit matches that index. More concretely, the probability at index 0 represents the probability that the input is a 0; the probability at index 1 represents the probability that the input is a 1, and so on.

Designing neural networks is often more art than science. You need to keep in mind certain principles and architectures that work well for specific problem types. However, designing an effective model often just takes some intuition and experimentation. The rest of this book will teach you broadly what kind of models to use in various situations, but you won't find any magic recipes for solving specific problems.

Inside the Model Representation

Assuming you ran this in a Livebook, you can visualize the Axon model using Kino and Axon's Axon.Display module:

```
template = Nx.template({1, 784}, :f32)
Axon.Display.as_graph(model, template)
```

Axon.Display.as_graph/2 traces the execution of the model and outputs a Mermaid graph so you can easily visualize the execution. You'll see the following output:

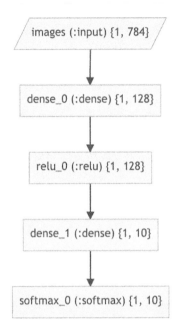

You can also display the model as a table using Axon.Display.as_table/2:

```
Axon.Display.as_table(model, template)
|> IO.puts
```

After running the code, you'll see this:

		Model		
Layer	Input Shape	Output Shape	Options	Parameters
images (input)	[]	{1, 784}	shape: {nil, 784} optional: false	
dense_0 (dense["images"])	[{1, 784}]	{1, 128}		kernel: f32[784][128] bias: f32[128]
relu_0 (relu["dense_0"])	[{1, 128}]	{1, 128}		
dense_1 (dense["relu_0"])	[{1, 128}]	{1, 10}		kernel: f32[128][10] bias: f32[10]
softmax_0 (softmax["dense_1"])	[{1, 10}]	{1, 10}		

Total Parameters: 101770
Total Parameters Memory: 407080 bytes

The description tells you layer names and inputs, layer shapes, trainable parameters, and options in each layer. If you're curious about what this model object actually is, you can inspect it again and pass structs: false:

```
IO.inspect model, structs: false
```

And you'll see a longer version:

```
%{
  __struct__: Axon,
  nodes: %{
    12 => %{
      __struct__: Axon.Node,
      args: [],
      hooks: [],
      id: 12,
      name: #Function<90.106397181/2 in Axon.unique_identifiers/2>,
      op: :input,
      op_name: :input,
      opts: [shape: {nil, 784}, optional: false],
      parameters: [],
      parent: [],
      policy: %{
        __struct__: Axon.MixedPrecision.Policy,
        compute: {:f, 32},
        output: {:f, 32},
        params: {:f, 32}
      },
      stacktrace: ...
    },
    ...
  },
  output: 20
}
```

The model is actually a regular Elixir struct. Axon models are mere representations of computation graphs that you can manipulate and compose before passing to Axon's execution and training APIs. You build the graph lazily and then use it when you actually need to.

This intermediate representation is useful because it allows Axon to accomplish all sorts of seemingly "magic" things. You'll get exposed to more and more of this magic throughout the rest of this book. It also allows Axon to convert to and from other neural network representations such as ONNX.[3] This comes in handy for deploying models and using models from the Python ecosystem, as you'll see in Chapter 8, Stop Reinventing the Wheel, on page 171.

---

3.   https://github.com/onnx/onnx

Training the Model

You now have data and a model in hand. The next step is to train your model on your training data. While you could write a gradient descent implementation from scratch, it would be cumbersome and error-prone. Fortunately, Axon has conveniences for training neural networks using gradient descent.

Axon's training abstraction lies in the Axon.Loop module. Axon.Loop contains functions for building up an %Axon.Loop{} data structure, which you can then run on input data using Axon.Loop.run/3. You can do some pretty complicated things with the loop API. But most of the time you only want to implement a simple supervised training loop:

```
trained_model_state =
  model
  |> Axon.Loop.trainer(:categorical_cross_entropy, :sgd)
  |> Axon.Loop.metric(:accuracy)
  |> Axon.Loop.run(train_data, %{}, epochs: 10, compiler: EXLA)
```

Axon.Loop.trainer/3 is a factory function for a supervised training loop that takes an Axon model, loss function, and optimizer as input. Note that "supervised" here means supervised in the machine learning sense, not the OTP sense. The trainer will optimize model by minimizing loss using optimizer. In this example, you pass the model you created earlier, the :categorical_cross_entropy loss function, which tells Axon you're working with a multi-class classification problem, and the :sgd optimizer, which tells Axon to use stochastic gradient descent.

Axon.Loop.metric/2 attaches metrics to the supervised training loop. This tells Axon to monitor and compute specific metrics throughout the training loop. For this example, you're primarily concerned with the accuracy of your predictions because you're dealing with a classification problem.

Finally, Axon.Loop.run/3 tells Axon to execute the given training loop on the given data with the given options. Axon will iterate through train_data for ten epochs, and finally output a trained model state. Passing compiler: EXLA ensures that Axon will JIT-compile intermediate train steps using EXLA. This will speed up training significantly. When you execute this cell, you'll see this model:

```
Epoch: 0, Batch: 750, accuracy: 0.9439270 loss: 0.9746160
Epoch: 1, Batch: 750, accuracy: 0.9759654 loss: 0.7108651
Epoch: 2, Batch: 750, accuracy: 0.9799850 loss: 0.5978507
Epoch: 3, Batch: 750, accuracy: 0.9817263 loss: 0.5321623
Epoch: 4, Batch: 750, accuracy: 0.9830977 loss: 0.4878981
Epoch: 5, Batch: 750, accuracy: 0.9840345 loss: 0.4553202
Epoch: 6, Batch: 750, accuracy: 0.9849032 loss: 0.4299005
```

```
Epoch: 7, Batch: 750, accuracy: 0.9856064 loss: 0.4092346
Epoch: 8, Batch: 750, accuracy: 0.9862743 loss: 0.3919075
Epoch: 9, Batch: 750, accuracy: 0.9868216 loss: 0.3770282
```

Notice how the model iterated through your dataset ten times, with each iteration leading to higher accuracy and lower loss. You might also notice that the training loop returned something that looks like this:

```
%{
  "dense_0" => %{
    "bias" => #Nx.Tensor<
      f32[128]
      EXLA.Backend<host:0, 0.2489291390.1016463368.89685>
      [...]
    >,
    "kernel" => #Nx.Tensor<
      f32[784][128]
      EXLA.Backend<host:0, 0.2489291390.1016463368.89686>
      [
        [...],
        ...
      ]
    >,
  },
  "dense_1" => %{...}
}
```

This is the trained_model_state. The Axon struct is a stateless representation of a neural network. It doesn't carry any of the model parameters or state internally. That means when performing inference and evaluation, you always need access to both the model and a model state compatible with the given model. Axon's supervised training loop will *always* output a model state that's compatible with the model you're training.

The model state is a nested map of namespaces and parameters. Each top-level map key represents an Axon namespace. Most models are namespaced by layers. In this example, you'll see that there's a key for each layer dense_0 and dense_1, and within each namespace, there's a key for each layer parameter kernel and bias.

Evaluating the Model

Remember, in machine learning, you're only concerned with your model's performance on an unseen test set. 98% accuracy on the training set isn't indicative of your model's true performance. Fortunately, Axon also offers conveniences for evaluating models against test data. To evaluate your model, implement the following supervised evaluation loop:

```
model
|> Axon.Loop.evaluator()
|> Axon.Loop.metric(:accuracy)
|> Axon.Loop.run(test_data, trained_model_state, compiler: EXLA)
```

Axon.Loop.evaluator/2 is a factory function, which creates a supervised evaluation loop using an Axon model and a model state. The evaluator tells Axon you want to evaluate model at the state trained_model_state. You also need to tell Axon what metrics you want to evaluate your model with. In this case, you attach accuracy to the loop, so Axon knows to track accuracy. Finally, you need to tell Axon to execute the loop on your test_data.

After running the code, you'll see this:

```
Batch: 156, accuracy: 0.9881768
```

This indicates your model correctly predicts around 99% of digits in the test data. That's pretty good. Of course, the purpose of a model is to actually make predictions on new data, so how can you do that with Axon?

Executing Models with Axon

Axon offers an execution API for compiling and running Axon models. Start by grabbing an individual batch of images from your test_data:

```
{test_batch, _} = Enum.at(test_data, 0)
```

To make things easier, take a single image from the test batch:

```
test_image = test_batch[0]
```

You can visualize the image using Nx.to_heatmap:

```
test_image
|> Nx.reshape({28, 28})
|> Nx.to_heatmap()
```

You'll see something that looks like the image on page 138.

In this example, the test image is a 3, so the model should predict 3 as the most probable label.

You now have everything you need to make predictions: a model, a compatible model state, and an input. The easiest way to query your model for predictions is to first build your model using Axon.build/2 and then call the returned predict function. Axon.build/2 converts your model into a tuple of {init_fn, predict_fn}. init_fn is an arity-2 function that can be used to initialize your model's parameters. predict_fn is an arity-2 function that takes model parameters and a tensor or collection of tensors as input and returns the result of running the full model.

Run the following code to try and query your model for predictions:

```
{_, predict_fn} = Axon.build(model, compiler: EXLA)
predict_fn.(trained_model_state, test_image)
```

You'll see the following error message:

```
** (Axon.CompileError) exception found when compiling layer
   Axon.Layers.dense/4 named dense_0:

  ** (ArgumentError) Axon.Layers.dense: expected input shape to have at
  least rank 2, got rank 1
  (axon 0.5.1) lib/axon/shared.ex:92: Axon.Shared.assert_min_rank!/4
  (nx 0.5.1) lib/nx/defn/compiler.ex:203: Nx.Defn.Compiler.__remote__/4
  (axon 0.5.1) lib/axon/layers.ex:125: Axon.Layers."__defn:dense_impl__"/4
```

What's going on here? Remember Axon requires input shapes to be somewhat static and to match the form you specified during model creation. In this case, your test_image is missing an additional dimension, so you can add one in using Nx.new_axis:

```
probabilities =
  test_image
  |> Nx.new_axis(0)
  |> then(&predict_fn.(trained_model_state, &1))
```

You'll see an output that looks like the following:

```
#Nx.Tensor<
  f32[1][10]
  EXLA.Backend<host:0, 0.4078460682.4224843782.56655>
  [
    [6.16645411355421e-5, 0.011110336519777775, 0.07432620227336884, ...]
  ]
>
```

Remember, your model outputs ten probabilities associated with the labels 0 to 9. You can get the discrete label from these probabilities by computing the Nx.argmax of the probabilities like so:

```
probabilities |> Nx.argmax()
```

This gives you the following output:

```
#Nx.Tensor<
  s64
  EXLA.Backend<host:0, 0.4078460682.4224843782.56658>
  3
>
```

What you see is the exact output you were looking for. Congratulations, you now have a model, a trained model state, and the ability to query the trained model using any inputs you'd like.

Wrapping Up

In this chapter, you were introduced to deep learning and why it's much more effective than other approaches to certain classes of problems. You broke down the anatomy of a neural network and implemented one of the most common types of neural networks: the basic feed-forward or dense network. You used Axon to create, train, and evaluate neural networks.

While feed-forward networks can be used to solve a number of complex problems, there are certain classes of problems where feed-forward networks are not enough. In the next few chapters, you'll solve problems in different areas where feed-forward networks come up short. You'll also implement different types of neural networks that overcome the limitations of basic feed-forward networks on specific classes of inputs.

## CHAPTER 7

Learn to See

In the previous chapter, you used Axon to create and train neural networks in Elixir, including one that recognizes handwritten digits. You also learned about the types of problems neural networks are well-suited to handle and why they outperform shallow machine learning approaches in many areas. More specifically, you implemented a type of neural network architecture known as the multi-layer perceptron (MLP) or deep feed-forward network.

While MLPs are capable of learning and modeling any kind of data, other deep learning architectures are even more powerful when applied to specific problem types. In this chapter, you'll implement domain-specific architecture known as the convolutional neural network (CNN) and learn how it outperforms traditional MLPs in computer vision.

Identifying Cats and Dogs

Imagine you run a social media website where users can post and view pictures of animals. To simplify the site as much as possible, you don't want users to attach any additional information to these images, such as whether or not the image is that of a dog or a cat. However, you do want users to be able to filter their feeds based on such criteria. So, how can you accomplish this without requiring users to tag their images with a specific category? You guessed it: machine learning.

In this example, you'll train a model to classify images into one of two categories:·cats or dogs. While you can easily extend the model to distinguish between any kind of animal, by reducing the number to two, you reduce the amount of data required to train the model—and in turn, the length of time to train that model.

Before you dive in, head over to Kaggle[1] and grab the Cats vs. Dogs training dataset. This dataset contains a directory of 25,000 images—12,500 images of cats and 12,500 images of dogs—nicely wrapped up in a single zip file. After you download the dataset, extract it to a train directory in a working directory of your choosing.

With the dataset downloaded and extracted, you're ready to fire up a Livebook and start training the model.

Installing Dependencies

First, you need to bring some dependencies into your notebook environment. Run the following code to install the dependencies needed to create an image classification model:

```
Mix.install([
  {:axon, "~> 0.5"},
  {:nx, "~> 0.5"},
  {:exla, "~> 0.5"},
  {:stb_image, "~> 0.6"},
  {:kino, "~> 0.8"}
])
```

By now, you should be familiar with all of the dependencies listed here.

With your dependencies set up, it's time to set some configuration defaults for Nx and EXLA. Run the following line to configure EXLA as the default Nx backend:

```
Nx.global_default_backend(EXLA.Backend)
```

That's all you need to do to configure your notebook environment for this example. The next step is to create a pipeline to load images from a directory into batches of tensors.

Building an Input Pipeline

As you saw in Training the Model, on page 135, to train an Axon model, you need to create a pipeline of input data for Axon to iterate through. While Axon can run a loop over any Enumerable, such as a list, there are often significant advantages to using lazy data structures, such as streams. Streams are lazy enumerables that generate elements one by one. Compared to an eager data structure (for example, a list), streams are often more performant as training input pipelines, especially when using an accelerator, such as a GPU. In practice, streams offer the following advantages over lists in a training pipeline: memory efficiency and overlapping execution.

---

1. https://www.kaggle.com/c/dogs-vs-cats

Memory Efficiency

Neural networks are *extremely* data-hungry. Practical datasets are often too large to fit entirely in memory. For example, the popular ImageNet[2] dataset is over 150GB in size. If you were using a list as your training pipeline, you would need to load all 150GB of that dataset into memory at once. Doing so is both impractical and inefficient. Streams only yield results when requested, which means you can consume batches of images one by one and avoid loading an entire dataset into memory.

Overlapping Execution

When using an external accelerator, such as a GPU, for training, the CPU is often idle for long periods of time as its only responsibility is feeding inputs to the GPU. Also, GPUs are so fast that data transfer is often the most expensive operation. For this reason, it's a good idea to run training and data loading concurrently to avoid *starving* the GPU. GPU starvation happens when the input pipeline is IO-bound rather than compute-bound. The biggest bottleneck is the GPU waiting for data, not the actual training computations.

Fortunately, you can combine streams with some of Elixir's concurrency primitives to create pipelines that maximize both the GPU and CPU usage. For example, you can make use of Elixir's Task.async_stream/3 to create a stream that processes inputs in parallel. This is especially useful when performing IO operations, such as reading files. You can build up preprocessing pipelines using stream operations, and Axon will consume the stream as batches become ready—overlapping input IO, preprocessing, and computation—maximizing the computing power available to you.

In this example, you'll create a lazy, parallel input pipeline using a stream. Start by creating a new module named CatsAndDogs:

```
defmodule CatsAndDogs do
end
```

Inside the CatsAndDogs module, create a function named pipeline/1 that accepts a list of input paths from which to create a pipeline:

```
def pipeline(paths) do
  paths
  |> Enum.shuffle()
end
```

---

2. https://www.image-net.org/

For now, this function simply shuffles a list of paths, which is an important step. You need to shuffle the dataset to avoid feeding your training algorithm only pictures of cats or only pictures of dogs for extended periods of time.

Now, run the following code outside of the declared module to test what you have so far:

```
train_path = Path.wildcard("train/*.jpg")

CatsAndDogs.pipeline(train_path)
```

And you'll see the following output:

```
["train/cat.11662.jpg", "train/dog.9221.jpg", "train/dog.10370.jpg",
  "train/cat.3705.jpg", "train/dog.3366.jpg", ...]
```

At this point in the pipeline, you have a list of image paths that you need to parse into tensors. You can accomplish this using StbImage. Start by creating a new private function in the CatsAndDogs module named parse_image/1:

```
defp parse_image(path) do
  label = if String.contains?(path, "cat"), do: 0, else: 1

  case StbImage.read_file(path) do
    {:ok, img} -> {img, label}
    _error -> :error
  end
end
```

This function parses paths into a tuple of {img, label}, where img is an %StbImage{} object and label is a 0 when the image is a cat or a 1 when the image is a dog. The label is determined directly from the file path. Notice that this function handles the possibility that some images are corrupt by returning :error atoms when StbImage encounters a file it can't successfully read. You can discard these errors later by applying a filter.

Next, you need to add this parsing to your pipeline. At this point, you could apply parse_image/1 with Enum.map/2, however, your pipeline should be both concurrent and lazy. To create a stream of parallel processes, you can use Task.async_stream/3, which returns a stream that runs a function concurrently on each element that it's given. You can add Task.async_stream/3 directly to your pipeline, like this:

```
def pipeline(paths) do
  paths
  |> Enum.shuffle()
  |> Task.async_stream(&parse_image/1)
end
```

Now, run the following code:

```
train_path = Path.wildcard("train/*.jpg")
CatsAndDogs.pipeline(train_path)
```

And you'll see this:

```
#Function<3.23692026/2 in Task.build_stream/3>
```

Notice that the pipeline doesn't yield any results; it simply returns a function that builds a stream data structure. To yield some results, you need to consume a part of the stream. Try consuming part of the pipeline by running the following code:

```
train_path = Path.wildcard("train/*.jpg")
train_pipeline = CatsAndDogs.pipeline(train_path)
Enum.take(train_pipeline, 5)
```

And you'll see something similar to this:

```
[
  ok: {%StbImage{
    data: <<127, 136, 133, 126, 135, 132, 126, ...>>,
    shape: {300, 399, 3},
    type: {:u, 8}
  }, 1},
  ok: {%StbImage{
    data: <<4, 4, 2, 4, 4, 2, 4, 4, 2, 4, 4, 2, ...>>,
    shape: {373, 500, 3},
    type: {:u, 8}
  }, 1},
  ...
]
```

Notice that Task.async_stream/3 wraps each result in an {:ok, result} tuple. This result is important to keep in mind as you add more steps to your pipeline because you'll need to handle success cases ({:ok, result}) and error cases ({:error, reason}) later on.

At this point, you have tuples of StbImage structs and integer labels. For training, Axon requires that your inputs are tuples of batched tensors. To get there, you need to implement some basic parsing for converting StbImage structs to tensors:

```
defp to_tensors({:ok, {img, label}}, target_height, target_width) do
  img_tensor =
    img
    |> StbImage.resize(target_height, target_width)
```

```
|> StbImage.to_nx()
|> Nx.divide(255)

label_tensor = Nx.tensor([label])

{img_tensor, label_tensor}
end
```

This function accepts a successful result from Task.async_stream/3, resizes each image to a uniform height and width, converts the image to a tensor, and scales the input pixel values to be between 0 and 1.

Recall from Chapter 2, Get Comfortable with Nx, on page 21, image tensors commonly order data in dimensions with color channels as the first or last dimension, which are denoted with channels first and channels last representations, respectively. StbImage yields tensors with channels last configurations, so there's no need to transpose the input data.

The to_tensor/3 function also converts integer labels to a tensor by wrapping the integer in a tensor before returning a tuple of {img_tensor, label_tensor}.

Of course, it's entirely possible that parse_image/1 didn't successfully load an image from a file. To prevent these errors from cascading down to to_tensors/3, you need to filter them out before applying to_tensors/3. You also need to add the target_height and target_width arguments to your pipeline, like this:

```
def pipeline(paths, target_height, target_width) do
  paths
  |> Enum.shuffle()
  |> Task.async_stream(&parse_image/1)
  |> Stream.filter(fn
    {:ok, {%StbImage{}, _}} -> true
    _ -> false
  end)
  |> Stream.map(&to_tensors(&1, target_height, target_width))
end
```

Notice that your filter function pattern matches on results that return {:ok, result} and discards everything else. Additionally, applying to_tensors/3 is as easy as using Stream.map/2. Run the following code to inspect what your pipeline looks like at this point:

```
train_path = Path.wildcard("train/*.jpg")
target_height = 96
target_width = 96

train_pipeline = CatsAndDogs.pipeline(
  train_path, target_height, target_width
)

Enum.take(train_pipeline, 5)
```

Notice you have to specify the additional target_height and target_width arguments. The choice of target_height and target_width is arbitrary. Just remember that lower resolutions encode less information than higher resolutions and might be more difficult for your neural network to train on, whereas higher resolutions require more processing power. After running this code, you'll see something similar to this:

```
[
  {#Nx.Tensor<
     f32[channels: 3][height: 96][width: 96]
     EXLA.Backend<cuda:0, 0.2231265192.3745644570.217183>
     [
       [
         [0.5490195751190186, 0.5647058486938477, 0.5568627119064331, ...],
         ...
       ],
       ...
     ]
   >,
   #Nx.Tensor<
     s64[1]
     EXLA.Backend<cuda:0, 0.2231265192.3745644570.217184>
     [0]
   >},
   ...
]
```

Your pipeline is almost finished. At this point, you have entries that are tuples of single image and label pairs. Rather than processing single images at once, it's often more efficient to process batches of images. Fortunately, you can implement batching relatively easily by chunking the input stream and applying a transformation to the chunks. Modify your pipeline to match the following:

```
def pipeline(paths, batch_size, target_height, target_width) do
  paths
  |> Enum.shuffle()
  |> Task.async_stream(&parse_image/1)
  |> Stream.filter(fn
    {:ok, {%StbImage{}, _}} -> true
    _ -> false
  end)
  |> Stream.map(&to_tensors(&1, target_height, target_width))
  |> Stream.chunk_every(batch_size, batch_size, :discard)
  |> Stream.map(fn chunks ->
    {img_chunk, label_chunk} = Enum.unzip(chunks)
    {Nx.stack(img_chunk), Nx.stack(label_chunk)}
  end)
end
```

Your pipeline now takes a batch_size argument, which controls the batch size of yielded entries in the stream. To generate batches, you chunk results using Stream.chunk_every/4 with a chunk size equal to the batch size, which yields a list of batch_size entries. You discard leftover images so you're never left with uneven batches. You then add a transformation, which uses Enum.unzip/1 to unzip the list of {img, label} tuples into two lists of tensors. Finally, you pass these lists to Nx.stack/1 to stack the list of tensors into a single tensor.

Now, run the following code to verify your pipeline is working as expected:

```
train_path =
  Path.wildcard("train/*.jpg")
  |> Enum.shuffle()

batch_size = 128
target_height = 96
target_width = 96

train_pipeline = CatsAndDogs.pipeline(
  train_path, batch_size, target_height, target_width
)

Enum.take(train_pipeline, 1)
```

And you'll see this:

```
[
  {#Nx.Tensor<
     f32[128][channels: 3][height: 96][width: 96]
     EXLA.Backend<cuda:0, 0.3445614888.3462266912.105686>
     [
       [
         [
           [0.9999999403953552, 0.9999999403953552, ...],
           ...
         ],
         ...
       ],
       ...
     ]
   >,
   #Nx.Tensor<
     s64[128][1]
     EXLA.Backend<cuda:0, 0.3445614888.3462266912.105719>
     [
       [1],
       [0],
       [0],
       [1],
```

```
        [0],
        [0],
        ...
      ]
    >}
]
```

Finally, you'll need to create a test set to test your results on. You can do this by shuffling the input paths and then splitting the train set:

```
{test_paths, train_paths} =
  Path.wildcard("train/*.jpg")
  |> Enum.shuffle()
  |> Enum.split(1000)

batch_size = 128
target_height = 96
target_width = 96

train_pipeline = CatsAndDogs.pipeline(
  train_paths, batch_size, target_height, target_width
)
test_pipeline = CatsAndDogs.pipeline(
  test_paths, batch_size, target_height, target_width
)

Enum.take(train_pipeline, 1)
```

Congratulations, the hardest part is over! You've successfully created an image input pipeline, and you're ready to start training a neural network.

Trying to See with MLPs

In Building the Model, on page 131, you created the simplest kind of neural network to recognize handwritten digits—a multi-layer perceptron (MLP) or dense feed-forward network. Your first instinct might be to try to apply an MLP to this problem—after all, it's just another image classification task, right?

As you'll see in this chapter, MLPs are not always the best choice for dealing with image data—but you'll still train one anyway so that you can establish a baseline level of performance.

Start by running the following code to create a new MLP model:

```
mlp_model =
  Axon.input("images", shape: {nil, target_height, target_width, 3})
  |> Axon.flatten()
  |> Axon.dense(256, activation: :relu)
  |> Axon.dense(128, activation: :relu)
  |> Axon.dense(1, activation: :sigmoid)
```

Forking Cells

The models you'll create and train in the next few sections are independent. To avoid adding an unnecessary dependency between individual training runs, you can tell Livebook that these sections only depend on the data section you defined previously. To do so, simply create a new Livebook section, and then specify that the section is forked from the section that contains your training pipeline.

You're welcome to add more hidden layers, adjust the hyperparameters of the hidden layers, and change the hidden activation. However, don't change the input or output layers.

Notice the input shape in this case is a tensor of {nil, target_height, target_width, 3}, where nil is the batch size and 3 is the number of color channels. The output layer is a dense layer with one unit and a :sigmoid activation function. Determining whether an image is a cat or a dog is a binary classification problem, which means you're trying to map inputs to one of two classes. Your output layer will return a single probability between 0 and 1, where probabilities closer to 0 map to the label cat and probabilities closer to 1 map to the label dog.

You should also notice the new layer Axon.flatten, which takes a two- or more-dimensional input and flattens the trailing dimensions into a single dimension. In this case, you want to pass a two-dimensional tensor to a dense layer so the flatten layer combines the channel, height, and width dimensions into a single dimension.

Now that you have data and a model, you need to implement the loop. The training loop for this problem should look similar to the one from Chapter 6, Go Deep with Axon, on page 117. Copy the following code to create and run a training loop for your MLP model:

```
mlp_trained_model_state =
  mlp_model
  |> Axon.Loop.trainer(:binary_cross_entropy, :adam)
  |> Axon.Loop.metric(:accuracy)
  |> Axon.Loop.run(train_pipeline, %{}, epochs: 5, compiler: EXLA)
```

If you compare this training loop to the one from Chapter 6, Go Deep with Axon, on page 117, you'll notice two slight differences:

- This training loop uses :binary_cross_entropy rather than :categorical_cross_entropy. Because this is a binary classification problem, :binary_cross_entropy is the appropriate loss function to use here.

- This training loop uses :adam as an optimizer rather than :sgd. :adam is a shortcut to tell Axon to use the *Adam* optimizer. Adam is a gradient-descent-based algorithm that makes slight adaptations to traditional gradient descent to improve convergence. Adam is an algorithm that may improve the training time of your neural network when compared to other optimizers.

The rest of this loop is identical to the one from Chapter 6, Go Deep with Axon, on page 117. You track :accuracy during training, pass your pipeline as input data, and train for five epochs—JIT-compiling train steps with the EXLA compiler.

After some time, you'll see this:

```
Epoch: 0, Batch: 150, accuracy: 0.5474960 loss: 1.0835106
Epoch: 1, Batch: 150, accuracy: 0.5723824 loss: 0.8659902
Epoch: 2, Batch: 150, accuracy: 0.6005284 loss: 0.7973230
Epoch: 3, Batch: 150, accuracy: 0.6123245 loss: 0.7604570
Epoch: 4, Batch: 150, accuracy: 0.6156876 loss: 0.7374102
```

Although your model improved after every epoch, it quickly plateaued at around 60% training accuracy. You may not care about training accuracy, but the inability of a model to perform well on training data is a tell-tale sign of underfitting, as you learned in Overfitting, Underfitting, and Capacity, on page 81. To see how well (or poorly), your model did, run the following code:

```
mlp_model
|> Axon.Loop.evaluator()
|> Axon.Loop.metric(:accuracy)
|> Axon.Loop.run(test_pipeline, mlp_trained_model_state, compiler: EXLA)
```

Eventually, you'll see this:

```
Batch: 0, accuracy: 0.5333334
```

What's going on here? Your model is *barely* doing better than random guessing. You might be tempted to go back and increase the capacity of your model by adding more layers or increasing the size of the existing hidden layers. You could spend hours on hyperparameter tuning, adding more layers and increasing the capacity of your model. While that might improve performance, increasing the size of the model isn't always the answer. Sometimes you need to change your approach or (in this case) change your model.

Scaling Laws

Recent advances in deep learning have suggested that adding more capacity to a model might have a direct positive correlation to model performance. Some of the large language models out of Google, OpenAI, and Facebook have hundreds of billions of parameters. Does this imply that scaling any old model will result in better performance? No, it implies that scaling the right model will lead to better performance.

Introducing Convolutional Neural Networks

MLPs are powerful enough to do well on many different problems, but they're not always the best choice. In the previous section, you saw how a basic MLP struggled to outperform random guessing when identifying images of cats and dogs. In this section, you'll see how you can do much better than an MLP by introducing a new type of neural network: the *convolutional neural network (CNN)*.

Convolutional neural networks are neural networks that replace traditional matrix multiplications in dense layers with *convolution* operations. If you have an engineering background, you're likely familiar with the convolution operation. Although the convolution operation used in neural networks is similar to the definition of a convolution you'd get from a pure mathematician or signals engineer, it differs slightly in some ways.

Imagine you have a two-dimensional input, such as an image without any color depth. You can represent this image as a grid, where each grid square is a pixel:

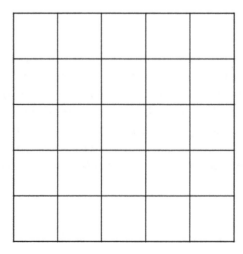

Now imagine you also have a two-dimensional *kernel*, which is a smaller grid:

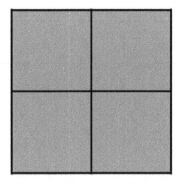

You can "slide" this kernel over each valid window in the input and map the input to a *feature map* using a relatively simple weighted sum operation. A single grid square in your new feature map is equal to the weighted sum of overlapping grid squares between the input grid and the kernel grid:

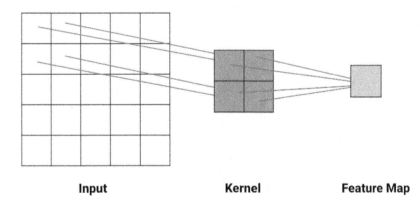

Input   **Kernel**   **Feature Map**

You can repeat this process for every valid, or full, window in the input grid. To traverse the grid, you move one grid square in the X direction until you reach the end, and then move one grid square in the Y direction, repeating this process until you've traversed the entire image. The size of each step you take is often referred to as the *stride* of the convolution. In the end, you'll have a fully transformed feature map.

So, what's the point of doing all of this? Well, if there's anything you should take away from this book, it's that a few seemingly simple matrix operations can produce magical results. You can think of your kernel as a filter. With some clever mathematics, you can design filters by hand that are capable of extracting useful representations from an input image. For example, try running the following code:

```
path = "train/dog.5.jpg"
img =
  path
  |> StbImage.read_file!()
  |> StbImage.to_nx()
  |> Nx.transpose(axes: [:channels, :height, :width])
  |> Nx.new_axis(0)
kernel = Nx.tensor([
  [-1, 0, 1],
  [-1, 0, 1],
  [-1, 0, 1]
])
kernel = kernel |> Nx.reshape({1, 1, 3, 3}) |> Nx.broadcast({3, 3, 3, 3})
img
|> Nx.conv(kernel)
|> Nx.as_type({:u, 8})
|> Nx.squeeze(axes: [0])
|> Nx.transpose(axes: [:height, :width, :channels])
|> Kino.Image.new()
```

And you'll see the following output:

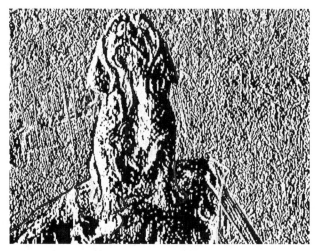

This code uses Nx.conv to implement a basic edge detector. In this instance, you can see how edges might be a useful set of features for a model to know. You can probably sit around and hand-engineer a number of feature detectors using convolutional operations by hand, but that would defeat the purpose of the machine learning process.

Remember, the power of deep learning is in its ability to learn useful representations for you. In a convolutional layer, you start with a randomly initialized kernel, and during training, the kernel starts to converge toward a parameterization capable of extracting useful features from the input. The key insight is that you can learn filters rather than engineer them by hand.

A real convolutional kernel for image data will have four dimensions. It will have two *spatial dimensions* that map directly to the X and Y coordinates of an input image. It will also have a depth or input channel dimension that corresponds to the color depth of the input image. In addition, it will have a number of *output filters*. Rather than learn a single filter per kernel, it's useful to learn multiple filters or multiple transformations of the input image. One filter can learn to extract edges, another can learn to extract corners, and so on. Typically, the output depth is considered the dimensionality of the convolutional layer.

Convolutional layers are powerful feature extractors, especially on data such as images, which have a natural grid-like structure. The convolutional layer is the fundamental unit of computation in a CNN, but there are a few other key pieces that increase the representational capacity of CNNs.

The Anatomy of a CNN

Technically speaking, a convolutional neural network is any type of neural network that contains one or more convolutional layers. However, most CNNs share a similar structure. They consist of one or more blocks or stages with a convolutional layer, an activation function, and a *pooling operation*. These blocks make up a convolutional base. The convolutional base is typically followed by a fully-connected network that takes learned features from the convolutional base and maps them to an output label. Let's have a closer look at each of these portions and what they do.

Convolutional Layers

You've already learned the ins and outs of the convolution operation and how convolutions extend to neural networks. A typical block in a convolutional base starts with a convolutional layer that performs a linear operation and forwards activations to a nonlinear activation function.

Activation Functions

As with feed-forward networks, you need to apply nonlinearities after a convolutional layer to unlock the true power of deep learning. Activation functions in the context of CNNs can be thought of as *detectors [GBC16]*—they fire on certain features. For example, in a CNN, one layer's activations might fire significantly on the presence of edges in an image, while another layer's activations might fire on the presence of certain colors.

Pooling Layers

Pooling layers aggregate spatial information in windows using some aggregate operation. Similar to convolutions, pooling layers slide a grid over an input tensor and compute an output tensor using the result of an aggregate operation for each valid spatial window in the tensor. Pooling operations share many of the same hyperparameters that control the size and traversal of a convolutional kernel, including kernel size, padding, and strides. Pooling layers, however, don't include a learned kernel. The intent of a pooling layer is to reduce the dimensionality of an input tensor while retaining some amount of useful information to be used in later layers.

Max pooling and average pooling are two of the most common pooling operations used in CNNs. Max pooling maps an input tensor to an output tensor by computing the max of every spatial window in the input. Average pooling maps an input tensor to an output tensor by computing the average of every spatial window in the input.

Fully-Connected Head

CNNs are commonly used as *feature extractors*. Remember that the strength of deep learning is in its ability to learn useful representations of inputs. Convolutional bases are *really* good at extracting features from certain types of data such as images. However, to make use of those features for practical problems, you typically need some type of fully-connected head to map features to labels. The head of a model is simply the final layer of the model. Most CNNs have a flatten or *global pooling* layer that aggregates the learned convolutional features into a form suitable for a dense network. As you'll see in Chapter 8, Stop Reinventing the Wheel, on page 171, the distinction between a feature extractor and a fully-connected classifier allows you to engineer neural networks that take advantage of the knowledge of more powerful models.

Implementing CNNs with Axon

At this point, you might be a bit overwhelmed trying to grok concepts like convolutions, padding, and pooling. It's okay if you don't fully understand these concepts yet—you don't need to have a deep understanding to take advantage of them in Axon.

The *convoluted* concepts of convolutions map to relatively simple APIs in Axon. To get the hang of how different operations in a CNN interact with an input, start by declaring a variable cnn_model that consists of a single Axon input layer:

```
cnn_model = Axon.input("images", shape: {nil, 96, 96, 3})
```

You can visualize the model by using Axon.Display.as_graph/2:

```
template = Nx.template({1, 96, 96, 3}, :f32)
Axon.Display.as_graph(cnn_model, template)
```

After running the code, you'll see this:

images (:input) {1, 96, 96, 3}

Axon.conv/3 is Axon's API for adding convolutional layers to a neural network. This API accepts an input Axon graph, a number of output filters, and a list of options that control the convolution. To see it in action, rebind the variable cnn_model to the following:

```
cnn_model =
  cnn_model
  |> Axon.conv(32,
    kernel_size: {3, 3},
    padding: :same,
    activation: :relu
  )
```

The arguments to Axon.conv/3 map directly to how the convolution operation transforms the input tensor. The first argument after the input graph represents the number of output filters this layer should learn, in this case, 32. The :kernel_size option controls the spatial size of the kernel. If you think of the spatial dimensions of the input as a matrix, the input tensor is a 96x96 matrix, while the kernel is a 3x3 matrix.

Padding controls how the input is altered before the convolution happens. In a valid or full convolution, the output feature map only has outputs for valid windows in the input tensor. The spatial size of the feature map will be smaller than the input. You can ensure the output of the convolution has the same size as the input by using :same padding.

Same padding tells the convolution to pad the input tensor's spatial dimensions such that the spatial size doesn't change. Padding simply adds new grid squares around the original input grid so the output has the same size as the original input.

Now, display the new model:

```
Axon.Display.as_graph(cnn_model, template)
```

And you'll see this graph:

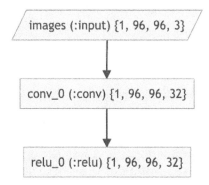

Do you notice how your model has changed? The graph now consists of an input, followed by a convolution, and then an activation function. What about the shapes? Notice the number of color channels or depth of the input tensor has gone from 3 to 32. Also, notice that the size of your spatial dimensions remained the same.

Next, rebind the variable cnn_model to the following:

```
cnn_model =
  cnn_model
  |> Axon.max_pool(kernel_size: {2, 2}, strides: [2, 2])
```

And display the model:

```
Axon.Display.as_graph(cnn_model, template)
```

After running it, you'll see this graph:

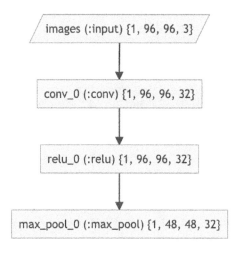

Once again, notice how your model changed. The graph has an additional max pooling layer, and the output height and width both are halved. You can repeat this process with more convolutional stages, and once again, observe how the model changes:

```
cnn_model =
  cnn_model
  |> Axon.conv(64, kernel_size: {3, 3}, activation: :relu, padding: :same)
  |> Axon.max_pool(kernel_size: {2, 2}, strides: [2, 2])
  |> Axon.conv(128, kernel_size: {3, 3}, activation: :relu, padding: :same)
  |> Axon.max_pool(kernel_size: {2, 2}, strides: [2, 2])
```

Now, use Axon.flatten to flatten the features and implement the fully-connected head:

```
cnn_model =
  cnn_model
  |> Axon.flatten()
  |> Axon.dense(128, activation: :relu)
  |> Axon.dense(1, activation: :sigmoid)
```

Overall, the entire model architecture is represented in the following code:

```
cnn_model =
  Axon.input("images", shape: {nil, 96, 96, 3})
  |> Axon.conv(32, kernel_size: {3, 3}, activation: :relu, padding: :same)
  |> Axon.max_pool(kernel_size: {2, 2}, strides: [2, 2])
  |> Axon.conv(64, kernel_size: {3, 3}, activation: :relu, padding: :same)
  |> Axon.max_pool(kernel_size: {2, 2}, strides: [2, 2])
  |> Axon.conv(128, kernel_size: {3, 3}, activation: :relu, padding: :same)
  |> Axon.max_pool(kernel_size: {2, 2}, strides: [2, 2])
  |> Axon.flatten()
  |> Axon.dense(128, activation: :relu)
  |> Axon.dense(1, activation: :sigmoid)
```

If you display this model as a table, you'll notice a few things.

One difference you'll notice between this model and your MLP model is that this model is significantly smaller in terms of the number of parameters and parameter size, even though the number of layers in your model has increased. CNNs take advantage of *sparsity*—a phenomenon you'll learn more about in Why CNNs Work, on page 160. You might be worried that this decrease in the number of trainable parameters will result in worse performance. However, it's important to know that bigger is only better if you've chosen the right tool for the job. A sledgehammer won't do better than a claw hammer at tightening a screw.

Now that you've finished building a CNN with Axon, you need to train it. You might be wondering if the change in architecture necessitates a change in the training loop. In some cases, changing the model requires changes to the training loop. However, in this case, you can copy the same training loop you used in Trying to See with MLPs, on page 149. But make sure you replace mlp_model with cnn_model:

```
cnn_trained_model_state =
  cnn_model
  |> Axon.Loop.trainer(:binary_cross_entropy, :adam)
  |> Axon.Loop.metric(:accuracy)
  |> Axon.Loop.run(train_pipeline, %{}, epochs: 5, compiler: EXLA)
```

After some time, you'll see this:

```
Epoch: 0, Batch: 150, accuracy: 0.6360207 loss: 0.6347136
Epoch: 1, Batch: 150, accuracy: 0.7611755 loss: 0.5627094
Epoch: 2, Batch: 150, accuracy: 0.8005486 loss: 0.5184103
Epoch: 3, Batch: 150, accuracy: 0.8290567 loss: 0.4833005
Epoch: 4, Batch: 150, accuracy: 0.8488207 loss: 0.4532791
```

Notice both training loss and training accuracy are significantly better than your MLP model—and it *seems* your model hasn't even plateaued. Of course, without the use of a validation set, it's difficult to know whether or not your model has started to overfit. Later in this chapter, you'll use some of Axon's out-of-the-box training tools to prevent overfitting. For now, verify your trained CNN outperforms your MLP model on the test set:

```
cnn_model
|> Axon.Loop.evaluator()
|> Axon.Loop.metric(:accuracy)
|> Axon.Loop.run(test_pipeline, cnn_trained_model_state, compiler: EXLA)
```

Eventually, you'll see this:

```
Batch: 6, accuracy: 0.8303571
```

Your test accuracy is significantly better than your MLP model. So, what's going on here? You know what a convolution is, what a typical CNN looks like, and how to implement a CNN in Axon, but you don't know why your CNN can solve this image classification problem so much better than a plain MLP.

Why CNNs Work

CNNs improve the performance of traditional MLPs on certain classes of input data, such as images, because they exploit prior knowledge about the structure of the input data.

Recall from Chapter 1, Make Machines That Learn, on page 3, that all models come with assumptions. CNNs make specific assumptions about the structure of input data and the types of relationships present in the input data. Mathematically speaking, CNNs make use of *sparse interactions*, *parameter sharing*, and *equivariant representations*. The spatial dimensions of the learned kernel in a convolutional layer are typically far smaller than the entire input image. The size of the input kernel enforces a measure of locality—a convolutional layer can only learn to extract features on a local scale. Additionally, the same kernel is applied over each valid region in the input data. Applying the same kernel to each valid region assumes that learned local representations are consistent globally. For example, the structure of an edge in an image largely remains the same regardless of whether it's in the top right corner or the bottom right corner. Convolutional layers exploit this fact and reuse the same weights for different spatial regions of the input.

Pooling layers further improve the performance of CNNs on certain classes of input data by making CNNs *translation invariant*. Translation invariance means that CNNs with pooling aren't affected by small translations in the input, which is useful because often you only care about the presence of a feature, but not necessarily where the feature is. If you have a CNN that detects images of dogs, the location of the dog in the input doesn't matter as much as the presence of the dog.

CNNs also appear to leverage the concept of cascading representations of the input data. If you were to inspect what features earlier convolutional layers identify, you'd likely find them activating on primitive features in the input, such as edges and colors. The deeper you go in the network, the higher-level extracted features become. For example, later layers in a CNN may appear to form higher-level representations of the visual representations of a dog or a cat. By composing more primitive extracted feature representations, CNNs are able to capture the complex spatial relationships present in images.

Intuitively, this learning process might make you think that it's possible to take advantage of a universal CNN for all image recognition tasks. After all, most images share many of the same primitive input features. As it turns out, it's possible to leverage feature detectors from pre-trained models in other models. You'll use pre-trained models in Chapter 8, Stop Reinventing the Wheel, on page 171.

Improving the Training Process

While a model that predicts cats and dogs with around 80% accuracy is pretty good, there's still a lot of room to improve. The winning model for this exact dataset achieved 98% accuracy in 2013. Since then, there have been significant advances in the field of computer vision, and you have yet to exhaust all of the training tricks in the book. In this section, you'll make a few small tweaks to your model and training process, and you'll see how they help you push your model toward 90% accuracy.

Augmenting Data

Right now you only have about 25,000 images total for training. For a typical deep learning problem, that's not a lot. You could go out and collect more labeled images of cats and dogs, but that's tedious and time-consuming. What if there was a way to artificially increase the size of your dataset, without needing to collect more images? As it turns out, there is. Introducing *data augmentation*.

Data augmentation is the process of slightly modifying input data to artificially increase the size of your dataset. While data augmentation is possible with all kinds of data, it's most common with images because images are mostly translation-invariant—a picture of a dog is still a picture of a dog, regardless of it being upside down or right side up.

With images, you can perform a small number of random translations and end up with an almost infinite number of different possible images. For example, if you randomly flip an input image upside down with some probability, you've essentially artificially doubled the size of your dataset. If you add another augmentation that randomly flips an image left or right, you've doubled the dataset again. Adding more augmentations leads to exponentially increasing variations of input data.

In addition to artificially increasing the size of data, data augmentation makes your model more resilient to transformations. In essence, you artificially challenge your model to learn relationships that capture the essence of a dog or the essence of a cat.

Fortunately, data augmentation is as easy as applying random transformations to each input in your pipeline. For this example, you will add transformations that randomly flip an input image up and down and left and right. You can introduce as many augmentations as you'd like, such as randomly setting the image hue, contrast, or brightness—but know that each augmentation incurs preprocessing cost.

Start by modifying your CatsAndDogs module to include the following augmentation methods:

```
defp random_flip({image, label}, axis) do
  if :rand.uniform() < 0.5 do
    {Nx.reverse(image, axes: [axis]), label}
```

```
    else
      {image, label}
    end
  end
end
```

This method randomly reverses the given axis with a probability of 0.5. Essentially, you flip a coin for each image and determine whether or not it gets flipped. Now, adjust your pipeline to include augmentations:

```
def pipeline_with_augmentations(
  paths,
  batch_size,
  target_height,
  target_width
) do
  paths
  |> Enum.shuffle()
  |> Task.async_stream(&parse_image/1)
  |> Stream.filter(fn
    {:ok, {%StbImage{}, _}} -> true
    _ -> false
  end)
  |> Stream.map(&to_tensors(&1, target_height, target_width))
  |> Stream.map(&random_flip(&1, :height))
  |> Stream.map(&random_flip(&1, :width))
  |> Stream.chunk_every(batch_size, batch_size, :discard)
  |> Stream.map(fn chunks ->
    {img_chunk, label_chunk} = Enum.unzip(chunks)
    {Nx.stack(img_chunk), Nx.stack(label_chunk)}
  end)
end
```

Now you can recreate your pipelines:

```
{test_paths, train_paths} =
  Path.wildcard("train/*.jpg")
  |> Enum.shuffle()
  |> Enum.split(1000)

batch_size = 128
target_height = 96
target_width = 96

train_pipeline = CatsAndDogs.pipeline_with_augmentations(
  train_paths,
  batch_size,
  target_height,
  target_width
)
```

```
test_pipeline = CatsAndDogs.pipeline(
  test_paths,
  batch_size,
  target_height,
  target_width
)

Enum.take(train_pipeline, 1)
```

Notice that you don't want to apply augmentations to your test pipeline. You don't want to make classification more difficult for your model at test time. Now, each image in the train set will be randomly flipped both horizontally and vertically in the training pipeline.

Tweaking the Model

In addition to updating the training pipeline, you can make some tweaks to your model to improve its overall performance, without changing the entire architecture. In Chapter 4, Optimize Everything, on page 73, you learned about the concept of regularization. Remember, regularization is any strategy applied to the training process designed to improve your model's generalization ability. Dropout is a form of regularization that seeks to prevent a model from overfitting by randomly masking some activations during training. For example, say you have a dense layer that outputs the following tensor:

```
#Nx.Tensor<
  f32[10]
  EXLA.Backend<cuda:0, 0.2231265192.3744595996.119072>
  [0.0, 1.0, 2.0, 3.0, 4.0, 5.0, 6.0, 7.0, 8.0, 9.0]
>
```

Applying dropout with a dropout probability or rate of 0.5 would *mask*, or set to 0, about half of the entries in the activation. So you might end up with a new activation tensor that looks like this:

```
#Nx.Tensor<
  f32[10]
  EXLA.Backend<cuda:0, 0.2231265192.3744595996.119072>
  [0.0, 1.0, 2.0, 0.0, 0.0, 5.0, 6.0, 0.0, 8.0, 0.0]
>
```

By dropping out intermediate activations, your model can no longer use them as a feature in subsequent layers, and thus your model needs to become more robust. It needs to learn a larger range of representations because, at any given time, a certain percentage of activations will be completely useless. Mathematically, you can think of dropout as forcing your model to learn an infinite ensemble of submodels—the applied mask changes during each training step, and thus each training step trains a fundamentally different model.

Geoffrey Hinton, one of the original authors of the *Dropout paper [SHKS14]*, said the idea for dropout came from security protocols in banks. According to Hinton, banks routinely switch a teller's shift to prevent any group of tellers from colluding to defraud the bank. Dropout routinely switches which activations are masked at any given time, preventing any group of activations from colluding to overfit to some feature in the training data.

It's important to note that dropout is only ever applied at training time. During model inference and evaluation, dropout layers are completely removed, meaning the model can make use of its entire capacity. Adding dropout layers to your model is relatively easy with Axon. Simply use Axon.dropout/2:

```
cnn_model =
  Axon.input("images", shape: {nil, 96, 96, 3})
  |> Axon.conv(32, kernel_size: {3, 3}, activation: :relu, padding: :same)
  |> Axon.batch_norm()
  |> Axon.max_pool(kernel_size: {2, 2}, strides: [2, 2])
  |> Axon.conv(64, kernel_size: {3, 3}, activation: :relu, padding: :same)
  |> Axon.batch_norm()
  |> Axon.max_pool(kernel_size: {2, 2}, strides: [2, 2])
  |> Axon.conv(128, kernel_size: {3, 3}, activation: :relu, padding: :same)
  |> Axon.max_pool(kernel_size: {2, 2}, strides: [2, 2])
  |> Axon.flatten()
  |> Axon.dense(128, activation: :relu)
  |> Axon.dropout(rate: 0.5)
  |> Axon.dense(1, activation: :sigmoid)
```

Notice this adjusts the original cnn_model by applying a dropout layer between the single hidden dense layer and the output layer. The :rate option controls the probability or rate of masking in the dropout layer. The higher the rate, the more difficult you make it for your model to learn. Also, note that you should only apply dropout after intermediate activations in hidden layers. You should *not* apply dropout on an output layer.

Early Stopping and Validation

When you first trained your CNN, you only allowed it to train for five epochs. You might have noticed that the model's training accuracy kept improving from epoch to epoch, indicating the model still had lots of room to improve even after five training epochs.

Hypothetically, you could increase the number of epochs to a large number like 100 and just let the model run. The problem is that your model will eventually overfit to the training data and likely perform worse than your underfit MLP model.

Fortunately, you can make two adjustments to the training loop that allow you to train your model indefinitely and automatically stop training when the model starts to overfit: early stopping and validation.

As you might remember from previous chapters, early stopping is a regularization technique that stops model training when the model appears to start overfitting. To determine whether a model is starting to overfit, you routinely check the model's performance against a holdout set. The holdout set is generally a small percentage of training data that's not shown to the model during training. If the model's performance on the validation data starts to dip, you know the model is probably starting to overfit, and you can stop training.

Axon offers loop *event handlers*, which takes care of early stopping and validation for you. In an Axon loop, certain events are "fired" periodically. For example, at the end of every epoch, the :epoch_completed event fires, and every handler registered to run on :epoch_completed executes. You can implement custom event handlers, but usually, you'll need only one of the few that Axon provides out of the box.

To add early stopping and validation to your training loop, you need only to make a few adjustments to your original training code. First, run the following code to split your original training pipeline into a train and validation pipeline:

```
{test_paths, train_paths} =
  Path.wildcard("train/*.jpg")
  |> Enum.shuffle()
  |> Enum.split(1000)

{test_paths, val_paths} = test_paths |> Enum.split(750)

batch_size = 128
target_height = 96
target_width = 96

train_pipeline = CatsAndDogs.pipeline_with_augmentations(
  train_paths,
  batch_size,
  target_height,
  target_width
)

val_pipeline = CatsAndDogs.pipeline(
  val_paths,
  batch_size,
```

```
    target_height,
    target_width
  )
test_pipeline = CatsAndDogs.pipeline(
  test_paths,
  batch_size,
  target_height,
  target_width
)

Enum.take(train_pipeline, 1)
```

Next, adjust your training loop code to match the following:

```
cnn_trained_model_state =
  cnn_model
  |> Axon.Loop.trainer(:binary_cross_entropy, Axon.Optimizers.adam(1.0e-3))
  |> Axon.Loop.metric(:accuracy)
  |> Axon.Loop.validate(cnn_model, val_pipeline)
  |> Axon.Loop.early_stop("validation_loss", mode: :min)
  |> Axon.Loop.run(train_pipeline, %{}, epochs: 100, compiler: EXLA)
```

You should notice two additional lines here when compared to your original training loop. Axon.Loop.validate/3 implements a supervised validation loop, tracking all of the metrics from the original training loop against the provided validation data with the provided model. The validation loop runs at the end of each epoch and tests the current model against the validation data it has yet to see. Immediately, the validation loop is Axon.Loop.early_stop/3. This handler implements early stopping. It monitors the metric "validation_loss" and stops if the metric hasn't improved. The :mode specifies which direction indicates improvement, with :min indicating you are looking to minimize loss. Note the order of these handlers is important. Axon.Loop.validate/3 registers validation metrics into the training state only after it runs, and thus if you add validation after early stopping, there won't be any valid criteria for early stopping to monitor.

You should also notice that rather than run for only five epochs, you can safely set :epochs to 100 and not have to worry about your model overfitting. The early stopping handler will trigger the alarm and stop the training loop from running at the first sign of overfitting. You can safely step away from the computer and let your model run for as long as it needs. Eventually, you'll see this:

```
...
Batch: 5, accuracy: 0.8711411 loss: 0.6648788
Epoch: 52, Batch: 150, accuracy: 0.9880484 loss: 0.1459639
Batch: 5, accuracy: 0.8589962 loss: 0.7372965
Epoch: 53, Batch: 150, accuracy: 0.9914632 loss: 0.1436956
Batch: 5, accuracy: 0.8685369 loss: 0.7409852
Epoch: 54, Batch: 150, accuracy: 0.9899628 loss: 0.1416151
```

```
Batch: 5, accuracy: 0.8683239 loss: 0.6846517
Epoch: 55, Batch: 150, accuracy: 0.9917219 loss: 0.1394880
Batch: 5, accuracy: 0.8726563 loss: 0.7095366
Epoch: 56, Batch: 150, accuracy: 0.9913080 loss: 0.1374808
Batch: 5, accuracy: 0.8626894 loss: 0.7270263
Epoch: 57, Batch: 150, accuracy: 0.9918253 loss: 0.1356151
Batch: 5, accuracy: 0.8605114 loss: 0.7936438
Epoch: 58, Batch: 150, accuracy: 0.9918253 loss: 0.1337494
```

Notice that at the first sign of overfitting your training loop stopped. Now, run the following code to validate that the tweaks you've made have actually improved your model's performance:

```
cnn_model
|> Axon.Loop.evaluator()
|> Axon.Loop.metric(:accuracy)
|> Axon.Loop.run(test_pipeline, cnn_trained_model_state, compiler: EXLA)
```

And you'll see the following output:

```
Batch: 5, accuracy: 0.8735322
```

So the few small tweaks you made resulted in a significantly better model. This final model is miles ahead of the original MLP model you started with. One thing you should take away from this is that training models is an iterative process of trial and error. In a practical setting, especially with large amounts of data, you want to test and prototype changes before implementing them on a full training run. Ideally, you add features one by one and only keep them if they show a demonstrable improvement over your previous model. As you train more and more models, you'll start to develop an intuition about what tweaks are necessary in certain situations. You'll also start to develop a standard process for prototyping and training models.

Going Beyond Image Classification

As you've seen in this chapter, CNNs are *really* good at learning to model image classification problems. In general, variants of CNN architectures are the go-to choice for any kind of computer vision task. But what other kinds of computer vision tasks can you expect to encounter in the wild?

Object Detection

Object detection is a computer vision problem in which the goal is to identify and locate the objects present in an image. Object detection can somewhat be seen as an extension of the image classification task. For example, you might have noticed in some of the training images in the cats vs. dogs dataset that a few images contained humans and other objects along with a dog.

Rather than attempt to classify an image as just a cat or dog, you could apply multiple labels to it such as human and dog or dog and toy. Object detection takes this task even further by assigning a *bounding box* to every object in a picture:

The standard object detection model in use today is *YOLO [RDGF16]*. Most variants of YOLO, short for "You Only Look Once," make use of CNNs for feature extraction and employ a number of additional strategies to achieve state-of-the-art performance on object detection tasks. Some new variants make use of *vision transformers* for feature extraction. You'll learn more about the power of transformers in Chapter 11, Model Everything with Transformers, on page 237.

Image Segmentation

Image segmentation or *semantic segmentation* is a computer vision task in which the goal is to classify every pixel in an image to some class. This extends the object detection task to an extreme level. Rather than draw a granular bounding box around each object in the image, the goal is to draw an exact mask around each object in an input image.

Perhaps the most famous architecture for image segmentation is *U-Net* *[RFB15]*, which employs a CNN for the semantic segmentation of biomedical imagery. Like in object detection, some modern architectures make use of vision transformers to achieve state-of-the-art performance on segmentation tasks.

Beyond Computer Vision

CNNs aren't only useful on image data. As you've learned in this chapter, you can effectively apply CNNs to anything with a grid-like topology. This includes audio data, video data, and even some representations of text. Intuitively speaking, CNNs can prove useful in any situation where there's a locality to the relationship being modeled.

Wrapping Up

In this chapter, you implemented a convolutional neural network (CNN) and compared its performance to a traditional MLP on computer vision tasks. You broke down the convolution operation, convolutional layers, and max pooling layers. You also learned why convolutional layers are able to learn to represent images so well. Finally, you used a few model training tricks in Axon to improve the performance of your model.

One thing you might have noticed throughout this chapter is that training neural networks can sometimes be tedious and time-consuming. Pushing the performance of your model into a state of the art is no joke. Wouldn't it be nice if you could save some training time and make use of someone else's hard work? Fortunately, you can. In the next chapter, you'll see how it's possible to stand on the shoulders of giants—or giant models—to achieve incredible performance on any task.

## CHAPTER 8

Stop Reinventing the Wheel

In the previous chapter, you implemented a new type of neural network: the convolutional neural network. You built and trained a convolutional neural network to accurately classify images of cats and dogs. After applying a few additional model training tricks, such as data augmentation and dropout, you were able to train a model to classify an image as a cat or a dog with 87% accuracy. While 87% accuracy is great, you can do even better still—with minimal changes to your training pipeline—by leveraging the power of *pre-trained models* and *transfer learning*. In this chapter, you'll discover what transfer learning is, when it's necessary, and how to perform transfer learning with Axon.

Identifying Cats and Dogs Again

To understand the powers of transfer learning, you'll make a few adjustments to your model training code from the previous chapter and compare the performance of your newly trained model with the performance of the models you trained previously. To start, fire up a Livebook and install the following dependencies:

```
Mix.install([
  {:axon_onnx, "~> 0.4"},
  {:axon, "~> 0.5"},
  {:nx, "~> 0.5"},
  {:exla, "~> 0.5"},
  {:stb_image, "~> 0.6"},
  {:kino, "~> 0.8"},
])
```

You should recognize all of these dependencies from the previous chapters of this book with the exception of :axon_onnx, which is a library for importing and exporting *Open Neural Network Exchange (ONNX)* models to and from

Axon. ONNX is a language-agnostic model serialization protocol that makes it perfect for bringing pre-trained models from the Python ecosystem into the world of Elixir. ONNX is supported by most major deep learning frameworks, and it has a number of runtime implementations that target edge, mobile, and server deployments. In Chapter 13, Put Machine Learning into Practice, on page 293, you'll get exposed to some additional usages of the ONNX format. In this chapter, you'll use ONNX as an intermediary between the Python and Elixir machine learning ecosystems.

ONNX

ONNX is a collaborative effort between Microsoft and Meta to provide a common model serialization format. The ONNX protocol[1] describes a graph-like data structure along with operator specifications which dictate arguments, behavior, and return types of a number of different nodes. While PyTorch and TensorFlow, two of the largest deep learning frameworks, have their own specialized model serialization protocols, both frameworks support serialization to ONNX.

You'll also want to set EXLA as the default backend:

```
Nx.global_default_backend(EXLA.Backend)
```

With the necessary dependencies installed, you can move on to implementing the same input pipeline as you did in the previous chapter. You don't need to make any adjustments to your pipeline implementation from the previous chapter, you simply need to add the following module to your Livebook:

```
defmodule CatsAndDogs do
  def pipeline(paths, batch_size, target_height, target_width) do
    paths
    |> Enum.shuffle()
    |> Task.async_stream(&parse_image/1)
    |> Stream.filter(fn
      {:ok, {%StbImage{}, _}} -> true
      _ -> false
    end)
    |> Stream.map(&to_tensors(&1, target_height, target_width))
    |> Stream.chunk_every(batch_size, :discard)
    |> Stream.map(fn chunks ->
      {img_chunk, label_chunk} = Enum.unzip(chunks)
      {Nx.stack(img_chunk), Nx.stack(label_chunk)}
    end)
  end
```

---

1.   https://github.com/onnx/onnx

```elixir
def pipeline_with_augmentations(
  paths,
  batch_size,
  target_height,
  target_width
) do
  paths
  |> Enum.shuffle()
  |> Task.async_stream(&parse_image/1)
  |> Stream.filter(fn
    {:ok, {%StbImage{}, _}} -> true
    _ -> false
  end)
  |> Stream.map(&to_tensors(&1, target_height, target_width))
  |> Stream.map(&random_flip(&1, :height))
  |> Stream.map(&random_flip(&1, :width))
  |> Stream.chunk_every(batch_size, :discard)
  |> Stream.map(fn chunks ->
    {img_chunk, label_chunk} = Enum.unzip(chunks)
    {Nx.stack(img_chunk), Nx.stack(label_chunk)}
  end)
end

defp random_flip({image, label}, axis) do
  if :rand.uniform() < 0.5 do
    {Nx.reverse(image, axes: [axis]), label}
  else
    {image, label}
  end
end

defp parse_image(path) do
  label = if String.contains?(path, "cat"), do: 0, else: 1

  case StbImage.read_file(path) do
    {:ok, img} -> {img, label}
    _error -> :error
  end
end

defp to_tensors({:ok, {img, label}}, target_height, target_width) do
  img_tensor =
    img
    |> StbImage.resize(target_height, target_width)
    |> StbImage.to_nx()
    |> Nx.divide(255)
    |> Nx.transpose(axes: [:channels, :height, :width])

  label_tensor = Nx.tensor([label])

  {img_tensor, label_tensor}
end
end
```

Recall from Building an Input Pipeline, on page 142, that this pipeline returns a Stream of tuples: {input, target}, where input is a tensor representation of a batch of images and target is a tensor representation of a batch of labels. You should also notice that this pipeline augments input images by randomly flipping them vertically and horizontally.

There's one minor difference between this pipeline and the pipeline you implemented on page 142. You're going to use a model that uses a channels first representation of images, and StbImage returns channels last representations. Therefore, you need to transpose the images to convert them to a channels first representation.

Now, to make sure you've copied everything over correctly, run the following code:

```
{test_paths, train_paths} =
  Path.wildcard("train/*.jpg")
  |> Enum.shuffle()
  |> Enum.split(1000)

{test_paths, val_paths} = test_paths |> Enum.split(750)

batch_size = 32
target_height = 160
target_width = 160

train_pipeline = CatsAndDogs.pipeline_with_augmentations(
  train_paths,
  batch_size,
  target_height,
  target_width
)

val_pipeline = CatsAndDogs.pipeline(
  val_paths,
  batch_size,
  target_height,
  target_width
)

test_pipeline = CatsAndDogs.pipeline(
  test_paths,
  batch_size,
  target_height,
  target_width
)

Enum.take(train_pipeline, 1)
```

You'll notice that in this snippet you've changed the target height and target width to 160. You can adjust the height and width to whatever you want, but the model you're going to use requires larger input images.

```
[
  {#Nx.Tensor<
     f32[32][channels: 3][height: 160][width: 160]
     EXLA.Backend<cuda:0, 0.2937518557.1715339297.110861>
     [
       [
         [
           [0.7450979948043823, 0.7372548580169678, 0.8078430891036987, ...],
           ...
         ],
         ...
       ],
       ...
     ]
   >,
   #Nx.Tensor<
     s64[32][1]
     EXLA.Backend<cuda:0, 0.2937518557.1715339297.110894>
     [
       [0],
       [0],
       [0],
       [0],
       [0],
       [1],
       ...
     ]
   >}
]
```

With your training pipeline in place, it's time to implement a model. In The
Anatomy of a CNN, on page 155, you learned about the typical architectural
pattern of a convolutional neural network—a convolutional base followed by
a fully-connected network. Remember that in this paradigm, the convolutional
base serves as a feature extractor, passing relevant features for use in
downstream tasks by the fully-connected network. Assuming that you have
a convolutional base that can extract useful features from your input data,
it doesn't matter where that convolutional base comes from, or what data it
was trained on.

In Chapter 7, Learn to See, on page 141, you trained your own convolutional
base from scratch on your own training data. In theory, there's nothing wrong
with training models from scratch, but trying to do so has disadvantages
when you're in a *low-data regime*. In other words, in the absence of *a lot* of
training data, training a model from scratch isn't necessarily a good idea. A
common solution to this problem is to use transfer learning. In the context
of computer vision, transfer learning often makes use of a pre-trained

convolutional base followed by a custom fully-connected network. The pre-trained convolutional base is usually trained on a large dataset like ImageNet[2] and serves as a general visual feature extractor. It doesn't matter that the convolutional base hasn't seen any of your training data because visual features are consistent. An edge is an edge, a face is a face, and a dog is a dog no matter the context in which they're presented.

Using a pre-trained model is kind of like buying some-assembly-required furniture from the store. While you might be able to build your own desk from scratch, you probably don't want to spend the time chopping down trees, designing and measuring different pieces, and hoping the final product turns out okay. Rather, you want to take advantage of the hard work somebody else has already done. All you need to do is put the pieces together—and there's still room to add some of your own flare.

While your final model from Tweaking the Model, on page 164, performed admirably, your dataset is small enough that you'll likely see improvements replacing your custom convolutional base with a pre-trained convolutional base. To do so, start by downloading the MobileNet[3] model from the official ONNX model repository.

MobileNet is a lightweight convolutional neural network specially designed for use on mobile devices. Although you can choose to use another—possibly more powerful model—MobileNet optimizes for maximum performance with minimal compute requirements and thus will be faster to work with.

After you've downloaded the mobilenetv2-7.onnx file, run the following code in your Livebook:

```
{cnn_base, cnn_base_params} = AxonOnnx.import(
  "mobilenetv2-7.onnx", batch_size: batch_size
)
```

This code imports the mobilenetv2-7.onnx model architecture and parameters into an Axon model and parameter map. You can inspect the architecture by running the following code:

```
input_template = Nx.template({1, 3, target_height, target_width}, :f32)
Axon.Display.as_graph(cnn_base, input_template)
```

The result is a lengthy output graph.

---

2.   https://www.image-net.org/
3.   https://github.com/onnx/models/blob/main/vision/classification/mobilenet/model/mobilenetv2-7.onnx

You might notice that the output shape of this model is {1, 1000}—that's because this model was pre-trained on ImageNet. The ImageNet classification task consists of images from 1,000 different classes. For this example, you want to train your own classification head, so you need to chop off the original one. Fortunately, Axon offers a robust graph manipulation API, which makes it easy to extract different portions of the graph. To chop off the original classification head, run the following code:

```
{_popped, cnn_base} = cnn_base |> Axon.pop_node()
{_popped, cnn_base} = cnn_base |> Axon.pop_node()
```

You can now reinspect the new convolutional base like so:

```
Axon.Display.as_graph(cnn_base, input_template)
```

You'll notice that the output shape of the model is {1, 1280, 1, 1} because you've removed the classification head from the original model.

cnn_base will serve as your model's pre-trained convolutional base. The output shape of the convolutional base is {batch_size, 1280, 1, 1}, which means you need to insert a fully-connected network on top of the convolutional base. The imported cnn_base is a regular Axon struct, which means you can build and manipulate it like you would if it were a model you built on your own. Before adding any additional layers, you will need to delineate the convolutional base from other components in your model. You can do this with an Axon *namespace.*

Axon namespaces are simple metadata layers that provide a mechanism for distinguishing between components of a model. Namespaces are simply a way to tell Axon to group the parameters and state of multiple layers into a single place. By default, all Axon layers belong to a root namespace. You can see this in the structure of the Axon model state, which is, essentially, a map.

Imagine you have a simple model with two layers named "foo" and "bar". The model state would look something like this:

```
%{
  "foo" => %{
    "param_name" => #Nx.Tensor<...>,
    "state_name" => #Nx.Tensor<...>
  },
  "bar" => %{
    "param_name" => #Nx.Tensor<...>
  }
}
```

If you add a namespace to the same model that wraps the layer named "foo", the model state takes on a form that looks something more like this:

```
%{
  "namespace" => %{
    "foo" => %{
      "param_name" => #Nx.Tensor<...>,
      "state_name" => #Nx.Tensor<...>
    },
  },
  "bar" => %{
    "param_name" => #Nx.Tensor<...>
  }
}
```

Notice how "foo" is no longer at the top level in the model state. That's because its state belongs to the namespace "namespace". At first glance, this might seem like a silly abstraction. But namespaces provide a simple and powerful way of initializing portions of a model from pre-trained checkpoints, applying different optimization mechanisms to different layers, and generally manipulating hierarchies of layers in your model. Axon differs explicitly from PyTorch and TensorFlow in that models aren't built from a hierarchy of modules, but rather composed into a graph-like data structure. This approach has some advantages, but it can be difficult to express ownership or hierarchy in a model. Namespaces offer a mechanism for expressing hierarchy and logical separation.

To wrap your convolutional base into its own namespace, you need to use the Axon.namespace/2 function:

```
cnn_base = cnn_base |> Axon.namespace("feature_extractor")
```

Axon.namespace/2 wraps all preceding nodes in the Axon graph under the given namespace. In this example, you give your convolutional base to the "feature_ extractor" namespace, which will come in handy later on.

In addition to namespacing your convolutional base, you need to *freeze* the convolutional base. When using pre-trained models, it's common to freeze or stop training for the pre-trained portion of your model to avoid *catastrophic forgetting* in the early stages of training. In other words, the pre-trained model remains entirely static during initial training, so it doesn't lose the knowledge it has already acquired. The early stages of training are typically the least stable, which means your pre-trained model is at risk of losing some of its value.

Freezing layers tells Axon to wrap a layer's parameters in stop_grad. This means that when updating the model during gradient descent, the gradient of frozen parameters will be 0 and therefore won't be updated. In Axon, freezing happens with respect to the model rather than the training loop or parameters. You can mark certain layers as frozen using the Axon.freeze/2 function. Axon.freeze/2 by default will freeze all proceeding layers. But it offers an API for more fine-grained freezing in models. For this example, you'll freeze your convolutional base like so:

```
cnn_base = cnn_base |> Axon.freeze()
```

You now have a frozen, pre-trained convolutional base wrapped in an identifiable namespace. The output shape of the model at this point is {batch_size, 1280, 1, 1}, so you need to flatten the features before passing them to a classification head. You can flatten the features using Axon.flatten/2, or you can use a global pooling layer. Because the amount of output features in this model is relatively large, a global pooling layer works better because it reduces the amount of input features to the classification head. Additionally, you'll want to add some regularization by using a dropout layer between your global average pooling and classification head. For this example, your classification head needs a single unit because this is a binary classification problem:

```
model =
  cnn_base
  |> Axon.global_avg_pool(channels: :first)
  |> Axon.dropout(rate: 0.2)
  |> Axon.dense(1)
```

Notice that you need to specify channels: :first for this example because the model you're using defaults to channels first representations. If you put all of these steps together, the code for building your model should look something like this:

```
{cnn_base, cnn_base_params} = AxonOnnx.import("mobilenetv2-7.onnx")
{_popped, cnn_base} = Axon.pop_node(cnn_base)
{_popped, cnn_base} = Axon.pop_node(cnn_base)

model =
  cnn_base
  |> Axon.namespace("feature_extractor")
  |> Axon.freeze()
  |> Axon.global_avg_pool(channels: :first)
  |> Axon.dropout(rate: 0.2)
  |> Axon.dense(1)
```

With your input pipeline and model in place, you can move forward with creating a training loop. By now, you should have a pretty good idea of how to create and manipulate Axon training loops. For this example, start by implementing the same training loop, as you did in Early Stopping and Validation, on page 165, with some minor adjustments:

```
loss = &Axon.Losses.binary_cross_entropy(&1, &2,
  reduction: :mean,
  from_logits: true
)
optimizer = Axon.Optimizers.adam(1.0e-4)

trained_model_state =
  model
  |> Axon.Loop.trainer(loss, optimizer)
  |> Axon.Loop.metric(:accuracy)
  |> Axon.Loop.validate(model, val_pipeline)
  |> Axon.Loop.early_stop("validation_loss", mode: :min, patience: 5)
  |> Axon.Loop.run(
    train_pipeline,
    %{"feature_extractor" => cnn_base_params},
    epochs: 100,
    compiler: EXLA
  )
```

When comparing this code to your previous training loop, you'll see a few differences.

First, you use a parametrized version of Axon.Losses.binary_cross_entropy/3 as your loss function. You may have noticed your output dense layer doesn't use a sigmoid activation—it doesn't squeeze the output to a probability between 0 and 1. The outputs for this dense layer are referred to as *logits* or *log-probabilities*. When you don't specify a final sigmoid activation (or softmax for multi-class classification problems), you need to tell your loss function that you are passing logits rather than probabilities. You can do this by passing from_logits: true to your loss function. There's no difference between using the logit form or probability form—other than you can skip the extra sigmoid activation. Axon actually has an optimization that internally always uses logits to compute the cross-entropy loss. When you use logits, you need to remember to apply a sigmoid or softmax to your predictions in order to compute a probability.

Another difference you'll see is the use of the Axon.Optimizers functional form to declare an optimizer. This is just to use a learning rate that differs from the Adam optimizer's default.

The final difference you'll see is that the empty map after train_pipeline has been replaced with a map containing the parameters for your model's feature extractor. This map represents your training loop's initial state.

In all of the previous chapters, you trained models from scratch, so you didn't need any initial state. Because you want to make use of a pre-trained model here, you need to tell Axon what pre-trained parameters to use. Axon will take this initial state and initialize a model with the given fixed parameters for your feature extractor.

You could provide all of the model's initial parameters here if you wanted to. Under the hood, Axon initializes all of the parameters not given in the initial state for you. The initial state argument is kind of like the accumulator for Axon's training loop. There's no difference between you initializing a model's parameters explicitly and providing them to a training loop and you letting Axon do it for you. Letting Axon do the work for you only saves you a little bit of boilerplate code.

It's important to understand that building on top of a pre-trained model doesn't necessarily need to change much about your model training process. Aside from a few tweaks in the model creation process, the addition of some initial state in the training loop, and some tweaks to the loss function and optimizer, not much has changed from the previous chapter. Many of the principles and strategies that apply when training a model from scratch also apply when training on top of a pre-trained model. You can take advantage of someone else's hard work with minimal changes.

As with any machine learning algorithm, you'll have to consider some caveats and limitations, which you'll learn about in Knowing When to Use Transfer Learning, on page 185. However, transfer learning is an incredibly powerful tool. In a lot of cases, it makes more sense to reach for a pre-trained model than to attempt to train one from scratch.

After some time running your training loop, you'll see the following output:

```
...
Batch: 23, accuracy: 0.9348959 loss: 0.1361023
Epoch: 15, Batch: 700, accuracy: 0.9220337 loss: 0.2185298
Batch: 23, accuracy: 0.9414064 loss: 0.1326849
Epoch: 16, Batch: 700, accuracy: 0.9208744 loss: 0.2164259
Batch: 23, accuracy: 0.9361981 loss: 0.1386008
Epoch: 17, Batch: 700, accuracy: 0.9210071 loss: 0.2145825
Batch: 23, accuracy: 0.9375002 loss: 0.1397082
Epoch: 18, Batch: 700, accuracy: 0.9189568 loss: 0.2129661
Batch: 23, accuracy: 0.9388022 loss: 0.1403071
```

Your model is touching 93-94% training and validation accuracy, but does it hold up on the test set? Run the following evaluation loop to find out:

```
eval_model = model |> Axon.sigmoid()

eval_model
|> Axon.Loop.evaluator()
|> Axon.Loop.metric(:accuracy)
|> Axon.Loop.run(test_pipeline, trained_model_state, compiler: EXLA)
```

In this example, you adjust your model by applying a sigmoid on top of the original model to output probabilities rather than logits.

After running the code, you'll see this result:

```
Batch: 23, accuracy: 0.9449407
```

Wow, by simply attaching a single dense output layer on top of a pre-trained model, you were able to significantly outperform your custom model. But there's still some performance left on the table. In the next section, you'll *fine-tune* your model for even better performance.

Fine-Tuning Your Model

In the previous section, you made use of a pre-trained model for feature extraction. You attached a classification head on top of a frozen pre-trained model—taking advantage of the general features extracted from the pre-trained model for your specific problem. Remember, freezing the model initially was important because the early stages of training are unstable and your model was at risk of losing all of its prior knowledge. But now that you have a trained model, you can unfreeze some of the layers of the pre-trained model and force them to learn features specific to your problem. This process is called fine-tuning.

Rather than freeze the entire pre-trained model, during fine-tuning you unfreeze the top-most layers of the pre-trained model. Remember that early layers of a convolutional neural network learn more general features, while later layers learn features specific to your dataset. By unfreezing a small amount of the top-most layers, you allow your model to learn features that are specific to your dataset. To start the fine-tuning process, run the following code to unfreeze the top-most layers of your convolutional base:

```
model = model |> Axon.unfreeze(up: 50)
```

This code unfreezes the top 50 layers of your model—meaning that the top 50 layers in your model will be trainable. Now, rewrite your training pipeline to look like this:

```
loss = &Axon.Losses.binary_cross_entropy(&1, &2,
  reduction: :mean,
  from_logits: true
)
```

```
optimizer = Axon.Optimizers.rmsprop(1.0e-5)

trained_model_state =
  model
  |> Axon.Loop.trainer(loss, optimizer)
  |> Axon.Loop.metric(:accuracy)
  |> Axon.Loop.validate(model, val_pipeline)
  |> Axon.Loop.early_stop("validation_loss", mode: :min, patience: 5)
  |> Axon.Loop.run(
    train_pipeline,
    trained_model_state,
    epochs: 100,
    compiler: EXLA
  )
```

This training pipeline is essentially identical to the one you implemented in the previous section. Only two minor differences exist. First, you changed the learning rate in the optimizer from 1.0e-4 to 1.0e-5 and switched to the RMSProp optimizer. When fine-tuning, it's important to keep the learning rate low—larger learning rates when fine-tuning make the model susceptible to overfitting and possibly unstable updates.

Finally, rather than only passing the pre-trained model's parameters, you pass the entire trained model state from the previous training iteration as the initial state of your loop. Again, this is just telling Axon that you don't want to start training from scratch—you already have a trained model and you want to use it.

After running the training loop, you'll see this:

```
...
Batch: 23, accuracy: 0.9739585 loss: 0.0710718
Epoch: 5, Batch: 700, accuracy: 0.9660777 loss: 0.1285189
Batch: 23, accuracy: 0.9739584 loss: 0.0710575
Epoch: 6, Batch: 700, accuracy: 0.9713383 loss: 0.1209094
Batch: 23, accuracy: 0.9765627 loss: 0.0717105
Epoch: 7, Batch: 700, accuracy: 0.9726299 loss: 0.1142527
Batch: 23, accuracy: 0.9778647 loss: 0.0800760
Epoch: 8, Batch: 700, accuracy: 0.9770432 loss: 0.1082386
Batch: 23, accuracy: 0.9752605 loss: 0.0922253
Epoch: 9, Batch: 700, accuracy: 0.9777576 loss: 0.1030978
Batch: 23, accuracy: 0.9709822 loss: 0.1120541
```

Your model already had some impressive performance after the previous iteration of training, and that shows in the training logs here. Your model recorded slight improvements on the training and validation data, but you need to see if fine-tuning increased its performance on the test set:

```
eval_model = model |> Axon.sigmoid()

eval_model
|> Axon.Loop.evaluator()
|> Axon.Loop.metric(:accuracy)
|> Axon.Loop.run(test_pipeline, trained_model_state, compiler: EXLA)
```

After running this cell, you'll see the following:

```
Batch: 23, accuracy: 0.9709823
```

Just when you start to think you can't do any better on this problem, you're able to squeeze even more performance out of your model. By fine-tuning the top layers of your pre-trained model, you were able to increase the performance of your model by a few percentage points.

Now that you've seen the power of transfer learning and fine-tuning, you might be wondering *why* they work so well, and if you should use them in every context. In the next section, you'll dive deeper into the intuition behind transfer learning and learn more about when you should use it.

Understanding Transfer Learning

Transfer learning is a technique for repurposing a pre-trained model for use on a related task. In the previous section, you saw transfer learning in the context of a deep learning problem—specifically a computer vision problem. It is possible to make use of transfer learning with other machine learning techniques and in other domains, but transfer learning is incredibly common in computer vision problems.

The power of transfer learning should make some intuitive sense. Rather than start from scratch for every problem, you inject a model with some past knowledge of the problem to speed up training. In Chapter 6, Go Deep with Axon, on page 117, you learned that the power of deep learning is all about learning useful representations of data. If you have a pre-trained model that already has some useful representations of input data that is similar to yours, it makes sense that it would allow your model to learn faster and with better final performance.

In this section, you'll dive deeper into why transfer learning works and when to use it.

Why Transfer Learning Works

Recall from Chapter 7, Learn to See, on page 141, that earlier layers in convolutional neural networks often appear to learn general features, such as edges in an image. These general features often apply to any image recognition task.

The features of an edge remain the same regardless of whether the purpose of the model is to identify cats and dogs or detect letters on street signs. What this means is that you can treat portions of pre-trained models as general feature detectors and apply them to your particular use case.

Pre-trained models are often trained on large datasets such as ImageNet, which means they are exposed to a wide range of input data. In other words, they are capable of generalizing to lots of different use cases because they've been trained on a broad range of data. In a sense, you can consider the representation learned by these models to be a general representation of visual data. But it might be a stretch to say these models apply to all classes of visual data. The implications of using a model which already has some useful representations of visual data are that your model doesn't have to spend time struggling to learn its own representations and instead can learn how to make use of those representations.

Consider the model you trained from scratch in the previous chapter. It was trained on around 25,000 images of cats and dogs. If you compare the features learned by your model from the previous chapter to the features learned by MobileNet—which was trained on 14 million images of 1,000 different image classes—what model do you think learned the most robust, generalizable features of visual data? Your trained-from-scratch model had to not only learn representations of visual data from a small amount of input data but also make use of those representations for making predictions. The model you trained in this chapter has a much simpler task—learn to make predictions from a robust representation. You can think of it as giving your model a significant head start in a race.

Understanding why transfer learning works so well might lead you to wonder if you should use pre-trained models for every problem you encounter. In the next section, you'll learn a little bit more about when it makes sense to use transfer learning and when it doesn't.

Knowing When to Use Transfer Learning

Like most questions in machine learning, there's no definitive answer to when to use transfer learning. The real answer is "it depends." It depends on many factors such as the kind of data you have, how much data you have, how many resources you have, and what your objectives are.

In some domains, such as computer vision and *natural language processing*, transfer learning is the standard approach to training new models on specialized applications. This is largely due to the abundance of general models and the significant performance increases they bring to a wide variety of problems—even without much data.

Generally speaking, if you don't have *a lot* of data, you'll probably benefit from making use of pre-trained models. Even if you do have a lot of data, you might still benefit from them. But certain domains necessitate novel approaches. Some domains don't have any useful pre-trained models.

It's also important to note you can't use any pre-trained model and expect it to work on your input data. For example, a MobileNet trained on ImageNet is a terrible choice for the convolutional base of a model intended for use on biomedical images. ImageNet doesn't have this imagery, and biomedical images don't share many similarities with other types of images. For transfer learning to work, you need to ensure you choose a model that was trained on data similar enough to your use case to be effective—you wouldn't expect a model trained on Portuguese to have a useful representation of the English language.

When choosing a pre-trained model, you need to consider the problem you're trying to solve and your success criteria for solving it. While you can choose the model with the best metrics on some common machine learning benchmark, that's not always the right thing to do. For example, if you're planning to deploy your model on mobile or edge devices, choosing the best model usually also means the model is larger and more compute-intensive, which means it will be slow. You need to take into account all of your performance objectives when choosing a pre-trained model.

Fortunately, pre-trained models are abundant in the machine learning ecosystem. But you might be wondering how it's even possible to use them considering the Elixir machine learning ecosystem is so new. Most pre-trained models you'll find were built in Python with Python-specific machine learning frameworks. How can you take advantage of these models in your problems? In the next section, you'll use some of the tools and repositories available in Python to bring models into your Elixir projects.

Taking Advantage of the Machine Learning Ecosystem

You may have noticed that the title of this chapter is a bit ironic given it appears in a book titled *Machine Learning in Elixir*. After all, isn't the Nx ecosystem a rehash of the Python machine learning ecosystem? In many ways, projects like Axon in the Elixir Nx ecosystem model themselves after their counterparts in the Python ecosystem—with sensible deviations and complete break-offs in design where necessary. The breaks from Python are deliberate, but that doesn't mean Elixir Nx completely shies away from the

Python ecosystem. From the beginning, Nx was designed for flexibility. Rather than depend entirely on projects with a popular Python front-end like Tensor-Flow or PyTorch, Nx implements a modular approach that makes it capable of taking advantage of *any* tensor manipulation library.

This philosophy of flexibility extends to libraries like Axon. The key feature of Axon is the Axon data structure, which represents neural networks in a graph-like data structure. You can manipulate and build this data structure directly from Elixir. The beauty is that if you know how to traverse the Axon graph, you know how to convert it to an external format. Similarly, if you have a serialized format from an external framework such as ONNX or TensorFlow, you can just as easily convert that into an Axon graph for use directly in Elixir. Axon isn't tied to any particular runtime, and thus you don't have to worry about being tied to a particular model format.

The Python ecosystem is *massive*, and just as there's an abundance of web frameworks and stacks to choose from across languages, there's an abundance of machine learning frameworks and stacks to choose from within the Python ecosystem. Axon and its related projects have an explicit goal of seamless import of any model from the Python ecosystem for use within Elixir without forcing you to implement a Port or tying you to a particular runtime.

Now you might be wondering how you can take advantage of existing models in your own projects. In the rest of this section, you'll convert existing models from popular frameworks into the ONNX format for use within Elixir.

Exporting Models from TensorFlow

TensorFlow's blessed serialized model format is the Saved Model,[4] though some older versions of TensorFlow Keras supported a variety of serialization formats for models and weights. This section focuses specifically on the saved model format.

Using tf2onnx

tf2onnx[5] is a Python library for converting TensorFlow models to the ONNX format. tf2onnx supports TensorFlow saved models, TensorFlow JS models, and TensorFlow Lite models. The easiest way to use tf2onnx is through the CLI. For example, if you have a TensorFlow saved model in a directory, you can run the following to convert it to an ONNX model:

---

4.   https://www.tensorflow.org/guide/saved_model
5.   https://github.com/onnx/tensorflow-onnx

```
$ python3 -m tf2onnx.convert |
  --saved-model path-to-model |
  --output model.onnx
```

To see tf2onnx in action, create a new Python file named save_tensorflow_model.py and copy the following code into a newly created file:

```
import tensorflow as tf

model = tf.keras.applications.ResNet50(weights="imagenet")

model.save("resnet")
```

Save the file you copied the code into as save_tensorflow_model.py. Then, run the script with this:

```
$ python3 save_tensorflow_model.py
```

This script imports a pre-trained ResNet50 model using the tf.keras.applications submodule. There are a number of other pre-trained models you can use under the Keras Applications[6] module. After importing ResNet50, the script saves the model using the saved model format to a directory resnet. You'll see the resnet directory in your working directory after running this script.

Next, run the following command to convert your model to ONNX:

```
$ python3 -m tf2onnx.convert |
  --saved-model resnet/ |
  --output resnet_tensorflow.onnx
```

After you run this script, you'll see the resnet_tensorflow.onnx file appear in your current working directory.

Now, create a new Elixir script named resnet.exs and copy the following code into the newly created file:

```
Mix.install([
  {:axon_onnx, "~> 0.4"},
  {:axon, "~> 0.5"}
])

{model, params} = AxonOnnx.import("resnet_tensorflow.onnx")

IO.inspect model
```

Then, in the terminal, run the following command:

```
$ elixir resnet.exs
```

---

6.   https://keras.io/api/applications/

Running this script installs Axon and AxonOnnx and imports the exported ResNet model into the Axon model format before inspecting the model. After running the command, you'll see the following output:

```
09:36:43.537 [warning] unk__613 has no specified dimension, assuming nil
#Axon<
  inputs: ["input_1"]
>
```

This output indicates that your model is ready for use from Elixir. The logged warning indicates that one of the dimensions has an unspecified size, so Axon filled it in as nil for you. In this case, the unk_613 is the model's batch dimension. If you see warnings like this and end up with errors during import, you can usually get rid of them by providing explicit values for these dimensions when importing your model:

```
{model, params} = AxonOnnx.import("resnet_tensorflow.onnx", unk__613: 32)
```

Once you pass an explicit value for a dimension, you must stick to using dimension sizes with the same value.

Finding Pre-trained Tensorflow Models

While this example made use of tf.keras.applications, you can find TensorFlow saved models in some other places too. TensorFlow Hub[7] is a TensorFlow-specific repository of pre-trained models for a variety of tasks. You can find models which are in a variety of different formats. Generally, most models are supported by tf2onnx, though you might need to dig into the tf2onnx documentation to ensure models export correctly from the variety of formats supported on TensorFlow Hub.

As you'll see in Exporting Models from HuggingFace, on page 191, you can also export saved models yourself from high-level application-specific libraries such as HuggingFace transformers.

Exporting Models from PyTorch

Because ONNX is an open collaborative between Microsoft and Meta, and PyTorch is a product of Meta's AI laboratory, PyTorch has first-class support for exporting models to ONNX. The torch.onnx[8] module provides functions for exporting models to ONNX. The documentation provides an in-depth overview of how to export models and some of the common sharp edges encountered

---

7. https://tfhub.dev/
8. https://pytorch.org/docs/stable/onnx.html

when exporting models. Given a pre-trained PyTorch module, you can typically export without issue using torch.onnx.export:

```
import torch

dummy_input = torch.randn(10, 3, 224, 224)

torch.onnx.export(model, dummy_input, "model.onnx")
```

All you need to do is provide an explicit input for PyTorch to use to build the ONNX graph. To see this in action, create a new Python script named save_pytorch_model.py and copy the following code into the newly created file:

```
import torch
import torchvision

dummy_input = torch.randn(10, 3, 224, 224)

model = torchvision.models.resnet50(pretrained=True)

torch.onnx.export(model, dummy_input, "resnet_pytorch.onnx")
```

Then run the script with this:

```
$ python3 save_pytorch_model.py
```

This script uses both PyTorch and TorchVision[9] to import a pre-trained ResNet and save it to the ONNX format using torch.onnx.export. After running the script, you'll see resnet_pytorch.onnx in your current working directory. Next, change your resnet.exs script to import your PyTorch version of the ResNet ONNX model:

```
Mix.install([
  {:axon_onnx, "~> 0.4"},
  {:axon, "~> 0.5"}
])

{model, params} = AxonOnnx.import("resnet_pytorch.onnx")

IO.inspect model
```

Then, run your script:

```
$ elixir resnet.exs
```

And you'll see this output:

```
#Axon<
  inputs: ["input.1"]
>
```

This output indicates that you've successfully imported a pre-trained model from PyTorch for use within Elixir.

---

9.   https://pytorch.org/vision/stable/index.html

Finding Pre-trained PyTorch Models

Similar to TensorFlow, there are a number of places to go for finding pre-trained models in PyTorch. For example, there are application-specific libraries, such as TorchVision,[10] TorchText,[11] and TorchAudio[12] with some pre-trained models available for export.

Generally, if you're able to find a PyTorch implementation of a pre-trained model on GitHub, you should be able to export the model to the ONNX format. As the PyTorch documentation mentions, there are a number of considerations when exporting models to ONNX, and not all implementations are written with these considerations in mind. You might have to make some minor modifications to certain models, but ONNX covers a significant percentage of the models you'd be interested in exporting.

Exporting Models from HuggingFace

Perhaps the most popular machine learning library in existence right now is HuggingFace Transformers.[13] This library provides conveniences and pre-trained implementations of *transformer models*. You'll use transformer models in Chapter 11, Model Everything with Transformers, on page 237. HuggingFace also has a pre-trained model hub that hosts models from a large number of organizations and individuals. Elixir has its own library which interfaces directly with the HuggingFace Hub known as Bumblebee.[14] Bumblebee provides native Elixir implementations of models, so they're a bit cleaner and more robust than the auto-imported versions you'd get from ONNX. If you want to use a model not available in Bumblebee, it's possible to export some transformer models from HuggingFace using the transformers.onnx Python module.

Assuming you have the transformers library installed, you only need to run a command like this from the CLI to extract an ONNX model from an implementation on HuggingFace:

```
$ python3 -m transformers.onnx --model=org/model path
```

org/model points to the specific model you'd like to export. Only a subset of all models on the hub are officially supported.[15] To see how exporting from

10. https://pytorch.org/vision/stable/index.html
11. https://pytorch.org/text/stable/models.html
12. https://pytorch.org/audio/stable/models.html
13. https://huggingface.co/docs/transformers/index
14. https://github.com/elixir-nx/bumblebee
15. https://huggingface.co/docs/transformers/serialization

transformers works hands-on, run the following command to export a pre-trained ResNet model from Microsoft:

```
$ python3 -m transformers.onnx --model=microsoft/resnet-50 resnet/
```

This code exports a pre-trained ResNet model with weights provided by Microsoft to the path resnset/model.onnx. Now you can modify your resnet.exs to import this model:

```
Mix.install([
  {:axon_onnx, "~> 0.4"},
  {:axon, "~> 0.5"}
])

{model, params} = AxonOnnx.import("resnet/model.onnx")

IO.inspect model
```

And then, run the script:

```
$ elixir resnet.exs
```

After running the script, you'll see the following output:

```
13:40:05.534 [warning] batch has no specified dimension, assuming nil

13:40:05.538 [warning] sequence has no specified dimension, assuming nil

#Axon<
  inputs: ["pixel_values"]
>
```

This output means that the import was successful. You now know how to import models from TensorFlow and PyTorch and how to take advantage of the largest model repository in existence from Elixir. This should set you on a path for using almost any pre-trained model you can find without having to jump through too many hoops.

Wrapping Up

In this chapter, you used pre-trained models to significantly improve your model performance over one trained from scratch. You made use of pre-trained models in Axon for feature extraction and fine-tuning, and you learned how to take most models from the Python ecosystem and use them in Elixir. Moving forward, you should always ask yourself if training a model from scratch is worth it, or if you can benefit from using a pre-trained model. More often than not, using a pre-trained model will save you time and improve the performance of your models.

In the previous few chapters, you learned quite a bit about deep learning and Axon. But you've been primarily focused on image data. Fortunately, many of the lessons you've learned in these chapters still apply, but there are some additional considerations when working with certain kinds of data. In the next two chapters, you'll apply deep learning to different types of sequential data—namely text and time-series data.

## CHAPTER 9

Understand Text

In the past few chapters, the problems you solved with neural networks have dealt exclusively with image data. While deep learning has had a significant effect on the field of computer vision, deep learning is versatile enough for use in a number of other domains. As a budding machine learning engineer, it's important to understand how to apply deep learning to solve different problems in different domains.

Natural language processing is one field that has significantly benefitted from the rise of deep learning. As a subfield of artificial intelligence and computer science, natural language processing deals with human language. If your problem deals with text, you're probably going to be doing some natural language processing.

Neural networks have resulted in significant breakthroughs in every language-understanding task, from text classification to question answering to machine translation. While most of these breakthroughs have come as a result of ever larger transformer models, it's still important to understand some of the foundational approaches to sequence processing—namely *recurrent neural networks (RNNs)*. RNNs are a class of deep learning models used specifically for processing sequences. In this chapter, you'll learn what RNNs are, why they're better than traditional feed-forward networks for sequence processing, and some of the pitfalls that lead to the rise of transformers.

Classifying Movie Reviews

Imagine you work for a movie theater, and your task is to decide which movies to show based on expert reviews about the movies. While you could spend the time sifting through all of these reviews, it's both time-consuming and tedious. Instead, you decide to create an algorithm that classifies movie reviews as positive or negative and then show only the movies with the most positive reviews. This problem is a textbook application of *sentiment analysis*.

The goal of sentiment analysis is to extract *sentiment* from natural language. Sentiment is simply the attitude of a given text. In other words, sentiment analysis is concerned with extracting the overall attitude or opinion of a given text. Typically, sentiment analysis deals with discrete labels, such as *positive*, *negative*, or *neutral*, as well as the sentiment of the text in the abstract rather than sentiment towards a certain topic. More advanced sentiment analysis tasks might focus on the degree of positivity or negativity of a text and also the object of the opinion.

For this problem, you're concerned with the sentiment of a given review toward a given movie. This is the ideal sentiment analysis problem—the object of the opinion is clear, and the reviews are explicitly meant to convey an opinion about a subject. To train your model, you'll be using the IMDB Movie Reviews Dataset.[1] The IMDB Movie Reviews Dataset contains 25,000 training reviews and 25,000 testing reviews. Each example includes an English language review and a sentiment label, such as this:

```
review = "The Departed is Martin Scorsese's best work, and anybody
who disagrees is wrong. This movie is amazing."

sentiment = 1
```

To get started, fire up a Livebook and add the following dependencies:

```
Mix.install([
  {:scidata, "~> 0.1"},
  {:axon, "~> 0.5"},
  {:exla, "~> 0.6"},
  {:nx, "~> 0.6"},
  {:table_rex, "~> 3.1.1"},
  {:kino, "~> 0.7"}
])
```

Nothing unexpected here. You're using SciData to download the IMDB dataset, Axon to create and train your neural network, EXLA to accelerate your computations, and Nx for some basic numerical computation and preprocessing. As a final bit of set up, run the following code to set EXLA as your default Nx backend:

```
Nx.default_backend(EXLA.Backend)
```

You know the drill. With your setup complete, it's time to move on to the data.

---

1. https://www.kaggle.com/datasets/lakshmi25npathi/imdb-dataset-of-50k-movie-reviews

Getting the Data

The IMDB Review Dataset is available as a module in SciData. Download the data by running the following code:

```
data = Scidata.IMDBReviews.download()
```

After running that code, you'll see the following output:

```
%{
  review: [
    "The story centers around Barry McKenzie who must go to England...,
    "'The Adventures Of Barry McKenzie' started life as a satirical...,
    ...
  ],
  sentiment: [1, 1, 1, 1, 1, 1, 1, 1, 1, ...]
}
```

Before continuing, you'll want to split the dataset into a training and test set:

```
{train_data, test_data} =
  data.review
  |> Enum.zip(data.sentiment)
  |> Enum.shuffle()
  |> Enum.split(23_000)
```

The dataset is a map of reviews and sentiment, with corresponding entries mapping to the same review. At this point, it might be unclear how you can map this raw text to numeric data. Extracting an informative numerical representation of text is a key challenge in natural language processing. There are many approaches. Perhaps the most common approach in deep learning is to *tokenize* and then *vectorize* the text.

Tokenization is the process of splitting text into discrete units known as tokens. You might be familiar with tokenization in the context of programming languages. Compilers generally tokenize a program into a sequence of tokens. The tokenization process is generally much easier because the rules of a programming language are well-defined. On the other hand, natural language is unstructured and differs in significant ways between languages. This implies that there are no universally superior tokenization strategies, but there are a few common ones.

Tokenizing on Whitespace

One of the most common tokenization strategies is to split text at each whitespace character. This is especially common in languages like English where whitespace is a semantically meaningful separator. This natural separation makes it easy to identify distinct tokens. Tokenizing on whitespace is not necessarily a good option for all types of text though. For example, Chinese doesn't give any significance to whitespace characters, so tokenizing on whitespace doesn't make any sense. An additional drawback is that whitespace tokenization leads to a large vocabulary of tokens. Depending on the corpus, the potential vocabulary size is unbounded.

Tokenizing on Characters

Another common strategy is to tokenize at the character level. In other words, each character, including whitespace, represents a distinct token. This is useful in a multilingual context, as you are able to capture distinct tokens across languages. Tokenizing at the character level also limits the size of your vocabulary, though tokens from character-based languages will end up representing a significant portion of your final vocabulary. One drawback of tokenizing at the character level, especially for languages like English, is that the length of your sequence increases significantly, which has significant disadvantages during training and inference. You'll learn more about these disadvantages later in Understanding Recurrent Neural Networks, on page 216.

Tokenizing on Bytes

Perhaps the simplest tokenization strategy is to treat each byte in a text sequence as an individual token. Similar to character-level tokenization strategies, this strategy is great for multilingual contexts. Additionally, the size of your vocabulary is fixed to 255. A lot of modern natural language algorithms tokenize at the byte level. Another advantage is that tokenization is simple—you only need to treat the raw text as a byte-string. Of course, this approach has the same shortcomings as tokenizing at the character level. The sequence length balloons and presents problems during training and inference.

Tokenizing on Pieces

Modern tokenization algorithms take a probabilistic approach and tokenize on pieces of sentences and words. Most modern algorithms employ a strategy based on *byte-pair encoding (BPE)*. They typically employ a pretokenization strategy, which may utilize one of the naive approaches presented in this chapter, to build a frequency map of words or tokens. Then, the algorithm splits each word in the frequency map into pieces and extracts the most likely pieces or chunks from the frequency maps. You'll see these more advanced tokenizers in action in Chapter 11, Model Everything with Transformers, on page 237.

Tokenizing and Vectorizing in Elixir

Given that all of your reviews are in English, it makes sense to tokenize on whitespace. If you're familiar with Elixir's String module, you know this can be accomplished with a simple String.split/2. Before you can go about splitting strings, you need to do some text normalization. If you were to split the text as is, you would end up with tokens that treat punctuation and casing as significant. In some problems, this makes sense. But in this problem, it doesn't. Notice that the following sentences have the same sentiment, regardless of punctuation and casing:

```
i didnt like this movie it was so bad nobody should ever watch it
I didn't like this movie. It was so bad; nobody should ever watch it.
```

In terms of sentiment, these sentences have identical meanings, and you want your model to understand that. If you went about splitting this sentence on whitespace, you'd end up with the following tokens:

```
["i", "didnt", "like", "this", "movie", "it", "was", "so", "bad",
"nobody", "should", "ever", "watch", "it"]
```

```
["I", "didn't", "like", "this", "movie.", "It", "was", "so", "bad;",
"nobody", "should", "ever", "watch", "it."]
```

Notice how many of the tokens in your sentence, which you know have the same meaning, end up getting treated differently by your model. Also, words with different casing get treated as different words. To fix these problems, you need to convert every character in the sentence to lowercase and remove the punctuation from each review. Fortunately, you can do this using String.downcase/1 and String.replace/3:

```
review = "I didn't like this movie.
It was so bad; nobody should ever watch it."
review |> String.downcase() |> String.replace(~r/[\p{P}\p{S}]/, "")
```

Running this code will first downcase all of the characters in the given binary and then replace all of the punctuation in the string with an empty string, effectively removing it from the sequence. If you inspect the output now, you'll see the following:

```
i didnt like this movie it was so bad nobody should ever watch it
```

Punctuation Matters

 English teachers are probably cringing at the assertion that punctuation means nothing to a machine learning engineer. You also can probably come up with any number of counterexamples where punctuation is significant to the sentiment of a piece of text. But in *most* cases it won't make a difference. You're not trying to design a model to catch every edge case here; you want something that handles only the common case.

Given what you've learned so far, you can implement a tokenization strategy that looks something like this:

```
review
|> String.downcase()
|> String.replace(~r/[\p{P}\p{S}]/, "")
|> String.split()
```

But, if you run this code, you will end up with only a list of tokens—the individual tokens don't map naturally to entries in a tensor. Instead, you need to apply a vectorization strategy. In this context, vectorization is any technique that converts the tokens you have into a vector. For example, you can replace each token with a vector from a pre-trained *word embedding*. Word embeddings map tokens to dense vector representations and give mathematical meaning to natural language. The quintessential example of mathematical relationships in word embeddings is that if you were to add the vector representations of the tokens "king" and "girl," the resulting vector would be very close to the vector for the word "queen."

Another approach is to convert each token to a sparse representation using one-hot encoding or as a simple index in a lookup table. The advantage of this approach over a pre-trained embedding is that you're able to learn a smaller specialized vocabulary and embedding.

So how can you turn your tokens into a sparse representation? All you need to do is map each unique token in your input to a unique integer index. But remember that one of the drawbacks of your tokenization strategy is that the vocabulary can grow incredibly large, so you'll want to limit the vocabulary to a certain size. You can do this by keeping the most frequent tokens in the corpus and discarding the rest. You can use the following code to get the frequencies of each token in the corpus:

```
frequencies =
  Enum.reduce(train_data, %{}, fn {review, _}, tokens ->
    review
    |> String.downcase()
    |> String.replace(~r/[\p{P}\p{S}]/, "")
    |> String.split()
    |> Enum.reduce(tokens, &Map.update(&2, &1, 1, fn x -> x + 1 end))
  end)
```

Notice that you tokenize each document and then accumulate token counts in a frequency map. If you run this code, you'll see something like this:

```
%{
  "diplomaswho" => 1,
  "egyptologists" => 1,
```

```
  "characther" => 1,
  "nearlyempty" => 1,
  "blobs" => 4,
  "doubletwist" => 1,
  "thingshe" => 1,
  "loleralacartelort7890" => 1,
  "placebo" => 1,
  "betterif" => 1,
  "smarttalk" => 1,
  "sorcererin" => 1,
  "celies" => 6,
  "tenancier" => 1,
  "ladies" => 284,
  ...
}
```

You can now create a vocabulary that only keeps the top tokens in your frequency map by sorting the inputs and keeping the top N most frequent tokens:

```
num_tokens = 1024

tokens =
  frequencies
  |> Enum.sort_by(&elem(&1, 1), :desc)
  |> Enum.take(num_tokens)
```

The number of tokens in your vocabulary is arbitrary. This example uses 1024 to limit the size of the final model. You still need to map each of the tokens in your vocabulary to a unique integer. The value of a single token represents a categorical variable without any significance in order or magnitude. In other words, you can assign any token to any integer as long as each unique token gets a unique integer. The easiest way to do this is to assign the index of each token in the vocabulary as its value:

```
tokens =
  frequencies
  |> Enum.sort_by(&elem(&1, 1), :desc)
  |> Enum.take(num_tokens)
  |> Enum.with_index(fn {token, _}, i -> {token, i} end)
  |> Map.new()
```

You can combine this vocabulary with your tokenization strategy to map each review to a list of integers:

```
review = "The Departed is Martin Scorsese's best work, and anybody
who disagrees is wrong. This movie is amazing."

tokenize = fn review ->
  review
  |> String.downcase()
  |> String.replace(~r/[\p{P}\p{S}]/, "")
```

```
|> String.split()
|> Enum.map(&Map.get(tokens, &1))
end
```

```
tokenize.(review)
```

This code tokenizes the inputs and then looks up each token in the token map you've prebuilt. If you run this code, you'll see the following output:

```
[1, nil, 6, nil, nil, 111, 159, 2, nil, 36, nil, 6, 361, 10, 18, 6, 465]
```

But wait, there are a bunch of nil values. You can't turn this into a tensor.

The issue, here, is by limiting the size of your vocabulary, you've created the possibility of encountering *out-of-vocab (OOV) tokens*. This is a common outcome when dealing with text and is easily solved by introducing a special value to represent OOV tokens. It's common for these special tokens to occupy the beginning of your vocabulary, so you need to slightly adjust your tokens and vectorization strategy:

```
review = "The Departed is Martin Scorsese's best work, and anybody
who disagrees is wrong. This movie is amazing."
```

```
unknown_token = 0
```

```
tokens =
  frequencies
  |> Enum.sort_by(&elem(&1, 1), :desc)
  |> Enum.take(num_tokens)
  |> Enum.with_index(fn {token, _}, i -> {token, i + 1} end)
  |> Map.new()
```

```
tokenize = fn review ->
  review
  |> String.downcase()
  |> String.replace(~r/[\p{P}\p{S}]/, "")
  |> String.split()
  |> Enum.map(&Map.get(tokens, &1, unknown_token))
  |> Nx.tensor()
end
```

```
tokenize.(review)
```

Here, you shift your vocabulary values to the right by one and provide a default value to Map.get/3. You also wrap the final tokenized list into an Nx tensor. After running this code, you'll see this:

```
#Nx.Tensor<
  s64[17]
  EXLA.Backend<host:0, 0.2532065982.2520645648.98884>
  [1, 0, 6, 0, 0, 114, 160, 2, 0, 36, 0, 6, 358, 10, 17, 6, 472]
>
```

Perfect! Now you can create an input pipeline that you can pass to Axon for training a model. To implement your input pipeline, copy the following code:

```
batch_size = 64

train_pipeline =
  train_data
  |> Stream.map(fn {review, label} ->
    {tokenize.(review), Nx.tensor(label)}
  end)
  |> Stream.chunk_every(batch_size, batch_size, :discard)
  |> Stream.map(fn reviews_and_labels ->
    {review, label} = Enum.unzip(reviews_and_labels)
    {Nx.stack(review), Nx.stack(label) |> Nx.new_axis(-1)}
  end)
test_pipeline =
  test_data
  |> Stream.map(fn {review, label} ->
    {tokenize.(review), Nx.tensor(label)}
  end)
  |> Stream.chunk_every(batch_size, batch_size, :discard)
  |> Stream.map(fn reviews_and_labels ->
    {review, label} = Enum.unzip(reviews_and_labels)
    {Nx.stack(review), Nx.stack(label) |> Nx.new_axis(-1)}
  end)
```

This code should feel similar to your input pipeline from the past few chapters. First, you zip reviews and sentiments, and then you do some preprocessing to convert reviews and sentiments to tensors. Next, you chunk adjacent entries in the Stream and stack them together to create batches of sequence and sentiment pairs. Now, you can run the following code to grab one batch from your input stream:

```
Enum.take(train_pipeline, 1)
```

And you'll see this:

```
** (ArgumentError) non-concat dims must be equal got 127 and 304
while concatenating on axis 0
```

What happened here? Well, if you were playing around with tokenizing different reviews, you might have noticed that each review has a different input length. Calling Nx.stack/1 doesn't work because it would result in what's called a *ragged tensor*—a tensor with nonuniform sizes for different entries in a given dimension. This problem arises often when dealing with sequences because they often have variable input lengths.

You had a similar problem when dealing with images, which was easily addressed by resizing the images to uniform shapes. Resizing in the context of images is a bit more natural because you can downsample, upsample, crop, or pad an input image, and it won't necessarily drastically change the content of the original image. Sequences, on the other hand, are a bit more difficult because it's possible to truncate a sequence and lose a lot of the original meaning of the sequence, so you need to be careful about choosing an appropriate sequence length.

While some frameworks support working with ragged tensors, Nx requires static shapes and doesn't support ragged tensors, so you need a strategy to convert all of your input reviews to a uniform shape. The most common way to do this is by padding or truncating each sequence to a fixed length. Padding is normally done by introducing a *pad token*, which is another special token in your vocabulary. You append each sequence with the number of pad tokens required to reach the desired sequence length.

Padding the Input Sequences

To introduce padding, you need to alter your original tokenization code:

```
pad_token = 0
unknown_token = 1

max_seq_len = 64

tokens =
  frequencies
  |> Enum.sort_by(&elem(&1, 1), :desc)
  |> Enum.take(num_tokens)
  |> Enum.with_index(fn {token, _}, i -> {token, i + 2} end)
  |> Map.new()

tokenize = fn review ->
  review
  |> String.downcase()
  |> String.replace(~r/[\p{P}\p{S}]/, "")
  |> String.split()
  |> Enum.map(&Map.get(tokens, &1, unknown_token))
  |> Nx.tensor()
  |> then(&Nx.pad(&1, pad_token, [{0, max_seq_len - Nx.size(&1), 0}]))
end
```

In this code, notice the addition of the pad token and how you shift each token index to the right again. But the real magic happens with this line:

```
|> then(&Nx.pad(&1, pad_token, [{0, max_seq_len - Nx.size(&1), 0}]))
```

This line adds padding with the value pad_token to the end of the sequence. The amount of padding is determined by max_seq_len - Nx.size(sequence), which means it will add enough padding for the original input sequence to be of length max_seq_len. You might be wondering what happens if the size of the original input sequence is greater than max_seq_len. In that case, the padding at the end of the sequence will be negative, and the semantics of Nx.pad/3 dictate the input tensor is truncated by the negative padding amount. This line works to pad or truncate your sequence to a fixed length regardless of the input size.

With the introduction of padding, you can reimplement and rerun your training pipeline:

```
batch_size = 64

train_pipeline =
  train_data
  |> Stream.map(fn {review, label} ->
    {tokenize.(review), Nx.tensor(label)}
  end)
  |> Stream.chunk_every(batch_size, batch_size, :discard)
  |> Stream.map(fn reviews_and_labels ->
    {review, label} = Enum.unzip(reviews_and_labels)
    {Nx.stack(review), Nx.stack(label) |> Nx.new_axis(-1)}
  end)

test_pipeline =
  test_data
  |> Stream.map(fn {review, label} ->
    {tokenize.(review), Nx.tensor(label)}
  end)
  |> Stream.chunk_every(batch_size, batch_size, :discard)
  |> Stream.map(fn reviews_and_labels ->
    {review, label} = Enum.unzip(reviews_and_labels)
    {Nx.stack(review), Nx.stack(label) |> Nx.new_axis(-1)}
  end)

Enum.take(train_pipeline, 1)
```

And you'll see this:

```
[
  {#Nx.Tensor<
    s64[64][64]
    EXLA.Backend<host:0, 0.3646858574.2605056008.58802>
    [
      [10, 208, 1, 57, 1, 1, 8, ...],
      ...
    ]
  >,
  #Nx.Tensor<
    s64[64][1]
    EXLA.Backend<host:0, 0.3646858574.2605056008.58868>
    [
      [0],
      [0],
```

```
      [1],
      ...
    ]
  >}
]
```

You've successfully put together an input pipeline for variable length sequences using a simple tokenization and vectorization strategy. Now, all you need is a model to train.

Trying to Read with MLPs

Before diving into the complex world of sequence processing with recurrent neural networks, you should start with something simple—like a basic feed-forward neural network:

```
model =
  Axon.input("review")
  |> Axon.embedding(num_tokens + 2, 64)
  |> Axon.flatten()
  |> Axon.dense(64, activation: :relu)
  |> Axon.dense(1)
```

The only unfamiliar layer here should be Axon.embedding/3. This layer takes a sparse collection of tokens like the ones you have in each of your sequences and maps them to a dense vector representation. The embedding operation is a relatively simple lookup, like the one depicted here:

Embeddings learn dense vector representations of text in your dataset. After embedding, you end up with a sequence of vectors or a three-dimensional input, so you need to flatten the input before passing the resulting embedding matrix to the next dense layer. Because your goal is to predict a binary label, your output layer is a dense layer with one output unit.

You could inspect this model as a table with the following code:

```
input_template = Nx.template({64, 64}, :s64)
Axon.Display.as_graph(model, input_template)
```

If you did so, after running the code, you'll see this:

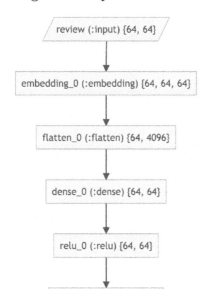

You can now train your model using the Axon.Loop API. Copy and run the following code to implement a supervised training loop using your model and input pipeline:

```
loss = &Axon.Losses.binary_cross_entropy(&1, &2,
  from_logits: true,
  reduction: :mean
)
optimizer = Axon.Optimizers.adam(1.0e-4)

trained_model_state =
  model
  |> Axon.Loop.trainer(loss, optimizer)
  |> Axon.Loop.metric(:accuracy)
  |> Axon.Loop.run(train_pipeline, %{}, epochs: 10, compiler: EXLA)
```

In this example, you pass in a parametrized form of Axon.Losses.binary_cross_entropy/3. You've used binary cross-entropy in the past so you should be familiar with it by now. The difference here is you need to specify from_logits: true. You might have noticed that your output dense layer didn't have an activation function. Previously, for binary classification problems, you had used a sigmoid activation to specify that a layer should output a probability between 0 and 1. In this instance, your output layer is going to learn to output logits or log-probabilities. This measure is literally only supposed to represent $\log(p)$ where p is an output probability.

Training with or without logits doesn't usually make a difference. Some loss implementations are more stable when using output logits vs. probabilities. But Axon's implementations use an optimization that always takes advantage of the stable path, so training with or without logits is a matter of personal preference.

After training, you'll see the following output:

```
Epoch: 0, Batch: 350, accuracy: 0.5002229 loss: 0.6860522
Epoch: 1, Batch: 350, accuracy: 0.6894144 loss: 0.6168785
Epoch: 2, Batch: 350, accuracy: 0.7786677 loss: 0.5573396
Epoch: 3, Batch: 350, accuracy: 0.8037750 loss: 0.5174768
Epoch: 4, Batch: 350, accuracy: 0.8238515 loss: 0.4877387
Epoch: 5, Batch: 350, accuracy: 0.8453078 loss: 0.4631703
Epoch: 6, Batch: 350, accuracy: 0.8648504 loss: 0.4411991
Epoch: 7, Batch: 350, accuracy: 0.8850605 loss: 0.4204423
Epoch: 8, Batch: 350, accuracy: 0.9082086 loss: 0.4002065
Epoch: 9, Batch: 350, accuracy: 0.9299769 loss: 0.3802384
```

Overall, your model performs decently but struggles to achieve over 90% training accuracy. You can see how this translates to the test set by running the following code:

```
model
|> Axon.Loop.evaluator()
|> Axon.Loop.metric(:accuracy)
|> Axon.Loop.run(test_pipeline, trained_model_state, compiler: EXLA)
```

After running the code, you'll see this:

```
Batch: 30, accuracy: 0.7676411
```

Overall, your model achieves 76% accuracy on the test set. This isn't bad, but you can definitely do better with a model designed for processing sequences. Enter the recurrent neural network (RNN).

Introducing Recurrent Neural Networks

You might be curious why basic feed-forward networks alone aren't ideal for processing sequences. The problem is that basic feed-forward networks don't have any way to account for *temporal dependencies*.

Temporal dependencies are simply dependencies on time. When dealing with sequences, it's common to refer to the entries in the sequence as individual timesteps, regardless of whether entries map to actual timesteps. A temporal dependency means that events that happen in the future are dependent on what has happened in the past, or what is currently happening. If you think about this in the context of natural language, it should make sense.

In a sequence of words from natural language, order matters. The order of words in a sentence can drastically alter the meaning of the sentence. Your dense network has no way of accounting for this. In essence, your dense neural network is learning to classify sentiment based on the *presence* of certain words, but not their location relative to other words in the sentence. This actually isn't a bad strategy, but it fails to capture the complex sequential relationships in each review. Consider the following review:

```
This movie was awfully good. I hated everything about it (not).
```

This review employs a couple of quirks of the English language that native speakers can understand easily but which might trick your naive sentiment analysis model. First, the phrase "awfully good" is an oxymoron. Additionally, the second sentence uses sarcasm in the form of a "not" joke. A human can understand that this is a positive review. But a model that doesn't account for temporal relationships in a review would struggle to classify this sequence correctly. Your models need to understand the significance of the modifiers, and without accounting for their position, it would struggle to classify this example correctly.

This is where recurrent neural networks come into play. Recurrent neural networks are neural networks that map a transformation over a sequence of input data, maintaining an internal state or memory that modifies outputs based on previous inputs. The term *recurrent* comes from the fact that recurrent neural networks implement a *recurrence relation*. In other words, the output of a recurrent neural network at step t depends on all of the entries in the sequence before t.

Recurrent neural networks are designed specifically for sequences. If you remember from Chapter 3, Harness the Power of Math, on page 47, the power of certain models is often thanks to the assumptions they make. Just as convolutional neural networks work well for data with a grid-like input structure, recurrent neural networks work well for data with a sequential structure. The assumptions of input structure allow CNNs and RNNs to perform significantly better on certain classes of inputs. Alternatively, feed-forward networks are more like a swiss army knife—they are universal function approximators, but they don't make significant assumptions about input structure and thus might struggle to learn on certain types of data.

There are many different kinds of RNNs in academia. But, in this book, you'll learn about two of the most common: *long short-term memory (LSTM)* and *gated recurrent units (GRU)*. Both are variants of recurrent neural networks that overcome the limitations of the basic or *simple RNN*. Axon offers out-of-the-box implementations of both LSTM and GRU recurrent neural networks, so you can easily plug them into your neural networks.

To see Axon's RNN implementations in action, you'll build one up from scratch and get a sense of what each output represents. To start, create an Axon input representing an input sequence from your movie review input pipeline:

```
sequence = Axon.input("review")
```

The shape of each input sequence is {batch_size, sequence_length}, and each entry in the sequence is an integer token drawn from your vocabulary. In your feed-forward network, you converted this sparse representation into a dense vector representation using an embedding layer. Axon's RNN implementations also require embedded inputs. However, you don't need to flatten them because RNNs are designed to work over an entire sequence. Thus, you should add an embedding layer to your network:

```
embedded = sequence |> Axon.embedding(num_tokens + 2, 64)
```

At this point, your neural network has shape {batch_size, sequence_length, 64}. In other words, for each token, you have a size 64 vector representation of that token. Next, you want to create a mask tensor from your input sequence by using Axon.mask/2:

```
mask = Axon.mask(sequence, 0)
```

Axon.mask/2 essentially works to tell your model to ignore certain tokens. Specifically, we ignore padding tokens because we don't want them to have any effect on the output of the model. Remember that in your input pipeline we had to pad inputs to the same length, which means your neural network would have to learn to be robust against padding tokens. You can help your network a bit by completely ignoring these tokens using Axon.mask/2. The 0 as the second argument indicates what value specifically should be ignored.

Now, with an embedded sequence and a mask, you can go about adding an LSTM layer using Axon.lstm/3:

```
{rnn_sequence, _state} = Axon.lstm(embedded, 64, mask: mask, unroll: :static)
```

The output form of Axon.lstm/3 is different than any of the layers you have encountered so far. That's because RNNs are different than any of the other layers you've seen so far. RNNs maintain a state or history from past entries in a sequence, which affects future outputs. RNNs perform an operation that is sometimes called a *scan* in functional programming. This operation is similar to Elixir's Enum.map_reduce operation. Enum.map_reduce performs a map operation which transforms values in an Enumerable, while also accumulating and eventually returning a final state.

The state output in the previous tuple represents the LSTM's final "memory." The rnn_sequence variable is a transformed sequence obtained from mapping the recurrent operation over the entire input sequence with the accumulated state. At this point, the output rnn_sequence has a shape {batch_size, sequence_length, 64}. In other words, rnn_sequence has taken your sequence of embedded tokens and transformed them into another sequence of embedded tokens. So what's the big deal?

Well, consider that your embedding layer simply looks up a vector associated with each individual token. It doesn't account for adjacent tokens. But your recurrent neural network maintains an internal state, which means it can account for previous tokens in the input. By the time you reach the last token in your sequence, your RNN can transform it in such a way that it encodes information from the *entire input sequence*. To better understand this, consider an easier problem. You have a list of strings and you want to alter the list of strings such that each entry in the list corresponds to the amount of times a specific string has occurred in the list up to that point. take for example the following magic word and input list:

```
magic_word = "sixers"
input = ["rockets", "mavericks", "sixers", "sixers",
"magic", "nets", "sixers"]
```

The output should be the following:

```
[0, 0, 1, 2, 2, 2, 3]
```

So, how would you solve this in Elixir? The easiest way is by using Enum.map_reduce:

```
{output, _} = Enum.map_reduce(input, 0, fn entry, count ->
  if entry == magic_word do
    {count + 1, count + 1}
  else
    {count, count}
  end
end)
```

In a way, this is exactly what your RNN is doing. The final token of your output sequence encodes all of the information from previous tokens in the sequence. But, rather than counting occurrences of certain tokens, your RNN is learning to output a useful representation for future layers. In this sentiment-analysis example, your RNN is learning to transform the sequence in such a way that the final token gives a good indication of sentiment based on all of the tokens in the input.

The implication here is that to make use of rnn_sequence, you need to extract the final token from the transformed sequence. You can do this with an Axon.nx/3:

```
final_token = Axon.nx(rnn_sequence, fn seq ->
  Nx.squeeze(seq[[0..-1//1, -1, 0..-1//1]])
end)
```

Axon.nx/3 allows you to utilize generic Nx functions as Axon layers. In this code, you use Nx.slice_along_axis/4 to grab the final token—at index max_seq_len - 1—from axis 1 or the temporal axis. At this point, you should have a good representation of the input sequence. Similar to convolutional neural networks, recurrent neural networks are typically followed by a fully-connected head specialized to whatever task you're trying to solve. In other words, you use the recurrent neural network to extract features and the fully-connected portion to inference on those features:

```
model =
  final_token
  |> Axon.dense(64, activation: :relu)
  |> Axon.dense(1)
```

Remember your final token contains an extracted representation of the entire sequence, so theoretically, it's useful for downstream tasks such as classification. Overall, your final model looks like this:

```
input_template = Nx.template({64, 64}, :s64)
Axon.Display.as_graph(model, input_template)
```

And you'll see the model as shown on page 213.

At this point, you have a model and an input pipeline, so you can move forward with implementing a training loop. Even though you're using a new architecture, you don't need to worry about adjusting your training loop. In fact, you can copy your training loop from your MLP sentiment analysis model:

```
loss = &Axon.Losses.binary_cross_entropy(&1, &2,
  from_logits: true,
  reduction: :mean
)
optimizer = Axon.Optimizers.adam(1.0e-4)

trained_model_state =
  model
  |> Axon.Loop.trainer(loss, optimizer)
  |> Axon.Loop.metric(:accuracy)
  |> Axon.Loop.run(train_pipeline, %{}, epochs: 10, compiler: EXLA)
```

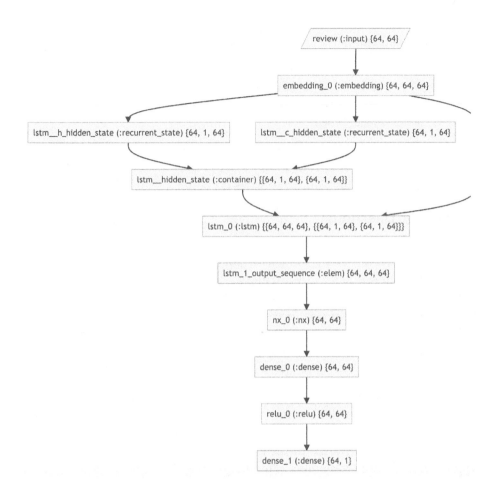

After running the code, you should see the following output:

```
Epoch: 0, Batch: 358, accuracy: 0.5121433 loss: 0.6840463
Epoch: 1, Batch: 358, accuracy: 0.7060410 loss: 0.6094189
Epoch: 2, Batch: 358, accuracy: 0.7469098 loss: 0.5683411
Epoch: 3, Batch: 358, accuracy: 0.7578339 loss: 0.5442138
Epoch: 4, Batch: 358, accuracy: 0.7610549 loss: 0.5284106
Epoch: 5, Batch: 358, accuracy: 0.7636232 loss: 0.5172608
Epoch: 6, Batch: 358, accuracy: 0.7654946 loss: 0.5089468
Epoch: 7, Batch: 358, accuracy: 0.7667568 loss: 0.5024669
Epoch: 8, Batch: 358, accuracy: 0.7686281 loss: 0.4972335
Epoch: 9, Batch: 358, accuracy: 0.7695855 loss: 0.4928872
```

This is a definite improvement over your simpler feed-forward model. Now, all you need is to evaluate your model. Copy and run your evaluation code from your MLP model:

```
model
|> Axon.Loop.evaluator()
|> Axon.Loop.metric(:accuracy)
|> Axon.Loop.run(test_pipeline, trained_model_state, compiler: EXLA)
```

After running the code, you'll see this:

```
Batch: 30, accuracy: 0.7510081
```

Overall, you were able to improve your sentiment-analysis model using a recurrent neural network. Your final model performance is decent, but you should know by now that you can always do better.

Going in Two Directions

Your current implementation makes use of a straightforward LSTM. As you know, your LSTM extracts a representation of the input sequence by transforming the input sequence forward along the temporal axis with an accumulated state or history. Intuitively, this makes sense. Humans generally understand sequences in one direction, so it's natural to enforce this constraint on neural networks as well. But neural networks aren't humans, and can significantly benefit from alterations that don't seem natural. One example of this is the use of *bidirectional recurrent neural networks*.

Bidirectional RNNs employ the same technique as traditional RNNs, but in two directions. Your previous neural network only transformed the sequence by unrolling or walking along the temporal axis in a forward direction. A bidirectional RNN transforms the sequence by unrolling or walking along the temporal axis in *both* directions. This might not make much sense to you. After all, reversing a movie review doesn't add any additional context to *your* understanding. How could it possibly help a neural network?

The reality is that for sequences that don't have an explicit *causal relationship*, the bidirectional transformation provides additional context for a recurrent neural network. They learn sequential relationships in both directions and are therefore more robust in nature. It's important to note that bidirectional RNNs are not valid for *all* sequential data. For example, you should *not* use bidirectional RNNs with time-series data because there's an explicit causal relationship you're trying to model. For text, working in both directions can help improve the generalization ability of your model.

Bidirectional RNNs are straightforward to implement from scratch with the Axon API. The following is a from-scratch implementation of a bidirectional LSTM:

```
backward_sequence = Axon.nx(forward_sequence, &Nx.reverse(&1, axes: [1]))

{forward_state, forward_out} = Axon.lstm(forward_sequence, 64)
```

```
{backward_state, backward_out} = Axon.lstm(backward_sequence, 64)
out_state = Axon.concatenate(
  forward_state,
  Axon.nx(backward_state, &Nx.reverse(&1, axes: [1]))
)
out_sequence = Axon.concatenate(
  forward_out,
  Axon.nx(backward_out, &Nx.reverse(&1, axes: [1]))
)
```

Notice that you need only to reverse the input sequence and apply the LSTM transformation in both directions. Then you merge the resulting states and sequences to get a final output state and sequence. You can choose another operation such as Axon.add/2 to merge forward and backward outputs, but concatenation is most common. The implication here is that if you want a bidirectional LSTM with 64 units, your output sequence will have 128 units as a result of the concatenation.

The Axon API offers a convenience around bidirectional RNNs with Axon.bidirectional/3. Using this, you can reimplement your RNN from the previous section:

```
sequence = Axon.input("review")
mask = Axon.mask(sequence, 0)
embedded = Axon.embedding(sequence, num_tokens + 2, 64)

{rnn_sequence, _state} =
  Axon.bidirectional(
    embedded,
    &Axon.lstm(&1, 64, mask: mask, unroll: :static),
    &Axon.concatenate/2
  )
final_token = Axon.nx(rnn_sequence, fn seq ->
  Nx.squeeze(seq[[0..-1//1, -1, 0..-1//1]])
end)

model =
  final_token
  |> Axon.dense(64, activation: :relu)
  |> Axon.dense(1)
```

Now, you can run your original training loop with this new model using the following code:

```
loss = &Axon.Losses.binary_cross_entropy(&1, &2,
  from_logits: true,
  reduction: :mean
)
optimizer = Axon.Optimizers.adam(1.0e-4)
```

```
trained_model_state =
  model
  |> Axon.Loop.trainer(loss, optimizer)
  |> Axon.Loop.metric(:accuracy)
  |> Axon.Loop.run(train_pipeline, %{}, epochs: 10, compiler: EXLA)
```

After running the code, you'll see this:

```
Epoch: 0, Batch: 350, accuracy: 0.5190082 loss: 0.6815987
Epoch: 1, Batch: 341, accuracy: 0.7035355 loss: 0.6067376
Epoch: 2, Batch: 332, accuracy: 0.7509853 loss: 0.5645106
Epoch: 3, Batch: 323, accuracy: 0.7610434 loss: 0.5400541
Epoch: 4, Batch: 314, accuracy: 0.7647320 loss: 0.5240928
Epoch: 5, Batch: 355, accuracy: 0.7672051 loss: 0.5114447
Epoch: 6, Batch: 346, accuracy: 0.7690023 loss: 0.5031880
Epoch: 7, Batch: 337, accuracy: 0.7696466 loss: 0.4966677
Epoch: 8, Batch: 328, accuracy: 0.7717992 loss: 0.4912724
Epoch: 9, Batch: 319, accuracy: 0.7726074 loss: 0.4866871
```

You should notice your model is performing slightly better, but it took a bit longer to train, which makes sense because you've added an additional LSTM layer to your network with the bidirectional transformation. Now you can test your model with your evaluation code:

```
model
|> Axon.Loop.evaluator()
|> Axon.Loop.metric(:accuracy)
|> Axon.Loop.run(test_pipeline, trained_model_state, compiler: EXLA)
```

And you'll see this:

```
Batch: 30, accuracy: 0.7641129
```

With the simple bidirectional transformation, you were able to eke out some extra accuracy from your model. At this point, you have a pretty solid understanding of how to implement recurrent neural networks in Axon, but now you need to understand a bit about what's going on under the hood. In the next section, you'll dive deeper into what's actually happening in a recurrent neural network, and we'll discuss some of their strengths and weaknesses.

Understanding Recurrent Neural Networks

You should already kind of understand the process behind RNNs through the lens of your string-counting implementation with Enum.map_reduce/3. RNNs transform input sequences with a similar operation. However, they make use of learned transformations via learned parameters. This visualization shows the simplest form of an RNN as shown in the diagram on page 217.

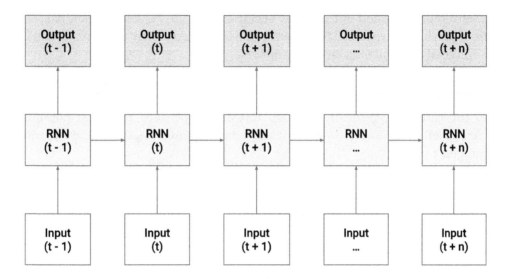

Notice that each subsequent state depends on the current token and previous output state—outputting a transformed token and new output state. This visualization shows an *unrolled* version of the RNN graph. Rather than depict loops in the computation graph, it shows the operations unrolled across all timesteps in the sequence. This unrolling operation also takes place in the RNN computation, either at compile-time or runtime. Axon makes the distinction by offering both :static and :dynamic unrolling of recurrent operation.

A :dynamic unroll makes use of a runtime loop, whereas a :static unroll inlines all of the RNN computations over a sequence at compile-time. The inlining works well for short sequences but often consumes too much memory for longer sequences. Regardless, the trip count for the recurrent loop is always known at compile-time, which means the gradient of the RNN transformation is straightforward to compute.

The actual recurrent transformation is often called the *recurrent cell*. You can think of the recurrent cell as the fn entry, acc -> ... end operation in Elixir's Enum.map_reduce. The most basic recurrent cell is often called a *simple RNN cell*. While powerful in theory, they aren't particularly useful in practice. This is because simple RNNs suffer from the *vanishing gradient problem*.

As you might remember, neural networks are trained with gradient descent. In order to learn to extract useful representations from sequences, recurrent neural networks need to send sufficient feedback signals during the training process. For longer sequences, timesteps in the simple RNN have decreasing sensitivity to the original inputs. In other words, they are unable to learn any useful representation of the input because they "forget" information passed from previous timesteps. LSTMs overcome this limitation by introducing some additional internal state and parameters.

The additional "gates" in the LSTM cell allow it to maintain information from previous states and thus overcome the limitations of traditional RNNs thanks to the vanishing gradient problem. LSTMs are perhaps the most popular variant of RNNs in use today but are also computationally expensive and difficult to scale.

The scalability issues and computational complexity of recurrent neural networks are part of the reason they've fallen out of favor in recent years. RNNs operate in an inherently sequential manner—this is part of what makes them so powerful. But it also makes them inefficient. You can only vectorize/parallelize RNNs along the batch dimension.

Wrapping Up

In this chapter, you were introduced to natural language processing with recurrent neural networks. You learned how to implement some basic text featurization and preprocessing with Elixir and how to implement and train recurrent neural networks in Axon. You also learned about some of the intuition behind recurrent neural networks and some of the fundamental shortcomings of recurrent neural networks, which have allowed them to be usurped by transformer models.

If you're familiar with the current state of natural language processing, you might have questioned the need to cover recurrent neural networks at all. However, to better understand the current state of the art, it's important to understand the previous state of the art—and why it ended up failing. While recurrent neural networks are no longer common in natural language processing, they still have some practical use in certain domains. Additionally, understanding how RNNs work and where they fail is important to better understand the rise of transformers.

Before completely closing the door on RNNs in favor of transformers, you'll explore one additional application of RNNs known as time-series data. In the next chapter, you'll dive deep into time-series analysis with neural networks.

CHAPTER 10

Forecast the Future

In the previous chapter, you were introduced to the concept of recurrent neural networks for learning on sequential data. Specifically, you created and trained recurrent neural networks on text data using Elixir and Axon. You saw how recurrent neural networks are capable of learning relationships in natural language far easier than traditional feed-forward networks due to their built-in memory and inherent sequential operation.

Recurrent neural networks are well-suited for processing text. However, that's not the only thing they're good for. Anything with a temporal nature presents challenges for traditional feed-forward networks and is better suited for recurrent neural networks. One example of such data is *time-series data*. Time-series data is any collection of data indexed in time order. At each timestep, there are one or many observations. You can see how time-series data lends itself naturally to working with recurrent neural networks.

In this chapter, you'll work with time-series data in Elixir, Nx, and Axon. You'll learn about some of the challenges of working with time-series data and a bit about why neural networks struggle so much with this data compared to other approaches. You'll also train both a convolutional and recurrent neural network on a time-series analysis problem, comparing the results and learning the benefits and drawbacks of each strategy.

Predicting Stock Prices

Perhaps one of the most obvious applications of time-series analysis is forecasting the direction of markets. Given enough historical data, you should be able to predict the future performance of a given equity or market, right? As you'll find out later in this chapter, the problem of forecasting markets is exceptionally difficult. If it were as easy as throwing a neural network at the problem, everybody would be doing it. Despite the challenges, attempting to forecast stock prices is a good exercise in time-series analysis and a good demonstration of the pitfalls of putting too much faith in a model.

In this example, you'll be working with the historical stock data for 30 companies in the Dow Jones Industrial Average between 2006 and 2018. The data is available for download on Kaggle.[1] After you download the data, you'll see a collection of CSVs that contain information for the prices of individual stocks and for all of the stocks. To simplify the problem, you'll create a model that predicts the future stock prices for a single stock, in this case, AAPL.

Start by firing up a new Livebook and adding the following dependencies:

```
Mix.install([
  {:explorer, "~> 0.5.0"},
  {:nx, "~> 0.6"},
  {:exla, "~> 0.6"},
  {:axon, "~> 0.5"},
  {:vega_lite, "~> 0.1.6"},
  {:kino, "~> 0.8.0"},
  {:kino_vega_lite, "~> 0.1.7"}
])
```

It's common to alias the VegaLite module to Vl, so run the following code in a new cell:

```
alias VegaLite, as: Vl
```

To simplify the process of working with the structured CSV data, you'll use *Explorer*, Elixir's DataFrame library. You'll use Nx and EXLA for numerical computing and acceleration, respectively, and you'll need Axon for the deep learning implementation. You'll also use VegaLite, Kino, and Kino.VegaLite for providing some functionality to visualize and summarize your dataset.

Before diving in, take some time to get familiar with the data. Start by loading it into a DataFrame using Explorer, like so:

```
csv_file = "all_stocks_2006-01-01_to_2018-01-01.csv"
df = Explorer.DataFrame.from_csv!(csv_file, parse_dates: true)
```

After running the code, you'll see the following output:

```
#Explorer.DataFrame<
  Polars[93612 x 7]
  Date string ["2006-01-03", "2006-01-04", "2006-01-05", ...]
  Open float [77.76, 79.49, 78.41, 78.64, 78.5, ...]
  High float [79.35, 79.49, 78.65, 78.9, 79.83, ...]
```

---

1. https://www.kaggle.com/datasets/szrlee/stock-time-series-20050101-to-20171231

```
  Low float [77.24, 78.25, 77.56, 77.64, 78.46, ...]
  Close float [79.11, 78.71, 77.99, 78.63, 79.02, ...]
  Volume integer [3117200, 2558000, 2529500, ...]
  Name string ["MMM", "MMM", "MMM", "MMM", "MMM", ...]
>
```

The dataset consists of opening, low, high, and closing prices on each trading day for a handful of stock tickers. You'll notice there's no intraday data and no *auxiliary information* aside from trading volume. Auxiliary information, or side information, is information you have access to outside of the target you're trying to predict. Rather than use side information, you're forced to make use only of past timesteps to predict future timesteps in an *autoregressive* manner. Autoregression means you're going to predict future values from existing values.

For this problem, you'll pay attention to only a ticker's closing prices, so you can filter out the other irrelevant information:

```
df = Explorer.DataFrame.select(df, ["Date", "Close", "Name"])
```

After doing so, you'll see the following output:

```
#Explorer.DataFrame<
  Polars[93612 x 3]
  Date string ["2006-01-03", "2006-01-04", "2006-01-05", ...]
  Close float [79.11, 78.71, 77.99, 78.63, 79.02, ...]
  Name string ["MMM", "MMM", "MMM", "MMM", "MMM", ...]
>
```

Next, run the following code to get a visualization of the various stock tickers using VegaLite:

```
Vl.new(title: "DJIA Stock Prices", width: 640, height: 480)
|> Vl.data_from_values(Explorer.DataFrame.to_columns(df))
|> Vl.mark(:line)
|> Vl.encode_field(:x, "Date", type: :temporal)
|> Vl.encode_field(:y, "Close", type: :quantitative)
|> Vl.encode_field(:color, "Name", type: :nominal)
|> Kino.VegaLite.new()
```

And you'll see the rendered image on page 222.

This image is, admittedly, a bit noisy. For this problem, you're only concerned with the price of the AAPL stock, so you can filter your data accordingly:

```
aapl_df = Explorer.DataFrame.filter_with(df, fn df ->
  Explorer.Series.equal(df["Name"], "AAPL")
end)
```

After you do so, you'll see the following output:

```
#Explorer.DataFrame<
  Polars[3019 x 3]
  Date string ["2006-01-03", "2006-01-04", "2006-01-05", ...]
  Close float [10.68, 10.71, 10.63, 10.9, 10.86, ...]
  Name string ["AAPL", "AAPL", "AAPL", "AAPL", "AAPL", ...]
>
```

Now, regenerate your original plot with only AAPL data:

```
Vl.new(title: "AAPL Stock Price", width: 640, height: 480)
|> Vl.data_from_values(Explorer.DataFrame.to_columns(aapl_df))
|> Vl.mark(:line)
|> Vl.encode_field(:x, "Date", type: :temporal)
|> Vl.encode_field(:y, "Close", type: :quantitative)
|> Kino.VegaLite.new()
```

And you'll see the rendered image on page 223.

Now it's time to start preparing the data for model training.

First, notice your dataset consists of unnormalized stock prices. Remember it's important to normalize data before you feed it into your neural network for training. Run the following code to normalize your DataFrame of AAPL stock prices:

```
normalized_aapl_df = Explorer.DataFrame.mutate_with(aapl_df, fn df ->
  var = Explorer.Series.variance(df["Close"])
  mean = Explorer.Series.mean(df["Close"])
  centered = Explorer.Series.subtract(df["Close"], mean)
  norm = Explorer.Series.divide(centered, var)
  ["Close": norm]
end)
```

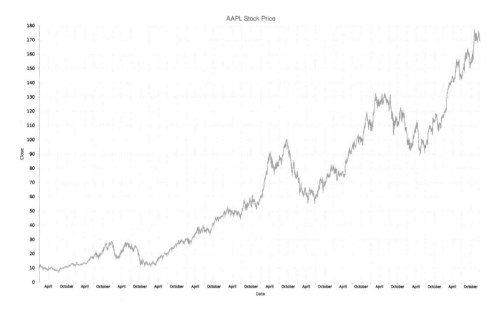

You can replot your graph to verify that the pattern remains the same despite the normalization:

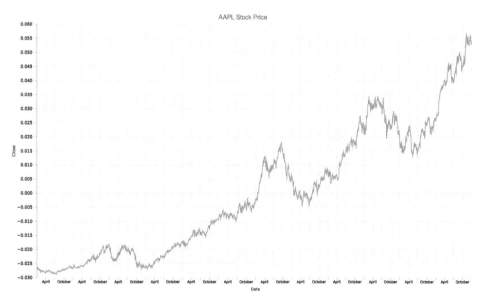

Next, you need to split your model between training and testing sets. In previous chapters, a clear delineation usually was made between input features and targets. That's not necessarily the case in this problem. In time-series analysis, your goal is to predict either a single step or multiple steps in the future. You can make this prediction based on a range of historical inputs or based on the current timestep. In this example, you'll perform single-step predictions using a range of historical values.

You'll also need to divide your dataset into training and test sets. Start by creating the following window/3 function in a new module:

```elixir
defmodule Data do
  def window(inputs, window_size, target_window_size) do
    inputs
    |> Stream.chunk_every(window_size + target_window_size, 1, :discard)
    |> Stream.map(fn window ->
      features =
        window
        |> Enum.take(window_size)
        |> Nx.tensor()
        |> Nx.new_axis(1)

      targets =
        window
        |> Enum.drop(window_size)
        |> Nx.tensor()
        |> Nx.new_axis(1)

      {features, targets}
    end)
  end
end
```

The window/3 method takes an Enumerable or stream, an input window size, and a target window size. It then returns a new stream, where each element is a tuple of tensors with features and targets.

The features tensor is comprised of window_size prices from the last window_size days. The targets tensor is comprised of target_window_size prices from target_window_size days after the input window. Notice that for both features and targets you need to add a new axis. Recall from Representing the World, on page 37, time-series data is typically represented in three dimensions with shape {batch, timesteps, features}. For this example, you only have a single feature—price—and you're only predicting a single feature—price.

Next, add the following batch/2 function to your data module:

```elixir
def batch(inputs, batch_size) do
  inputs
  |> Stream.chunk_every(batch_size, :discard)
  |> Stream.map(fn windows ->
    {features, targets} = Enum.unzip(windows)
    {Nx.stack(features), Nx.stack(targets)}
  end)
end
```

The batch/2 method converts your input windows into batches of input windows by stacking features and targets on top of one another. You can now use these methods to create new training and testing sets. But how do you split up your data into training and test sets?

In the past, you randomly split your dataset into some percentage of training and testing data. You're able to split your dataset somewhat naively because your data doesn't have any temporal dependencies. With a time-series dataset, you have a bunch of potentially overlapping dependencies, which means you can leak information about your test set into the training process. Leakage isn't good, and it can result in overconfidence and the deployment of bad models.

An alternative approach is to split your dataset temporally. For this example, you have ten years' worth of data, so you can take the first eight years as training data and the last two years as testing data. While this approach is better, it's important to understand that there are still drawbacks. Certain time-series analysis problems, like stock price prediction, are often dependent on unseen macro windows. Your model may appear quite good at predicting the price of a stock because the market was in the middle of a very consistent bull run. However, if that fundamental macro trend changes for the test set, you'll have a garbage model.

A challenge with time-series analysis is there are often *confounding variables* at play, and without access to that information, it can be difficult to get an accurate model. You need to be extremely careful when evaluating time-series models to ensure you've eliminated most of the possible sources of bias.

For this example, after looking at the plot of AAPL stock over the last ten years, you can see the general trend: AAPL stock goes up. The macro trends between the training and testing sets are relatively similar. However, that doesn't necessarily mean you'll end up with a model that's good at predicting stock prices for 2023 or 2024. One consideration when doing time-series analysis is that you'll constantly need to retrain and update trends. The world is chaotic, and the future isn't easy to predict.

To split your data into training and test sets, run the following code:

```
train_df = Explorer.DataFrame.filter_with(normalized_aapl_df, fn df ->
  Explorer.Series.less(df["Date"], Date.new!(2016, 1, 1))
end)
test_df = Explorer.DataFrame.filter_with(normalized_aapl_df, fn df ->
  Explorer.Series.greater_equal(df["Date"], Date.new!(2016, 1, 1))
end)
```

After doing so, you'll see the following output:

```
#Explorer.DataFrame<
  Polars[503 x 3]
  Date date [2016-01-04, 2016-01-05, 2016-01-06, 2016-01-07, ...]
  Close float [105.35, 102.71, 100.7, 96.45, 96.96, ...]
  Name string ["AAPL", "AAPL", "AAPL", "AAPL", "AAPL", ...]
>
```

Now, convert your DataFrames to batches of windowed tensors using your data module by running the following code:

```
window_size = 5
batch_size = 32

train_prices = Explorer.Series.to_list(train_df["Close"])
test_prices = Explorer.Series.to_list(test_df["Close"])

single_step_train_data =
  prices
  |> Data.window(window_size, 1)
  |> Data.batch(batch_size)

single_step_test_data =
  prices
  |> Data.window(window_size, 1)
  |> Data.batch(batch_size)
```

You can confirm you've correctly created your datasets by taking samples from each. Run the following code in a new cell:

```
Enum.take(single_step_train_data, 1)
```

And you'll see this:

```
[
  {#Nx.Tensor<
    f32[32][5][1]
    [
      [
        [-0.027216043323278427],
        [-0.027200918644666672],
        [-0.02724125050008297],
        [-0.02710512839257717],
        [-0.027125295251607895]
      ],
      ...
    ]
  >,
  #Nx.Tensor<
    f32[32][1][1]
    [
      [
```

```
          [-0.026777423918247223]
        ],
        [
          [-0.026555592194199562]
        ],
        ...
    >}
]
```

Now you have a dataset of training inputs and training outputs. Your inputs are a sample of five days of closing prices, with the target being a single closing price.

Now that you've built a dataset, it's time to start training some neural networks.

Using CNNs for Single-Step Prediction

Recall from Chapter 7, Learn to See, on page 141, that the convolutional neural networks take advantage of locality and weight sharing to effectively learn patterns on image data. Images naturally have local structure—features that are close together spatially in an image are often related. Additionally, convolutional neural networks apply the same set of parameters across an entire sliding window. That means convolutional neural networks learn to extract the same set of features from multiple regions in the input.

The properties that make convolutional neural networks useful for image data also make them useful for time-series data. With time-series data, local relationships matter because adjacent timesteps are likely related. Additionally, when you have situations with multiple features per time window, convolutions are capable of extracting information across both your feature dimension and temporal dimension. That means you can use one-dimensional convolutions and treat the temporal or time axis as the spatial dimension to extract useful representations of the input. Feed-forward networks fall short here because they don't have the same built-in assumptions about input data as convolutions.

To create a new convolutional neural network, run the following code in a new Livebook cell:

```
cnn_model =
  Axon.input("stock_price")
  |> Axon.nx(&Nx.new_axis(&1, -1))
  |> Axon.conv(32, kernel_size: {window_size, 1}, activation: :relu)
  |> Axon.dense(32, activation: :relu)
  |> Axon.dense(1)
```

Then, run the following code to inspect your network:

```
template = Nx.template({32, 10, 1}, :f32)
Axon.Display.as_graph(cnn_model, template)
```

And you'll see the following output:

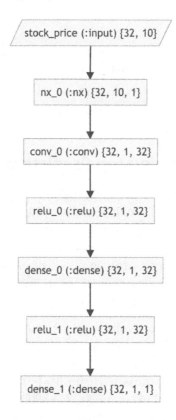

Notice that the output shape is {32, 1, 1}. Specifically, you'll notice that with this model, you're predicting a single step. To achieve this effect, you need to ensure your convolutional kernel size is the same size as your temporal window size. The convolution will transform your temporal window into a single timestep. You can now train your model on the single-step training data. But what metric and loss function should you use here?

Most commonly, time-series models use mean squared error or root mean squared error as the loss function. Both of these loss functions penalize large errors, which is beneficial when you're trying to closely predict the correct next values in a sequence. In addition to mean squared error, it's common to use mean absolute error because it's more readily interpretable than mean squared error. You immediately know that a mean absolute error of 10 means your prediction was $10 off the actual next day's closing price of AAPL stock on a given day.

The training loop for time-series data is exactly the same as every other training loop you've written so far. Run the following code to train your convolutional neural network:

```
cnn_trained_model_state =
  cnn_model
  |> Axon.Loop.trainer(:mean_squared_error, :adam)
  |> Axon.Loop.metric(:mean_absolute_error)
  |> Axon.Loop.run(single_step_train_data, %{}, epochs: 10, compiler: EXLA)
```

After training, you'll see the following output:

```
Epoch: 0, Batch: 50, loss: 16.0255032 mean_absolute_error: 3.1325140
Epoch: 1, Batch: 72, loss: 14.3411617 mean_absolute_error: 2.1435401
Epoch: 2, Batch: 44, loss: 11.9783182 mean_absolute_error: 1.2704648
Epoch: 3, Batch: 66, loss: 12.3826933 mean_absolute_error: 1.9970336
Epoch: 4, Batch: 38, loss: 11.7019396 mean_absolute_error: 1.2344553
Epoch: 5, Batch: 60, loss: 11.8652802 mean_absolute_error: 1.9007618
Epoch: 6, Batch: 32, loss: 11.5063419 mean_absolute_error: 1.1604406
Epoch: 7, Batch: 54, loss: 11.4728088 mean_absolute_error: 1.7184598
Epoch: 8, Batch: 76, loss: 11.6156797 mean_absolute_error: 2.1458588
Epoch: 9, Batch: 48, loss: 11.1360197 mean_absolute_error: 1.4754609
```

You can now evaluate your model on the test set using the following code:

```
cnn_model
|> Axon.Loop.evaluator()
|> Axon.Loop.metric(:mean_absolute_error)
|> Axon.Loop.run(
  single_step_test_data,
  cnn_trained_model_state,
  compiler: EXLA
)
```

After you do so, you'll see the following output:

```
Batch: 13, mean_absolute_error: 0.0035810
```

You can use the mean and variance of AAPL stock prices you computed earlier to get a more accurate estimate of what this normalized error represents:

```
0.0035810
|> Kernel.*(
  :math.sqrt(Explorer.Series.variance(aapl_df["Close"]))
)
|> Kernel.+(
  Explorer.Series.mean(aapl_df["Close"])
)
```

After running the code, you'll see the following output:

```
64.82237670703707
```

You can interpret the result as meaning that over the course of two years, your model had an absolute error of $64 off the next day's closing stock price across each batch. This seems pretty bad. You can put this more into perspective by visualizing your single-step predictions against the AAPL chart and seeing how well the curves line up. Start by creating the following module:

```
defmodule Analysis do
end
```

Add the following function to the Analysis module:

```
defmodule Analysis do
  def visualize_predictions(
    model,
    model_state,
    prices,
    window_size,
    target_window_size,
    batch_size
  ) do
    {_, predict_fn} = Axon.build(model, compiler: EXLA)

    windows =
      prices
      |> Data.window(window_size, target_window_size)
      |> Data.batch(batch_size)
      |> Stream.map(&elem(&1, 0))

    predicted = Enum.flat_map(windows, fn window ->
      predict_fn.(model_state, window) |> Nx.to_flat_list()
    end)

    predicted = List.duplicate(nil, 10) ++ predicted

    types =
      List.duplicate("AAPL", length(prices))
      ++ List.duplicate("Predicted", length(prices))

    days =
      Enum.to_list(0..length(prices) - 1)
      ++ Enum.to_list(0..length(prices) - 1)

    prices = prices ++ predicted

    plot(%{
      "day" => days,
      "prices" => prices,
      "types" => types
    }, "AAPL Stock Price vs. Predicted, CNN Single-Shot")
  end
```

```
  defp plot(values, title) do
    Vl.new(title: title, width: 640, height: 480)
    |> Vl.data_from_values(values)
    |> Vl.mark(:line)
    |> Vl.encode_field(:x, "day", type: :temporal)
    |> Vl.encode_field(:y, "prices", type: :quantitative)
    |> Vl.encode_field(:color, "types", type: :nominal)
    |> Kino.VegaLite.new()
  end
end
```

The function visualize_predictions/6 will run through the entire AAPL dataset and produce predictions for every valid window. It will then produce a plot of the side-by-side predictions with the actual data—so you can see how far off you actually are. With your module created, run the following code to visualize your CNN model's predictions:

```
Analysis.visualize_predictions(
  cnn_model,
  cnn_trained_model_state,
  Explorer.Series.to_list(aapl_df["Close"]),
  window_size,
  1,
  batch_size
)
```

After running the code, you'll see the following plot:

Your single-shot CNN model tends to follow the trend, but you'll notice it misses some drastic drops and spikes in price, and thus it's very off in many places. Of course, this plot is a bit intentionally misleading. At first glance, you might think you have the key to riches on your hand as your CNN outputs seem to track AAPL's stock price pretty well. Realistically, you do your model a favor and self-correct it with the next day's actual stock price, so it can never be too far off. If you were to rerun this analysis and feed the model its own inputs, it would diverge from AAPL's actual stock price rather quickly. Single-step predictions are generally easier than multi-step predictions because you don't drift too far from the initial conditions you're modeling against.

In a multi-step prediction, you create a feedback loop in the model so it learns to make multiple predictions from its own predictions. As your model predicts more and more outputs in a multi-step prediction, it drifts further from true values.

Convolutional neural networks are perfectly suitable for modeling time-series problems. However, they don't have any temporal assumptions built into them like recurrent neural networks. In the next section, you'll create and train a recurrent neural network on the same problem, and you'll see how it stacks up against the convolutional neural network.

Using RNNs for Time-Series Prediction

Recall from Chapter 9, Understand Text, on page 195, the reason recurrent neural networks are so powerful with text is they model temporal dependencies. The same assumptions built into RNNs that make them good for text also make them good for time-series data. In a time-series dataset, inputs at time t-1 obviously have an impact on inputs at time t. Recurrent neural networks are quite good at capturing what the relationship is between timesteps.

You should have some familiarity with implementing recurrent neural networks in Axon from the previous chapter. You can start by creating a new recurrent model, like this:

```
rnn_model =
  Axon.input("stock_prices")
  |> Axon.lstm(32)
  |> elem(0)
  |> Axon.nx(& &1[[0..-1//1, -1, 0..-1//1]])
  |> Axon.dense(1)
```

You should be familiar with LSTMs from Chapter 9, Understand Text, on page 195. This model takes a time series of stock prices as input, runs them through a single LSTM layer, and extracts the final token from the LSTM. The model then passes the LSTM output to a dense layer with 1 output unit. Run the following code to visualize the LSTM as shown on page 233.

```
template = Nx.template({32, 10, 1}, :f32)
Axon.Display.as_graph(rnn_model, template)
```

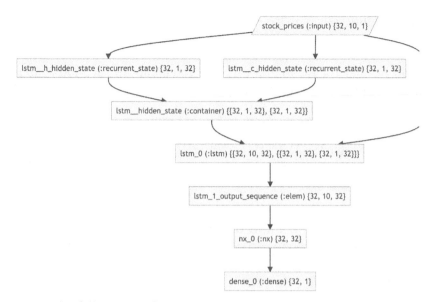

Now, use the following code to run your single-step RNN:

```
rnn_trained_model_state =
  rnn_model
  |> Axon.Loop.trainer(:mean_squared_error, :adam)
  |> Axon.Loop.metric(:mean_absolute_error)
  |> Axon.Loop.run(single_step_train_data, %{}, epochs: 50, compiler: EXLA)
```

After a while, you'll see the following output:

```
Epoch: 40, Batch: 70, loss: 0.0000170 mean_absolute_error: 0.0032365
Epoch: 41, Batch: 43, loss: 0.0000170 mean_absolute_error: 0.0035252
Epoch: 42, Batch: 66, loss: 0.0000169 mean_absolute_error: 0.0027809
Epoch: 43, Batch: 39, loss: 0.0000168 mean_absolute_error: 0.0030578
Epoch: 44, Batch: 62, loss: 0.0000166 mean_absolute_error: 0.0023700
Epoch: 45, Batch: 35, loss: 0.0000165 mean_absolute_error: 0.0026432
Epoch: 46, Batch: 58, loss: 0.0000162 mean_absolute_error: 0.0021020
Epoch: 47, Batch: 31, loss: 0.0000161 mean_absolute_error: 0.0023653
Epoch: 48, Batch: 54, loss: 0.0000158 mean_absolute_error: 0.0019592
Epoch: 49, Batch: 27, loss: 0.0000157 mean_absolute_error: 0.0023374
```

With a trained model, you can use Axon's evaluation API to evaluate it against your test data:

```
rnn_model
|> Axon.Loop.evaluator()
|> Axon.Loop.metric(:mean_absolute_error)
|> Axon.Loop.run(
  single_step_test_data,
  rnn_trained_model_state,
  compiler: EXLA
)
```

After running this code, you'll see the following output:

```
Batch: 13, mean_absolute_error: 0.0032470
```

Again, you can use the mean and variance you computed previously to get a more interpretable version of this metric:

```
0.0032470
|> Kernel.*(
  :math.sqrt(Explorer.Series.variance(aapl_df["Close"]))
)
|> Kernel.+(
  Explorer.Series.mean(aapl_df["Close"])
)
```

So your single-shot RNN performed slightly better than the CNN. But the difference between model errors is near negligible, so it's difficult to say which of these models between the CNN and RNN is better. If you were making a decision between deploying the RNN or CNN, you would likely need to do more tests or use other criteria such as storage and compute cost of each model, to determine which to use.

You can repeat the analysis you ran in Using CNNs for Single-Step Prediction, on page 227, to get a better visualization of how your model fits the data overall:

```
Analysis.visualize_predictions(
  rnn_model,
  rnn_trained_model_state,
  Explorer.Series.to_list(aapl_df["Close"]),
  window_size,
  1,
  batch_size
)
```

After running the code, you'll see the image as shown on page 235.

And again, you'll notice there are negligible differences between how well your RNN and CNN fit to the data. Both an RNN and CNN may be appropriate for conducting time-series analysis on this particular dataset when making inferences over a single timestep.

Tempering Expectations

After running these small experiments on stock prices, you might feel there's some promise in using neural networks to predict the future. After all, both of the neural networks you've trained do a pretty good job of following the trend line of AAPL's stock price over the course of ten years. In reality, forecasting the future is *really* challenging.

Neural networks are powerful *interpolators*. Interpolation is the process of filling in unknown data points within a fixed domain. Interpolation is explicitly different from extrapolation because in extrapolation we attempt to fill in unknown data points from outside a fixed domain. What does this have to do with time-series analysis?

Well, you may have noticed that your neural networks were decent at predicting AAPL's stock prices for the time-period you had access to. You have two neural networks that are decent models of the *past*, but they have no information about the future. You can attempt to extrapolate information about the future from past patterns, but the patterns may change drastically.

When doing time-series analysis, you're always at risk of drawing incorrect conclusions from incomplete information from the past. That's not to say you cannot exploit certain patterns in the past to use in the future, but you should always be aware of potential catastrophic failures in relying too much on old patterns.

Wrapping Up

In this chapter, you implemented two types of neural networks to predict the prices of AAPL stock in the future. You created and trained both a convolutional and recurrent neural network to perform single-step time-series prediction on AAPL stock prices. You learned a bit about the challenges of modeling time-series data. You used Explorer for normalizing your input data and VegaLite for visualizing your input data.

In the previous two chapters, you spent a lot of time working with recurrent neural networks. Recurrent neural networks are powerful, but in the past five years, they've been completely blown away by an even more powerful class of models.

In the next chapter, you'll come face-to-face with the *transformer*, the architecture which powers some of the most powerful models in use today including ChatGPT[2] and Whisper.[3]

2.   https://openai.com/blog/chatgpt/

3.   https://openai.com/blog/whisper/

## CHAPTER 11

Model Everything with Transformers

At this point in the book, you've worked with many different types of data, such as structured data, visual data, text data, and time-series data. For each of these specific applications of machine learning, you used a new approach or architecture to solve the problem. With each of these new models or architectures, you saw firsthand how building a model with some simple assumptions and slight tweaks can drastically impact its performance.

In Chapter 7, Learn to See, on page 141, you used convolutions with learned kernels to drastically increase the ability of your model to extract features from image inputs. Convolutional neural networks work well because they *assume* your inputs have a grid-like structure.

In Chapter 8, Stop Reinventing the Wheel, on page 171, you improved performance on low-data problems with pre-trained models. You *assume* your chosen pre-trained model acts as a superior feature extractor to anything you can train from scratch.

In Chapter 9, Understand Text, on page 195, you applied recurrent architectures to sequential problems. Recurrent neural networks work well because they *assume* your inputs have temporal dependencies.

When making assumptions in machine learning, you also make trade-offs. Linear models are simple, but they can't capture nonlinear relationships. Convolutional neural networks work well on images but are generally not as strong as recurrent neural networks on sequences.

In an ideal world, you wouldn't need to construct a distinct architecture for each input modality. Up until recently, the promise of a universally *good* or preferred model architecture was somewhat of a fantasy. Remember from Chapter 1, Make Machines That Learn, on page 3, that this fantasy stems from the no-free lunch theorem. However, in recent years, *transformers* have proven extremely generalizable on a wide range of input modalities.

Transformers are a class of deep learning models that were originally designed for natural language processing. Over time, transformer models have emerged as not only the most powerful models in natural language processing, but also as some of the most powerful models in audio processing, computer vision, and more. There's seemingly no limit to the power of a carefully crafted transformer model and *a lot* of input data.

Transformers aren't necessarily the best model for modeling *everything*, but they do pretty well at modeling *a lot of things*. For example, when dealing with text, transformers are a good choice. When dealing with certain kinds of image problems, such as image-to-image search, transformers are still a good choice. When working with multiple modalities, and one of those modalities is text, you guessed it, use transformers. Are there exceptions? Of course. But if there was a competition for the most universally good model, transformer models would probably be at the top of the list.

Transformers are revolutionizing nearly every domain of artificial intelligence and machine learning. The last few years have seen the emergence of a new transformer ecosystem in which libraries, infrastructure, hardware, and even companies are built entirely on the promises of transformers. Understanding transformers is vital to being successful as a machine learning engineer in today's world. In this chapter, you'll apply transformers on three different problems using Nx, Axon, and Bumblebee.[1] Bumblebee is an Elixir library that consists of pre-trained Axon models as well as out-of-the-box pipelines for solving machine learning problems. You'll use Bumblebee to simplify the process of creating, training, and using transformer models—and you'll see how effective transformers can be at modeling everything.

Paying Attention

To understand transformers, you first need to understand *attention*. The key feature of transformers is in how they apply attention. But what is attention, and where does attention come from?

First, consider you're trying to train a model to translate text between English and German. You have a large corpus of text pairs with a source sentence in English and a target sentence in German. This is a classic example of *machine*

---

1. https://github.com/elixir-nx/bumblebee

translation, and more specifically in the context of deep learning, *neural machine translation.*

In neural machine translation, the goal is to map a source sequence to a target sequence. From what you know so far, this sounds like a perfect application of recurrent neural networks. Remember, recurrent neural networks are capable of taking a source sequence and transforming it into some output sequence. Intuitively, it seems reasonable to believe that you can transform the input sequence with one or many LSTM or GRU blocks. After all, they are designed for processing sequences and mapping sequences to convenient sequence representations.

However, this problem isn't that easy. There's no guarantee the source sequence and target sequence have the same length. Additionally, syntax between languages differs drastically—you can't just map source tokens to the translated variants and expect the translation to be correct. As it turns out, this task is pretty difficult for a single RNN. To address this problem, researchers introduced *sequence-to-sequence models.*

Sequence-to-sequence models are designed specifically for problems in which the objective is to map a source sequence to a target sequence. Sequence-to-sequence models consist of an encoder and a decoder. The encoder is responsible for summarizing the information present in the source sequence in a *context vector.* The decoder is initialized with the context vector and produces the target sequence. The context vector is a convenient representation of the input sequence. If you consider what a context vector is in the context of machine translation, you can think of it as the meaning of the source sentence. The goal of a translation is to capture the meaning of the sentence in the source language in the target language.

Sequence-to-sequence models break the process of mapping source to target sequences into two steps. First, the encoder extracts meaning from the source sequence, and then the decoder uses this meaning to generate a target sequence. In Axon, the implementation of a sequence-to-sequence model looks like this:

```
source = Axon.input("source")
cur_target = Axon.input("target")

{_, context_vector} = Axon.lstm(source, 64)
{out_target, _} = Axon.lstm(cur_target, context_vector, 64)

Axon.dense(out_target, vocab_size)
```

Notice that the context vector is the final hidden state produced by the LSTM layer. You use this context vector as the initial hidden state of the decoder to produce a transformed representation of the sequence. Notice that you don't transform source but rather cur_target, which is the current target sequence. In a sequence-to-sequence model, rather than try to output an entire sequence at once, you generally predict one token at a time. You can almost think of it as a game of filling in the blanks. You're given a source sentence, such as this:

```
I love cats
```

The source comes with a partial sequence, like this:

```
Ich liebe
```

The goal is to predict the next token that produces the next translation, which, in this case, is Katzen.

Sequence-to-sequence models work really well, and in theory, can learn to map any sequence to any other sequence. In practice, they have some limitations. Most notably, sequence-to-sequence models struggle to remember information from long sequences. Remember, the state in an RNN is accumulated from the beginning of the sequence to the end. With long sequences, it's common for the latter portions of the sequence to be overrepresented in the final state, while earlier portions are forgotten.

To overcome the problem of forgetting, you can introduce a shortcut that computes the alignment between source and target sentences. This is the *attention mechanism*. Attention was originally designed as a shortcut between the context vector and the source input—it provides a map that indicates how much each hidden state should be weighed into each output token. You might see this called an *alignment score*, the *attention matrix*, or the *attention weights*. The attention matrix essentially tells you how important each word in the source sequence is to the target sequence. For a translation task, you can think of this as mapping which words in the source sequence best relate to words in the target sequence. For example, the alignment score between cats and Ich should be relatively low whereas the alignment between cats and Katzen should be relatively high.

Much like you can visualize intermediate activations in convolutional neural networks, you can also visualize attention weights to provide a bit of insight into the relationships your model is learning. For example, you can see the visualized attention matrix for an English-to-French translation on page 241.

Notice how words whose meanings are more closely aligned are more active in the attention map. Attention enables a model to learn to selectively *pay attention* to certain tokens in the input. This small addition to recurrent models turns out to be pretty powerful. But it still depends on a recurrent neural network.

	I	love	cats
Ich	0.8	0.0	0.2
liebe	0.0	1.0	0.0
Katzen	0.1	0.0	0.9

So how do you go from a recurrent neural network with attention to an attention-only transformer?

Going from RNNs to Transformers

Attention provides a shortcut between source and target sequences. This helps a recurrent model learn longer sequences by highlighting which portions of the context vector map to portions of the target sequence. The learned attention matrix encodes information about the relationships between tokens in source and target sequences. But you still need to rely on a recurrent network for extracting context from the source sequence.

Recall from Chapter 9, Understand Text, on page 195, that it's common practice to extract the last token from a sequence transformed by an RNN such as an LSTM. This is because this token contains a representation that encodes information about the entire sequence. The sequential nature of RNNs restricts their ability to make connections between nonadjacent tokens in a sequence. The recurrent process works on a single timestep in the forward or reverse direction, so it's difficult to capture relationships between nonadjacent tokens. Fortunately, you already know how to address this problem using attention.

Rather than weight the relationships between a source and target sequence, you can use attention to weight the relationships between a source sequence and itself. Using the same process in the original attention mechanism, you initialize and learn an attention matrix, which highlights the relationship between words in a single sentence. This is known as *self-attention*, and it highlights relationships between words in a sequence. This allows you to learn which words most relate to one another and which words provide the most context to the input sequence. At this point, you might ask yourself, "Isn't this what a recurrent neural network is supposed to do? Isn't the point of a recurrent neural network to extract temporal relationships between tokens in sequences?" Yes. But in this case, you've managed to model these relationships without the need for a recurrent neural network. In fact, *Attention is All You Need. [VSPU17]*

The typical transformer architecture makes use of an encoder-decoder architecture on a *masked language modeling task.* The masked language-modeling task is best described as an elementary school vocabulary assignment. In other words, transformers learn to model language by predicting the next word most likely to appear in a sequence.

The encoder in a transformer typically consists of a collection of multiple encoder layers and operates on a representation of the source sequence. Each encoder layer is identical and consists of some form of self-attention and some series of output projections. The actual variant of self-attention in use in a transformer is typically *multi-headed self-attention,* which is identical to self-attention with one slight exception.

In single-headed self-attention, the model computes one attention matrix, which means it learns to weight the relationships between tokens in one way. In multi-headed self-attention, the model computes multiple (typically 12) different attention matrices (heads). This means the model learns an ensemble of relationships between tokens in the input. Encoders pass the encoded representation on to subsequent encoder layers.

The decoder in a transformer model typically consists of a collection of multiple decoder layers and operates on a representation of the target sequence—usually, the source sequence shifted to the right by one token—and some information about the source sequence from the encoder. Each decoder layer also consists of some variant of self-attention, but the decoder also makes use of cross-attention. The decoder layer computes multi-headed self-attention on the target sequence. The decoder layer also computes multi-headed cross-attention between information provided by the encoder and the target sequence. This is similar to attention in the traditional sense you learned about earlier. Cross-attention provides a shortcut in context between the encoder and the decoder. You can see a high-level visual overview of cross-attention in the diagram on page 243.

One issue with using attention to model temporal data is that transformers have no way of representing temporal dependencies. To overcome this limitation, most transformers introduce a positional embedding or positional encoding which injects information about positional relationships into the model.

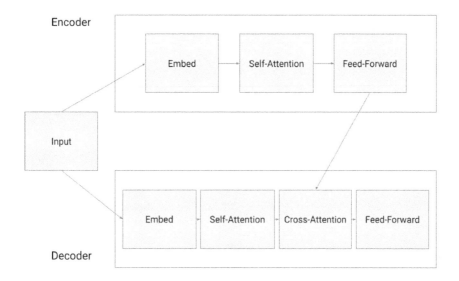

Most transformers consist of hierarchies of encoder layers and decoder layers stacked on top of one another. While there are many variants of the traditional transformer architecture, essentially all of them follow this same pattern. If you look at the transformer implementations in Bumblebee, you'll find that many of them are nearly identical. Most models are differentiated only by slight tweaks in specific parts such as the attention implementation, the positional encoding used, or the training process.

The typical transformer architecture produces a high-dimensional representation of sequences, which are useful on downstream tasks. Transformers, more or less, eliminate the need for recurrent neural networks in the context of natural language processing. In fact, in almost every case, transformers prove significantly more powerful than their recurrent counterparts. Additionally, transformers are readily parallelizable and are significantly more scalable than an equivalent recurrent neural network. Combined with massive amounts of data, transformers have proven to be one of the most important innovations in deep learning.

Using Transformers with Bumblebee

To really appreciate the power of transformers, you'll put a few into practice using the Bumblebee library. Bumblebee is a library that contains implementations of popular deep learning architectures in Axon. Bumblebee interacts directly with the HuggingFace hub and is even capable of loading parameters directly from pre-trained PyTorch checkpoints. Bumblebee allows you to rapidly use some of the most powerful open-source models in existence with a few lines of Elixir. To demonstrate the power of transformers and the simplicity of Bumblebee, you'll use Bumblebee to solve three different kinds of problems.

Installing Dependencies

To get started, fire up a Livebook and add the following dependencies:

```
Mix.install([
  {:bumblebee, "~> 0.5"},
  {:axon, "~> 0.6"},
  {:nx, "~> 0.7"},
  {:kino, "~> 0.8"},
  {:kino_bumblebee, ">= 0.0.0"},
  {:exla, ">= 0.0.0"}
])
```

The only new dependencies here are Bumblebee and KinoBumblebee. KinoBumblebee provides some conveniences for using Bumblebee in Livebook. You can actually implement a number of the tasks demonstrated in this chapter without having to write any code using the smart cells provided by KinoBumblebee.

You'll also need Axon for performing inference and fine-tuning on pre-trained models, Nx for basic tensor manipulations, and EXLA for hardware acceleration. Before continuing, set the default backend to EXLA to ensure all of your computations are accelerated:

```
Nx.global_default_backend(EXLA.Backend)
```

Zero-Shot Classification with BART

To get your toes wet with Bumblebee, you'll start by implementing some basic *zero-shot classification* tasks using Bumblebee and Axon. Zero-shot classification is a technique that associates text with labels without the need to specialize a model on specific input domains. Some models are trained on general enough data that they're able to classify closely related natural language labels to portions of text without needing to see any examples of input-target pairs. With zero-shot classification, you can take advantage of a model without needing to gather input data.

As a practical example, imagine you're tasked with automating the process of filing customer support tickets for an airline. In this example, users enter their inquiries in natural language, and your model is responsible for filing the requests under the appropriate tags: "New Booking," "Update Booking," "Cancel Booking," or "Refund." Up until this point in the book, you wouldn't have had any way to solve this problem without access to a sufficient amount of training data. Fortunately, with zero-shot classification, you don't necessarily need training data.

First, copy and run the following code to import a pre-trained model and tokenizer with Bumblebee:

```
{:ok, model} = Bumblebee.load_model(
  {:hf, "facebook/bart-large-mnli"}
)
{:ok, tokenizer} = Bumblebee.load_tokenizer(
  {:hf, "facebook/bart-large-mnli"}
)
```

This code uses the Bumblebee module to load a pre-trained model and tokenizer directly from the HuggingFace hub. Bumblebee is designed to support multiple model hubs, which is why you need to specify the tuple {:hf, path} in both load_model/1 and load_tokenizer/1. load_model/1 returns the pre-trained model and parameters, as well as the model's configuration. The configuration will tell you exactly what model architecture you've loaded from the given path. In this case, bart-large-mnli is an instantiation of the BART transformer architecture from Facebook. BART is a large language model pre-trained by Facebook for text generation, translation, and comprehension. The MNLI variant is trained on *natural language inference* tasks, which attempt to predict the probability a given hypothesis is true based on some input text.

load_tokenizer/1 serves the same purpose as load_model/1, but with tokenizers. Bumblebee depends on a low-level tokenizers library that binds HuggingFace's Rust tokenizer implementations. Recall from Chapter 9, Understand Text, on page 195, that some sophisticated tokenization strategies rely on probabilistic methods to learn vocabularies with fixed sizes. Most of the transformer models in Bumblebee employ these kinds of tokenization strategies and come with a pre-trained tokenizer. It's important that you use a model's corresponding pre-trained tokenizer because it will encode text in the same manner the model was exposed to during training.

model is actually a map with :model, :spec, and :params keys. You can inspect each key in the map to see what it represents, but for now, inspect the :model key in model:

```
IO.inspect model.model
```

You'll see this:

```
#Axon<
  inputs: %{
    "attention_head_mask" => {12, 16},
    "attention_mask" => {nil, nil},
    "cache" => nil,
    "cross_attention_head_mask" => {12, 16},
    "decoder_attention_head_mask" => {12, 16},
    "decoder_attention_mask" => {nil, nil},
    "decoder_input_embeddings" => {nil, nil, 1024},
    "decoder_input_ids" => {nil, nil},
    "decoder_position_ids" => {nil, nil},
    "encoder_hidden_state" => {nil, nil, 1024},
    "input_embeddings" => {nil, nil, 1024},
    "input_ids" => {nil, nil},
    "position_ids" => {nil, nil}
  }
  outputs: "container_64"
  nodes: 1956
>
```

Notice how model is a regular Axon model. Under the hood, Axon pulls the specified model's configuration from the HuggingFace hub and delegates to a module that builds the Axon implementation with the given configuration. This means you can use model like you would any other Axon model. Bumblebee provides conveniences; it doesn't change how you interact with Axon models.

Next, run the following Livebook cell:

```
labels = ["New booking", "Update booking", "Cancel booking", "Refund"]

zero_shot_serving =
  Bumblebee.Text.zero_shot_classification(
    model,
    tokenizer,
    labels
  )
```

Running this cell creates an %Nx.Serving{} struct which runs a zero-shot classification task end-to-end. Nx.Serving is a high-level serving API that encapsulates preprocessing, inference, and postprocessing. Bumblebee works directly with the serving API, offering serving factories that return end-to-end pipelines for tasks such as image and text classification.

This code makes use of a natural language inferencing (NLI) model for zero-shot classification. NLI models are commonly used for understanding whether two sentences are entailments, contradictions, or neutral. In other words, you can propose a premise and a hypothesis, and the model will tell you if the hypothesis contradicts or goes along with the premise. With these kinds of models, you can build the hypothesis in such a way that it's useful for zero-shot classification. In this case, you always build your hypothesis as This example is #{label}, which fills in the hypothesis with the given label. The model spits out a probability for each label that the premise (input sequence) goes along with the hypothesis. At the end, you have a list of labels and their corresponding probabilities, which you can extract the maximum value from.

In addition to a model and tokenizer, Bumblebee's zero-shot classification function accepts labels to assign to zero-shot queries. That's all you need to start making zero-shot classifications. To try out your zero-shot classification pipeline, you can use Nx.Serving.run/2. Try running the following code in a new cell and observe the output:

```
input = "I need to book a new flight"

Nx.Serving.run(zero_shot_serving, input)
```

Your model will output the following:

```
%{
  predictions: [
    %{label: "New booking", score: 0.5991652011871338},
    %{label: "Update booking", score: 0.3455488979816437},
    %{label: "Refund", score: 0.028283976018428802},
    %{label: "Cancel booking", score: 0.027001921087503433}
  ]
}
```

You can try a few more examples to get a feel for how powerful this zero-shot classification task is:

```
inputs = [
  "I want to change my existing flight",
  "I want to cancel my current flight",
  "I demand my money back"
]

Nx.Serving.run(zero_shot_serving, input)
```

Your model will output the following:

```
[
  %{
    predictions: [
      %{label: "New booking", score: 0.43927058577537537},
```

```
        %{label: "Update booking", score: 0.4268641471862793},
        %{label: "Cancel booking", score: 0.10792690515518188},
        %{label: "Refund", score: 0.02593844011425972}
    ]
  },
  %{
    predictions: [
      %{label: "Cancel booking", score: 0.5605528950691223},
      %{label: "Refund", score: 0.3020733594894409},
      %{label: "Update booking", score: 0.09756755083799362},
      %{label: "New booking", score: 0.03980622440576553}
    ]
  },
  %{
    predictions: [
      %{label: "Refund", score: 0.913806140422821},
      %{label: "Cancel booking", score: 0.04736287519335747},
      %{label: "Update booking", score: 0.02491646446287632},
      %{label: "New booking", score: 0.013914537616074085}
    ]
  }
]
```

Notice you can pass batches of inputs to the Nx.Serving API, which means you can easily batch-process inputs.

Without any training data, and in under five lines of Elixir, you have a model that's capable of filing customer service requests with appropriate tags. You can also augment or extend this pipeline to allow for multiple labels for each input. For example, you might add tags related to the urgency of the request. Thanks to the power of transformers, you're limited mostly by your imagination and needs.

Making Conversation

More than likely, you have been exposed to the incredible coherence of AI-generated text. Models such as GPT-3, OPT-3, and BLOOM are capable of incredible feats. These *large language models* are adept at *sentence completion* tasks. You feed a large language model a prompt, and it completes the prompt with what it thinks is the most reasonable sequence. If you engineer the prompt in a clever way, you can get some pretty impressive behavior. One application of a completion or generation task such as this one is a chat bot. With some prompt engineering, you can have a transformer model that maintains coherent conversations in a few lines of code.

To start, you'll need to import a new model and tokenizer:

```
repo = {:hf, "google/gemma-2b-it"}
{:ok, model} = Bumblebee.load_model(repo)
{:ok, tokenizer} = Bumblebee.load_tokenizer(repo)
{:ok, generation_config} = Bumblebee.load_generation_config(repo)

generation_config =
  Bumblebee.configure(generation_config,
    max_new_tokens: 256,
    strategy: %{type: :multinomial_sampling, top_p: 0.6}
  )
```

Next, create a new generation serving using Bumblebee.Text.generation/4:

```
serving =
  Bumblebee.Text.generation(
    model_info,
    tokenizer,
    generation_config,
    compile: [batch_size: 1, sequence_length: 1028],
    stream: true,
    defn_options: [compiler: EXLA]
  )

Kino.start_child({Nx.Serving, name: Gemma, serving: serving})
```

This serving encapsulates all of the logic necessary for using large-language models to generate text. Next, you'll want to implement an interface for querying the large language model.

Add the following code to a new Livebook cell:

```
user_input = Kino.Input.textarea("User prompt", default: "Who are you?")

user = Kino.Input.read(user_input)

prompt = """
<start_of_turn>user
#{user}
<start_of_turn>model
"""

Nx.Serving.batched_run(Gemma, prompt)
|> Enum.each(&IO.write/1)
```

This code renders an input, which prompts the user to initiate the conversation. It then formats a prompt in the particular style required by the Gemma LLM. Then, it uses Nx.Serving.batched_run/2 to generate text, and it streams the generated text out using IO.write/1.

Certain models, such as the Gemma model used here, support generation out of the box in Bumblebee by implementing a generation behavior. By default, Bumblebee uses a greedy text generation strategy to generate tokens from a sequence. The greedy strategy generates one token of the sequence at a time by predicting the most probable next token. Bumblebee also supports more complex generation strategies out of the box, but they're often more compute-intensive. You'll find when working with large language models that generation strategies and hyperparameters often have a significant impact on the quality of generations.

After generating the bot's response given the chat history, the chat bot outputs the text to the screen using Kino and waits for the next input.

After running this cell, you'll see a Kino input form with a large submit button. You can type in any text you want to converse with the large language model. With only a few lines of Elixir code, you're able to interact with some extremely powerful language models.

Classifying Images

As the title of this chapter implies, transformers are also not just limited to text data. You can also apply them effectively to the visual domain. To demonstrate the seemingly universal dominance of transformers, you'll implement a simple image classifier using a pre-trained transformer.

Start by creating a new cell and running the following code:

```
{:ok, model_info} =
  Bumblebee.load_model({:hf, "google/vit-base-patch16-224"})

{:ok, featurizer} = Bumblebee.load_featurizer(
  {:hf, "google/vit-base-patch16-224"}
)

serving =
  Bumblebee.Vision.image_classification(model_info, featurizer,
    top_k: 1,
    compile: [batch_size: 1],
    defn_options: [compiler: EXLA]
  )
```

You should be pretty familiar with this workflow by now. The only difference in this example is that you've changed load_tokenizer to load_featurizer. Much like tokenizers are used to extract features from text, featurizers are used to extract features from images. In this example, you're using the *Vision Transformer (ViT)*. The ViT is a pre-trained transformer architecture that achieves a state-of-the-art performance on ImageNet.

With your model loaded, you can load an image file, such as this one:

You'll use the following code:

```
image_input = Kino.Input.image("Image", size: {224, 224})
form = Kino.Control.form([image: image_input], submit: "Run")
frame = Kino.Frame.new()

form
|> Kino.Control.stream()
|> Stream.filter(& &1.data.image)
|> Kino.listen(fn %{data: %{image: image}} ->
  Kino.Frame.render(frame, Kino.Markdown.new("Running..."))
  image =
    image.file_ref
    |> Kino.Input.file_path()
    |> File.read!()
    |> Nx.from_binary(:u8)
    |> Nx.reshape({image.height, image.width, 3})
  output = Nx.Serving.run(serving, image)

  output.predictions
  |> Enum.map(&{&1.label, &1.score})
  |> Kino.Bumblebee.ScoredList.new()
  |> then(&Kino.Frame.render(frame, &1))
end)

Kino.Layout.grid([form, frame], boxed: true, gap: 16)
```

This cell will make use of Kino form controls again. The code creates an image upload component and listens for input. Once you upload an image, the code parses the image data into an Nx tensor and passes it through the serving you declared in the previous cell. The serving returns scores for the top k labels. You then use Kino to render these scores and labels into a scorecard. After the cell runs, you'll see this:

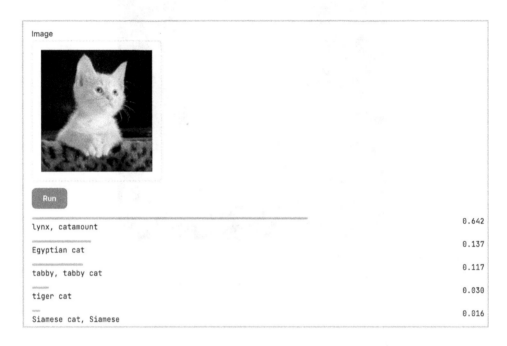

Again, with only a few lines of code you're able to make use of a powerful image classification model.

Fine-Tuning Pre-trained Models

All of these examples demonstrate the practicality of Bumblebee for inference tasks, which are well-suited to using pre-trained models without any need for additional training. But what happens if you have a use case which requires additional training? Fortunately, as you learned in Chapter 8, Stop Reinventing the Wheel, on page 171, it's possible to fine-tune pre-trained models in Axon to your specific use case. Models imported from Bumblebee are no exception.

As with pre-trained image models, it's common to make use of pre-trained language models as a base representation for more specific language tasks. In this example, you'll fine-tune a pre-trained Transformer to categorize Yelp

Reviews.[2] Each review consists of the actual review text and the rating associated with the review. This should feel similar to the problem you solved in Chapter 9, Understand Text, on page 195—classifying movie reviews. In this case, however, each rating belongs to one of five possible categories. Start by downloading the dataset from here.[3]

Next, import a pre-trained transformer with the following code:

```
{:ok, spec} = Bumblebee.load_spec({:hf, "distilbert-base-cased"},
  module: Bumblebee.Text.Distilbert,
  architecture: :for_sequence_classification
)
spec = Bumblebee.configure(spec, num_labels: 5)

{:ok, %{model: model, params: params}} = Bumblebee.load_model(
  {:hf, "distilbert-base-cased"},
  spec: spec
)

{:ok, tokenizer} = Bumblebee.load_tokenizer({:hf, "distilbert-base-cased"})
```

In this example, you're using the DistilBERT[4] model. DistilBERT is a smaller, faster version of BERT, which trades off compute and storage for a small dip in accuracy. Bidirectional encoder representations of text (BERT) is one of the most famous transformer implementations originally developed at Google. When it was originally integrated in 2017, BERT proved so powerful in practice that it caused one of the most significant changes to the Google search algorithms in years. While you can adjust this example to make use of a more powerful model such as BERT, you should note that larger models are more expensive and slower to train.

Before actually loading the model, you use load_spec/2, which loads the model configuration before loading the actual model. You can then edit the configuration using Bumblebee.configure/2. In this example, you configure the spec to accept num_labels: 5, and in load_model/2, you specify the architecture as :for_sequence_classification. Additionally, you pass the reconfigured spec with the :spec option to tell Bumblebee to create a sequence classification model with five output classes.

Next, you'll need to create an input pipeline. If you extract the dataset into a local directory, you'll notice it consists of both train and test CSVs. You can stream a CSV line by line and parse the ratings and review into batches of Tensors using this code:

2. https://huggingface.co/datasets/yelp_review_full/tree/main
3. https://s3.amazonaws.com/fast-ai-nlp/yelp_review_full_csv.tgz
4. https://huggingface.co/docs/transformers/model_doc/distilbert

```
batch_size = 32
max_length = 128

train_data =
  File.stream!("yelp_review_full_csv/train.csv")
  |> Stream.chunk_every(batch_size)
  |> Stream.map(fn inputs ->
    {labels, reviews} =
      inputs
      |> Enum.map(fn line ->
        [label, review] = String.split(line, "|",\"")
        {String.trim(label, "|""), String.trim(review, "\"")}
      end)
      |> Enum.unzip()

    labels = labels |> Enum.map(&String.to_integer/1) |> Nx.tensor()
    tokens = Bumblebee.apply_tokenizer(tokenizer, reviews, length: max_length)

    {tokens, labels}
  end)
```

This code will stream the file line by line in chunks of 32. Each chunk gets split into a label and review. Each label is parsed to an integer, and each review is tokenized using Bumblebee. Reviews are padded or truncated to a max sequence length of 128 characters. You can take the first sample from your training data and inspect it like this:

```
Enum.take(train_data, 1)
```

You'll see the following:

```
[
  {#Nx.Tensor<
    s64[32]
    [5, 2, 4, 4, 1, 5, 5, 1, 2, 3, 1, 1, 4, 2, ...]
  >,
  %{
    "attention_mask" => #Nx.Tensor<
      s64[32][128]
      [
        [1, 1, 1, 1, 1, 1, 1, 1, 1, 1, 1, 1, 1, 1, 1, 1, ...],
        ...
      ]
    >,
    "input_ids" => #Nx.Tensor<
      s64[32][128]
      [
        [101, 173, 1197, 119, 2284, 2953, 3272, 1917, ...],
        ...
      ]
    >,
```

```
      "token_type_ids" => #Nx.Tensor<
        s64[32][128]
        [
          [0, 0, 0, 0, 0, 0, 0, 0, 0, 0, 0, 0, 0, 0, 0, ...],
          ...
        ]
      >
    }}
]
```

Now, you need to tweak your model a little bit. The models returned from Bumblebee return outputs in addition to those you care about for training. In this instance, the model output is a map consisting of :attentions, :hidden_states, and :logits. You can verify this by running the following:

```
Axon.get_output_shape(model, %{"input_ids" => Nx.template({32, 128}, :s64)})
```

And you'll see this output:

```
%{
  attentions: #Axon.None<...>,
  hidden_states: #Axon.None<...>,
  logits: {32, 5}}
```

You only care about :logits in this case. Before passing the model to a training loop, you'll need to extract logits specifically. You can do so by adding the following layer to your model:

```
model = Axon.nx(model, fn %{logits: logits} -> logits end)
```

This will create a new model that only returns :logits.

Now all you need to do is create a training loop. This problem is a multi-class classification problem, so you should be pretty familiar with how to solve it. You can implement your loop with the following code:

```
optimizer = Axon.Optimizers.adamw(5.0e-5)
loss = &Axon.Losses.categorical_cross_entropy(&1, &2,
  from_logits: true,
  sparse: true,
  reduction: :mean
)
trained_model_state =
  model
  |> Axon.Loop.trainer(loss, optimizer, log: 1)
  |> Axon.Loop.metric(:accuracy)
  |> Axon.Loop.run(train_data, params, epochs: 3, compiler: EXLA)
```

And that's all you need. Note that transformers are often significantly larger and more expensive to run than the other types of models you've implemented

in this book. You may end up waiting for a while for results. You can validate
your training process by only training on a small portion of the original
dataset. After running this code, you'll see this:

```
Epoch: 0, Batch: 249, accuracy: 0.3605000 loss: 1.1831361
Epoch: 1, Batch: 249, accuracy: 0.5363751 loss: 1.0118284
Epoch: 2, Batch: 249, accuracy: 0.6470000 loss: 0.8826395
```

After your model finishes training, you can create a test pipeline with the
given test data and evaluate your trained model with the following code:

```
model
|> Axon.Loop.evaluator()
|> Axon.Loop.metric(:accuracy)
|> Axon.Loop.run(test_data, params, compiler: EXLA)
```

And you'll see this:

```
Batch: 49, accuracy: 0.3675000
```

Note that the 36% accuracy shown here demonstrates the accuracy of the
model after training on a small subset of the original data. For a more powerful
classifier, you can continue training for a longer duration. With a few lines
of code, you fine-tuned a powerful pre-trained model into a powerful classifier
capable of categorizing Yelp reviews.

Only the Beginning

While this section specifically highlights four different use cases of Bumblebee,
the actual number of practical use cases far exceeds that. As you continue
your ML journey, you'll encounter transformers in use everywhere for search
applications, image generation, document classification, text summarization,
machine translation, and more. The chances are also good that you'll be able
to make use of the same models you find others using simply by importing
a pre-trained implementation with Bumblebee.

Wrapping Up

In this chapter, you harnessed the power of transformers on a variety of
machine learning tasks. You learned about what transformers are and where
the intuition behind transformers comes from. You learned about attention
and how slight modifications to the original attention mechanism lead to the
power of transformers. You used Bumblebee to make use of powerful pre-
trained transformers to solve a variety of different tasks. You put Bumblebee
in action on inference tasks, and you fine-tuned a pre-trained model with
Bumblebee and Axon.

At this point, you've implemented the majority of the most important types of deep learning models in use. You know how to solve almost any type of problem on any type of data using Axon. Of course, almost every one of the problems you've solved so far assumes access to a large amount of labeled data. But what happens if you don't have any input data?

In the next chapter, you'll explore some approaches to deep unsupervised learning and generative modeling with Axon. This will wrap up your journey into deep learning with Axon, and you'll be ready to move on to putting machine learning into practice with Nx, Axon, and Elixir.

## CHAPTER 12

Learn Without Supervision

Throughout this book, you've primarily been focused on problems that fall in the domain of supervised learning. Remember, a supervised learning problem is one where you have access to labeled data at training time. Algorithms for supervised learning problems are great in theory because they typically have well-established solutions and are often easier to interpret and understand.

Unfortunately, the reality is that a majority of the data you encounter is unlabeled. Equally problematic is that labeling data is an expensive, tedious, and time-consuming task. While most machine learning solutions would benefit from some level of supervision, this isn't possible to achieve in all cases. In these cases, it's necessary to take advantage of unsupervised learning.

Recall from Chapter 1, Make Machines That Learn, on page 3, that unsupervised learning is learning to capture relationships in data without supervision signals. Essentially, you learn from data without labels. In this chapter, you'll apply *deep unsupervised learning*, which is a subset of unsupervised learning that depends on the power of neural networks, to solve compression and *generative modeling* problems. Specifically, you'll implement three types of unsupervised neural networks: *autoencoders*, *variational autoencoders*, and *generative adversarial networks*. You'll use these networks to generate images of handwritten digits.

Compressing Data with Autoencoders

If you're familiar with compression, you already know a bit about unsupervised learning. A somewhat close relationship exists between the objectives of compression and the objectives of unsupervised learning. In a compression algorithm, your goal is to reduce the size of the original data—typically by taking advantage of patterns and structures of the input data. In an unsupervised learning problem, your goal is to capture or model the patterns and structures of the input data.

If you consider a compression algorithm as an Elixir behavior, the contract look something like this:

```
@callback compress(data) :: compressed_data

@callback decompress(compressed_data) :: data
```

Recall from Chapter 6, Go Deep with Axon, on page 117, that neural networks are function approximators. Because neural networks simply approximate functions, you can use them to approximate functions for compression and decompression. Your neural network learns to compress data, and then you can train an additional neural network to decompress the compressed form. This type of neural network is known as an autoencoder.

An autoencoder is a neural network that consists of an *encoder* and a *decoder*. The encoder learns a *latent representation* of input data. A latent representation is a compressed representation of input data in which similar items are close together in space. For example, if you had a latent representation of animals, the latent representations of a tiger and a cat would be more similar than the latent representations of an alligator and a human. The decoder learns to reconstruct input data from the latent representation. The goal of an autoencoder is to map an input to a latent representation and back with minimal information loss. The output of the decoder should resemble the input as much as possible.

To see how autoencoders work in practice, fire up a Livebook and install the following dependencies:

```
Mix.install([
  {:scidata, "~> 0.1"},
  {:axon, "~> 0.5"},
  {:exla, "~> 0.5"},
  {:nx, "~> 0.5"},
  {:kino, "~> 0.8"}
])
```

Nothing new here. With your dependencies installed, you can get started working on an input pipeline. To simplify this example, you'll use the MNIST dataset. You've worked with MNIST a few times throughout this book, so you should be pretty familiar with it by now. MNIST requires minimal preprocessing. You just need to convert the massive binary to a stream consumable by your training loop:

```
batch_size = 64

{{data, type, shape}, _} = Scidata.MNIST.download()

train_data =
  data
  |> Nx.from_binary(type)
  |> Nx.reshape({:auto, 28, 28, 1})
  |> Nx.divide(255)
  |> Nx.to_batched(batch_size)
```

This code downloads MNIST data and metadata using Scidata and then processes the data into batches of 64 images. MNIST images are 28x28 grayscale
images, so each input has one color channel with a height and width of 28
pixels.

You can now move forward with implementing your model. First, run the
following code:

```
defmodule Autoencoder do
  def encoder(input) do
    input
    |> Axon.flatten()
    |> Axon.dense(256, activation: :relu, name: "encoder_dense_0")
    |> Axon.dense(128, activation: :relu, name: "encoder_dense_1")
  end

  def decoder(input) do
    input
    |> Axon.dense(256, activation: :relu, name: "decoder_dense_0")
    |> Axon.dense(784, activation: :sigmoid, name: "decoder_dense_1")
    |> Axon.reshape({:batch, 28, 28, 1})
  end
end
```

This code implements an autoencoder module with two functions: encoder/1
and decoder/1. The encoder flattens the input for consumption by two dense
layers. Each dense layer is followed by a ReLU activation function. It's
important to note that the final encoder shape will be {batch_size, 128}. You
should notice that the 128-length vector is smaller than the original dimensionality of each input. Remember, the point is to compress the input. The
output of the encoder is the latent representation of the input or the latent
space. You might find it useful to mess around with different latent configurations to see how they affect the overall model.

The decoder takes an input and transforms it with two dense layers followed
by a final reshape to match the original shape of the input. The final dense
layer consists of a sigmoid activation. The final activation is important because
your input pipeline scales input pixels to be between 0 and 1, so you need

your output to also have pixel values between 0 and 1. Notice that the output dimensionality matches the input dimensionality.

Now, you can use your helpers to declare your joint autoencoder model:

```
model =
  Axon.input("image")
  |> Autoencoder.encoder()
  |> Autoencoder.decoder()

model
```

The model will look like this:

```
#Axon<
  inputs: %{"image" => nil}
  outputs: "reshape_0"
  nodes: 11
>
```

Your model implementation is relatively small, but it's the first time you've used a module and helper functions to implement a model. While in some instances it makes sense to declare a model as a sequence of Axon function calls, in other cases it makes sense to extract reusable blocks into helper functions. In this instance, your model has two clear sub-architectures that might be useful on their own, so it's best to declare them separately for later use. The important thing to understand is that *Axon is still just a regular Elixir library*. You should embrace Elixir patterns when using Axon.

Now you can focus on implementing your training loop. The goal of your autoencoder is to produce a network that encodes the original input into a lower-dimensional representation and decodes the representation into an output that's identical to the input. Following this logic, you can see that you can kind of turn this into a supervised learning problem by treating your original input as both your input data and output labels. You have plenty of experience implementing supervised training loops. But what should your loss function be?

You want a loss function that, when minimized, minimizes the distance between your input and autoencoder output. If you treat the distance between input and output as the pairwise distance between pixels, it follows that you should use :mean_squared_error:

```
trained_model_state =
  model
  |> Axon.Loop.trainer(:mean_squared_error, Axon.Optimizers.adam(1.0e-3))
  |> Axon.Loop.run(
    Stream.zip(train_data, train_data),
```

```
  %{},
  epochs: 5,
  compiler: EXLA
)
```

Notice that the training loop is similar to many of the training loops you've implemented in this book. By treating the input as both the input and label, you've turned this unsupervised learning problem into a supervised learning problem. Now, you could run this loop and watch the loss decrease, but it's difficult to interpret how this loss corresponds to how well your model is reconstructing compressed inputs. A much more interpretable measure of progress is a periodic visualization of your model's outputs on some example data. You can accomplish this with Axon event handlers.

The Axon.Loop reduction fires deterministic events at different points in the loop cycle. For example, at the beginning and end of each epoch, the :epoch_started and :epoch_completed events fire. You can register handlers with each of these events to trigger custom functions to run inside the loop. This gives you more fine-grained control over what happens during the loop.

Handlers are arity-1 functions that take a loop state and return a control-flow/ state tuple: {:continue | :halt_epoch | :halt_loop, state}. Internally, Axon.Loop aggregates a struct Axon.Loop.State which contains loop metadata, metrics, and step state. When a handler is triggered after an event fires, the handler receives the current Axon.Loop.State struct. A handler can then use this state to perform side-effecting operations such as saving loop or model checkpoints, inspecting model metrics, or, in this case, visualizing a model's predictions. Handlers can also choose to terminate a loop based on some criteria, by passing the control-flow term :halt in the control-flow/state tuple.

You already have experience with some event handlers that Axon offers out of the box including checkpoints and early stopping. These handlers are implemented on top of the more general and readily-customizable event-handler API. Your custom event handler needs to visualize your model's predictions—which you can do using Kino's built-in image and rendering functionality. Copy the following code to implement your custom event handler:

```
test_batch = Enum.at(train_data, 0)
test_image = test_batch[0] |> Nx.new_axis(0)

visualize_test_image = fn
  %Axon.Loop.State{step_state: step_state} = state ->
    out_image = Axon.predict(
      model,
      step_state[:model_state],
```

```
        test_image,
        compiler: EXLA
      )
    out_image =
      out_image
      |> Nx.multiply(255)
      |> Nx.as_type(:u8)
      |> Nx.reshape({28, 28, 1})

    Kino.Image.new(out_image) |> Kino.render()
    {:continue, state}
end
```

Your visualization handler needs to make a prediction on your test image and then convert the floating point result to an unsigned 8-bit integer tensor. That's because Kino.Image expects image tensors to be created from u8 tensors. To cast from float to u8, you can multiply the image by 255 and use Nx.as_type/2. Note that this approach is lossy as you're going from a 32-bit to an 8-bit tensor; but for this example, that won't matter much.

To get the predictions from your model, you need the model, its parameters, and an input. To get the most up-to-date model parameters, you need to access the :model_state within the loop state's step state. That's a bit of a mouthful, but it's easy to understand with a little understanding of how the Axon.Loop API works.

The Axon.Loop API is an abstraction for building the kind of reductions commonly encountered in machine learning applications. These reductions iterate over datasets and aggregate state—whether it be metrics or actual model state. At the core, this reduction looks something like this:

```
def run(data) do
  state = init_state()

  Enum.reduce(data, state, fn batch, state ->
    step(batch, state)
  end)
end
```

What you care about at the end of this loop is the final value of state. For a supervised training loop, this state contains the model state, but it also contains some additional metadata such as internal optimizer state, aggregate loss, and more. The Axon.Loop API aggregates this state for you. But to generalize better to other types of loops, it needs to track some additional metadata. This metadata is baked into the Axon.Loop.State struct. The meat and potatoes of this struct is the step_state which maps directly to state in the run/1 implementation shown previously. In most custom handlers, you'll only ever touch the step_state portion of the Axon.Loop.State struct. But the additional metadata is there for you—if you need it.

With your handler implemented, you need to make some slight adjustments to your training loop to register your event handler:

```
trained_model_state =
  model
  |> Axon.Loop.trainer(:mean_squared_error, Axon.Optimizers.adam(1.0e-3))
  |> Axon.Loop.handle_event(:epoch_completed, visualize_test_image)
  |> Axon.Loop.run(
    Stream.zip(train_data, train_data),
    %{},
    epochs: 5,
    compiler: EXLA
  )
```

Axon.Loop.handle/3 registers an event handler to run on the given event. In this example, you register visualize_test_image to run on each :epoch_completed event. This means that after each epoch, you'll get a nice visualization of an example model output—giving you a good idea of how well your model is able to deconstruct and then reconstruct an input example.

After running this code, you'll see the following output:

```
Epoch: 0, Batch: 900, loss: 0.0251183

5

Epoch: 1, Batch: 912, loss: 0.0163151

5

Epoch: 2, Batch: 924, loss: 0.0127149

5

Epoch: 3, Batch: 936, loss: 0.0106826

5

Epoch: 4, Batch: 398, loss: 0.0100536
```

At this point, you might be thinking that, while your model is able to compress and decompress images pretty well, training a neural network to do this seems like overkill when there are much more efficient ways to solve the compression problem. And you're absolutely right—so what's the point?

Well, if you think about it, you've accidentally trained a *deep generative model*. A deep generative model is a deep learning model designed to generate data from some distribution. In this example, your decoder is actually kind of a generative model—it takes a latent representation and produces an output. Hypothetically, you can skip the encoder altogether and give the decoder some random latent representation, and it should give you an output that resembles a handwritten digit:

```
decoder_only =
  Axon.input("noise")
  |> Autoencoder.decoder()

key = Nx.Random.key(42)
{noise, _key} = Nx.Random.normal(key, shape: {1, 128})

out_image = Axon.predict(decoder_only, trained_model_state, noise)
upsampled = Axon.Layers.resize(out_image, size: {512, 512})
out_image =
  upsampled
  |> Nx.reshape({512, 512, 1})
  |> Nx.multiply(255)
  |> Nx.as_type(:u8)

Kino.Image.new(out_image)
```

This code is pretty much identical to your visualization handler; however, you add a function to upsample the input using Axon's resize layer. This will resize the input image to be much larger than the original 28x28. After running this code, you'll see the following output:

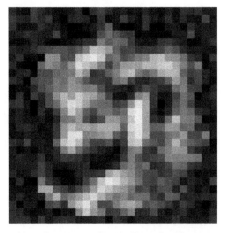

That's definitely not a handwritten digit. So what's going on here?

In spirit, your decoder would make a great generative model with access to the right latent representations. Unfortunately, you didn't force your model to have a latent space with structure. The structure of your encoded representations is at the mercy of a neural network and gradient descent. You can't pass random uniform or normal noise to your decoder and expect coherent output because your decoder only knows how to handle latent representations produced by the encoder. But what if there was a way to force your encoder to learn a structured representation, which you can easily query later on? Fortunately, there is. Enter the variational autoencoder.

Learning a Structured Latent

While trying to implement a basic compression algorithm, you've managed to stumble upon a strategy for generating arbitrary input data. But to make it work, you need to tame the latent space. Remember, a latent space is a representation of data where similar inputs lie closely together in the space. For example, word embeddings and sentence embeddings from Chapter 9, Understand Text, on page 195, and Chapter 11, Model Everything with Transformers, on page 237, are examples of a learned latent space for text.

Unfortunately, the emphasis here is that your latent space is *learned*. That is to say that it's difficult to query the latent space without access to information from the encoder. To generate images, you need access to a target image—which defeats the purpose of the generative model. You need a way to force your model to learn a *structured latent space*. This means you force your model to follow some input distribution, such as a normal distribution. Variational autoencoders are designed to do just that.

Variational autoencoders are the same as autoencoders—with a slight twist. Rather than project inputs down to some lower-dimensional vector representation, variational autoencoders learn to project inputs down to the parameters of a distribution. You can easily sample inputs from this distribution and use these inputs to generate examples. With some small modifications, you can turn a basic autoencoder into a generative model.

In a new cell, create a new module named VAE:

```
defmodule VAE do
  import Nx.Defn
end
```

Next, add the following function to implement the encoder:

```
def encoder(input) do
  encoded =
    input
    |> Axon.conv(32,
      kernel_size: 3,
      activation: :relu,
      strides: 2,
      padding: :same
    )
    |> Axon.conv(32,
      kernel_size: 3,
      activation: :relu,
      strides: 2,
      padding: :same
    )
    |> Axon.flatten()
    |> Axon.dense(16, activation: :relu)

  z_mean = Axon.dense(encoded, 2)
  z_log_var = Axon.dense(encoded, 2)
  z = Axon.layer(&sample/3, [z_mean, z_log_var], op_name: :sample)

  Axon.container({z_mean, z_log_var, z})
end
```

This encoder implementation is somewhat different than your first encoder implementation. Rather than using dense layers for feature extraction, this implementation uses some convolutional layers. Remember, the goal of your encoder is to extract a useful representation from the input so your decoder can use it to reconstruct the output. As you learned in Chapter 7, Learn to See, on page 141, convolutional layers are powerful feature extractors for images. It follows that adding convolutional layers to encode the input will likely result in a more useful latent representation.

In addition to some slight architectural modifications, you slightly modified the encoder output. Axon.container/1 is an Axon construct that allows you to wrap layers into Elixir collections such as tuples, maps, and structs. Containers are most commonly used as output layers—like in this example. Your encoder will output a tuple of three variables: z_mean, z_log_var, and z. Rather than encode the input into a single dense vector, your new encoder returns the parameters of a distribution. These parameters are the result of learned transformations of the input. From the parameters z_mean and z_log_var, your model produces a latent z using a custom Axon layer.

Custom layers in Axon are defined with the Axon.layer/3 function. You can remember the form of Axon.layer/3 by keeping in mind that it's nearly identical to Elixir's `apply`. You pass a function, typically defined with `defn`, and a list of inputs. Axon.layer/3 also accepts some additional metadata options for defining the layer's name and what operation it performs. You might be wondering, why is `sample/3` an arity-3 function if you're only giving it two inputs. Each Axon layer takes an additional `opts` argument. Every layer must accept at least the `:mode` option—which changes the layer behavior between training and inference.

Now, add the following `sample/3` implementation to your module:

```
defnp sample(z_mean, z_log_var, _opts \\ []) do
  noise_shape = Nx.shape(z_mean)
  epsilon = Nx.random_normal(noise_shape)
  z_mean + Nx.exp(0.5 * z_log_var) * epsilon
end
```

This method implements what is known as the *reparameterization trick.* Remember, your goal is to learn a structured latent. In this instance, you've estimated two parameters of a normally distributed latent space: its mean and log-variance. Ideally, you could just use these parameters to sample from a normal distribution with Nx.random_normal/3. But you cannot take the gradient of a random node. If you tried to sample just from Nx.random_normal/3 and then attempted to train this model with gradient descent, there would be no feedback signal to `z_mean` and `z_log_var`. The reparameterization trick makes the sampling a function of `z_mean` and `z_log_var` in such a way that your model still produces a normally distributed latent, but `z_mean` and `z_log_var` can learn from signals during gradient descent.

One thing to note here is that the pattern of pairing custom layers with `defn` implementations is the best way to add custom functionality to your model. This is actually how Axon behaves under the hood. Every Axon layer has a backend implementation in the Axon.Layers module, with a frontend interface in the Axon module.

Next, add the following function to your module to implement the decoder:

```
def decoder(input) do
  input
  |> Axon.dense(7 * 7 * 64, activation: :relu)
  |> Axon.reshape({:batch, 7, 7, 64})
  |> Axon.conv_transpose(64,
    kernel_size: {3, 3},
    activation: :relu,
    strides: [2, 2],
    padding: :same
  )
```

```
  |> Axon.conv_transpose(32,
    kernel_size: {3, 3},
    activation: :relu,
    strides: [2, 2],
    padding: :same
  )
  |> Axon.conv_transpose(1,
    kernel_size: {3, 3},
    activation: :sigmoid,
    padding: :same
  )
end
```

This decoder implementation is also slightly different from your previous one. Both decoder implementations use convolutional layers instead of dense layers. The difference is that this decoder implementation uses transposed convolutions instead of plain convolutions. Transposed convolutions behave somewhat similarly to traditional convolutions, but they can be used as a strategy for upsampling rather than downsampling. If you want to inspect the layer-by-layer shape of your decoder, you use this:

```
template = Nx.template({1, 128}, :f32)
Axon.Display.as_graph(VAE.decoder(Axon.input("latent")), template)
```

And you'll see the output as shown in the image on page 271.

The size of each spatial dimension increases by a factor of 2 after each subsequent call to Axon.conv_transpose/3. You'll often see Axon.conv_transpose/3 used in generative architectures such as this one.

At this point, you've successfully implemented a variational autoencoder. Now, you need to train it.

In the previous section, you were able to turn your unsupervised learning problem into a supervised learning problem by using the inputs as labels. This meant you could make use of Axon's out-of-the-box APIs for supervised training loops. Unfortunately, that won't work for training your variational autoencoder. Variational autoencoders require some specific tweaks for the training process to work. You'll need to write your first custom training loop.

Writing a custom training loop in Axon is easier than you think and is a good exercise in understanding what Axon does for you under the hood. To start, look at what Axon.Loop.trainer/3 returns for you on a dummy model by entering this:

```
model = Axon.input("foo")
```

```
loop = Axon.Loop.trainer(model, :binary_cross_entropy, :sgd)
IO.inspect loop, structs: false
```

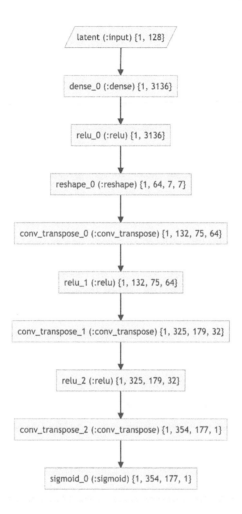

You'll see the following output:

```
%{
  __struct__: Axon.Loop,
  attached_state: nil,
  handlers: %{
    completed: [],
    epoch_completed: [
      {#Function<24.105974664/1 in Axon.Loop.log/5>,
        #Function<5.105974664/1 in Axon.Loop.build_filter_fn/1>}
    ],
    epoch_halted: [],
    epoch_started: [],
    halted: [],
```

```
  iteration_completed: [
    {#Function<24.105974664/1 in Axon.Loop.log/5>,
     #Function<3.105974664/1 in Axon.Loop.build_filter_fn/1>}
  ],
  iteration_started: [],
  started: []
},
init: #Function<136.105575625/2 in Nx.Defn.wrap_arity/2>,
metrics: %{
  "loss" => {#Function<12.116147200/3 in Axon.Metrics.running_average/1>,
    #Function<6.105974664/2 in Axon.Loop.build_loss_fn/1>}
},
output_transform: #Function<37.105974664/1 in Axon.Loop.trainer/4>,
step: #Function<136.105575625/2 in Nx.Defn.wrap_arity/2>
}
```

Most of this is internal information Axon uses to control the execution of the loop. The most important fields here are :init and :step. Every single Axon loop needs an initialization function for initializing the step state and a step function for updating the step state from the current input and current step state. Axon.Loop.trainer is a factory that generates these for you. In reality, Axon.Loop .trainer makes use of the step factory Axon.Loop.train_step which implements initialization and step functions for a supervised training loop. The big takeaway here is that all you need to do to implement a custom training loop is implement an initialization and step function.

It's easiest to start by implementing a single train step. This function takes the current batch and the current step state and returns an updated step state. You can think of it as the inner function in an Enum.reduce/3. Your train_step needs to do the following:

1. Determine the gradient of the model with respect to some objective function
2. Scale gradients using an optimizer and a current state
3. Apply scaled gradients to obtain a new model state
4. Return the updated state

For tracking purposes, you'll also want to keep a running average of the loss. With all of this in mind, you can take a shot at implementing your custom train step within the VAE module:

```
defn train_step(encoder_fn, decoder_fn, optimizer_fn, batch, state) do
  {batch_loss, joint_param_grads} = value_and_grad(
    state[:model_state],
    &joint_objective(encoder_fn, decoder_fn, batch, &1)
  )

  {scaled_updates, new_optimizer_state} = optimizer_fn.(
    joint_param_grads,
```

```
    state[:optimizer_state],
    state[:model_state]
  )
  new_model_state = Axon.Updates.apply_updates(
    state[:model_state], scaled_updates
  )
  new_loss =
    state[:loss]
    |> Nx.multiply(state[:i])
    |> Nx.add(batch_loss)
    |> Nx.divide(Nx.add(state[:i], 1))
  %{
    state
    | i: Nx.add(state[:i], 1),
      loss: new_loss,
      model_state: new_model_state,
      optimizer_state: new_optimizer_state
  }
end
```

While it seems like a lot is going on here, it actually follows perfectly from the steps you just outlined. First, you take the gradient of some joint_objective/4 on batch with respect to :model_state within state. Notice you need to parameterize joint_objective/4 on encoder_fn and decoder_fn. The functions represent the predict functions for the encoder and decoder, respectively.

Next, you use the given optimizer_fn to scale the joint_param_grads with the given :optimizer_state and :model_state in state. optimizer_fn is an update function that scales the gradients according to some algorithm such as Adam before you use them to update your model state.

The next line actually applies the scaled updates to :model_state using Axon.Updates .apply_updates. The rest of the implementation is for tracking purposes—you need to update the loss according to the given batch loss and then return an entirely new state.

Notice that train_step/5 is a defn. You want to try as much as possible to implement loop initialization and step functions as defn in order to take advantage of hardware acceleration and JIT compilation during the training process.

Now, you need to implement the joint_objective/4 defined in train_step/5. Add the following function to your VAE module:

```
defnp joint_objective(encoder_fn, decoder_fn, batch, joint_params) do
  %{prediction: preds} = encoder_fn.(joint_params["encoder"], batch)
  {z_mean, z_log_var, z} = preds
```

```
%{prediction: reconstruction} = decoder_fn.(joint_params["decoder"], z)
  recon_loss = Axon.Losses.binary_cross_entropy(
    batch, reconstruction, reduction: :mean
  )
  kl_loss = -0.5 * (1 + z_log_var - Nx.power(z_mean, 2) - Nx.exp(z_log_var))
  kl_loss = Nx.mean(Nx.sum(kl_loss, axes: [1]))

  recon_loss + kl_loss
end
```

This code implements a joint-objective function using both the encoder and decoder. First, you get an encoded representation from the encoder by calling encoder_fn/2 on the "encoder" parameters in joint_params and the current batch. This returns the tuple {z_mean, z_log_var, z}. Next, you reconstruct the input from the encoded latent output z by calling decoder_fn. Both encoder_fn and decoder_fn return a map—this is the case for all Axon models which are called in training mode. The training mode output is a map with a key :prediction representing the output and a key :state for the updated internal layer state for stateful layers such as Axon.batch_norm/3. Your model doesn't have any stateful layers, so you can safely ignore layer state.

The joint-objective function uses all of the model's outputs to form a joint-loss. The first part of the loss is a reconstruction loss which measures how well your decoder reconstructs the original batch of images from the encoded representation. The second part of the loss is a regularization which penalizes the model from drifting too far away from a normal distribution. It basically measures the difference of the distribution defined by the given parameters z_mean and z_log_var from a normal distribution with mean 1 and variance 0. This term helps coerce your encoder into learning to encode your data as a normal distribution.

Now that you've implemented your training step, you can implement your initialization function. From your training step, it follows that you need to track the current iteration i, the current loss :loss, the current model state :model_state, and the current optimizer state :optimizer_state:

```
defn init_step(
  encoder_init_fn,
  decoder_init_fn,
  optimizer_init_fn,
  batch,
  init_state
) do
  encoder_params = encoder_init_fn.(batch, init_state)
  decoder_params = decoder_init_fn.(Nx.random_uniform({64, 2}), init_state)
  joint_params = %{
```

```
    "encoder" => encoder_params,
    "decoder" => decoder_params
  }
  optimizer_state = optimizer_init_fn.(joint_params)

  %{
    i: Nx.tensor(0),
    loss: Nx.tensor(0.0),
    model_state: joint_params,
    optimizer_state: optimizer_state,
  }
end
```

This function uses the initialization functions for both the encoder and decoder. The function initializes separate encoder and decoder parameters inside a joint parameter map. Then, you combine the encoder and decoder parameters into a single map, joint_params. It's necessary to join the parameters because you want to use a single optimizer for both models, so both sets of parameters must be within a single structure. Next, you call optimizer_init_fn on your joint parameters to initialize the optimizer state before finally returning the initial state.

You now have everything you need to define a training loop for your VAE. To see how all of this comes together, start by defining your encoder and decoder:

```
encoder = Axon.input("image") |> VAE.encoder()
decoder = Axon.input("latent") |> VAE.decoder()
```

Currently, both your encoder and decoder are Axon structs. To make use of them within defn, you need to build them into their {init_fn, predict_fn} tuples using Axon.build/2:

```
{encoder_init_fn, encoder_fn} = Axon.build(encoder, mode: :train)
{decoder_init_fn, decoder_fn} = Axon.build(decoder, mode: :train)
```

Next, you can define your optimizer:

```
{optimizer_init_fn, optimizer_fn} = Axon.Optimizers.adam(1.0e-3)
```

You've actually constructed optimizers in this way before. But you've never decomposed them into distinct parts. Every optimizer is a tuple of {init_fn, update_fn}. With all of your components, you can build parameterized initialization and train steps:

```
init_fn = &VAE.init_step(
  encoder_init_fn,
  decoder_init_fn,
  optimizer_init_fn,
  &1,
  &2
)
```

```
step_fn = &VAE.train_step(
  encoder_fn,
  decoder_fn,
  optimizer_fn,
  &1,
  &2
)
```

With an initialization and step function, you can create a loop using the Axon.Loop.loop/2 factory, and then you can work with and execute this loop in the ways you're already familiar with. For this example, you'll also want to add some functionality for displaying generated samples after each epoch. You already know how to do this with an event handler. Additionally, you'll want to add some basic logging. You can take care of this with Axon.Loop.log/4:

```
step_fn
|> Axon.Loop.loop(init_fn)
|> Axon.Loop.handle(:epoch_completed, &VAE.display_sample(&1, decoder_fn))
|> Axon.Loop.log(:iteration_completed, fn
  %Axon.Loop.State{epoch: epoch, iteration: iter, step_state: state} ->
  "\rEpoch: #{epoch}, batch: #{iter}, loss: #{Nx.to_number(state[:loss])}"
end, :stdio)
|> Axon.Loop.run(train_data, %{}, compiler: EXLA, epochs: 10)
```

Notice you need to implement the event handler display_sample/2. Additionally, you use Axon.Loop.log/4 to attach a log event to the loop. This logs the string returned from the given function on the given event to the given device. In this instance, you simply write some loop metadata such as the current epoch, iteration, and loss. Before executing this loop, add the following code to your VAE module:

```
def display_sample(
  %Axon.Loop.State{step_state: state} = out_state,
  decoder_fn
) do
  latent = Nx.tensor([[0.0, 0.0], [0.5, 0.5], [1.0, 1.0]])
  %{prediction: out} = decoder_fn.(state[:model_state]["decoder"], latent)
  out_image = Nx.multiply(out, 255) |> Nx.as_type(:u8)
  upsample = Axon.Layers.resize(
    out_image,
    size: {512, 512},
    channels: :first
  )
  for i <- 0..2 do
    Kino.Image.new(Nx.reshape(upsample[i], {512, 512, 1})) |> Kino.render()
  end
  {:continue, out_state}
end
```

This event handler implementation will sample three outputs from the decoder and convert them to a heatmap before displaying the output. Now, you can execute the loop. After a while you'll see this:

```
Epoch: 9, batch: 937, loss: 0.5638180375099182
```

You'll also see periodic images that look like this:

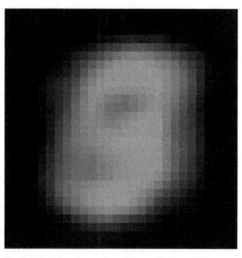

Whoa. Those actually look like handwritten digits. The quality isn't great, but it's apparent the generated output is similar to what your inputs look like. Now the question is, can you do better? Of course, you can.

Your VAE, while impressive, is nowhere near the quality of modern generative models. You need only look at DALL-E 2 to understand that deep generative models are capable of amazing things.[1] DALL-E 2 is an example of a *diffusion model* that internally makes use of a VAE and a few other models to generate incredibly realistic images. Before DALL-E and diffusion models, VAEs were mostly an afterthought. Up until recently, a different kind of model ruled the generative AI game.

Generating with GANs

Variational autoencoders are somewhat impressive generative models for how easy they are to train; but up until recently, they weren't seen as all that useful for generative AI. Before diffusion models, the most popular and most powerful generative models were variants of generative adversarial networks or GANs.

---

1. https://openai.com/dall-e-2/

Diffusion Models

Recent developments in generative modeling using diffusion have lead to incredible breakthroughs. Stable Diffusion, a specific type of diffusion model, has quickly become one of the most popular deep learning models on the internet. For many image generation tasks, you'll find a pre-trained diffusion model like stable diffusion is much more powerful than a pre-trained GAN.

Generative adversarial networks are deep generative models that make use of a dueling network architecture with a *generator* and *discriminator*. The generator is responsible for transforming a latent representation into something that resembles inputs from the training data. The discriminator attempts to differentiate real inputs from generated inputs, and in turn, it provides feedback to the generator to improve its generations.

The classic analogy for the relationship between a generator and a discriminator in a generative adversarial network is the relationship between an art counterfeiter and a critic. The generator is akin to an art counterfeiter who attempts to create forgeries of famous paintings. The discriminator is the critic who attempts to determine if a painting is counterfeit. The critic provides feedback signals to the counterfeiter which improve the counterfeiter's next work until the counterfeiter generates art that the critic cannot differentiate from the real thing.

Generative adversarial networks have some interesting theoretical guarantees, and in practice, they've proven capable of generating incredible images. But they can be difficult to train when compared to VAEs. More recent evolutions of generative adversarial networks attempt to alleviate some of these training difficulties. But the reality is that training a generative adversarial network successfully can involve more art than science. Even so, with enough data and the right training recipe, GAN outputs can be truly incredible.

To get a better sense of how GANs work in practice, you'll implement a GAN that generates handwritten digits—just like your VAE.

You should already have a Livebook open with all of the dependencies you need. Start by defining a new module in a new cell:

```
defmodule GAN do
  import Nx.Defn
end
```

Next, copy the following code into the module to implement your discriminator:

```
def discriminator(input) do
  input
  |> Axon.conv(32,
    activation: :mish,
    kernel_size: 3,
    strides: 2,
    padding: :same
  )
  |> Axon.layer_norm()
  |> Axon.conv(64,
    activation: :mish,
    kernel_size: 3,
    strides: 2,
    padding: :same
  )
  |> Axon.layer_norm()
  |> Axon.flatten()
  |> Axon.dropout(rate: 0.5)
  |> Axon.dense(1, activation: :sigmoid)
end
```

Remember the goal of your discriminator is to determine if an input image is from the real training data or the generator. This should sound a lot like a straightforward image classification task—so your discriminator only needs to be a powerful enough image classification model. This example makes use of some convolutional layers followed by layer normalization layers to extract features from the input image before passing them to a dense classifier.

Now you need to implement your generator. You already have some experience implementing a model that generates image outputs from a latent representation from the last example. The principles for creating a generator for a GAN aren't that different from creating a decoder for a VAE. You can copy the following code into your GAN module to implement the GAN generator:

```
def generator(input) do
  input
  |> Axon.dense(128 * 7 * 7, activation: :mish)
  |> Axon.reshape({:batch, 7, 7, 128})
  |> Axon.resize({14, 14})
  |> Axon.conv(128, kernel_size: 3, padding: :same)
  |> Axon.layer_norm()
  |> Axon.relu()
  |> Axon.resize({28, 28})
  |> Axon.conv(64, kernel_size: 3,padding: :same)
  |> Axon.layer_norm()
  |> Axon.relu()
  |> Axon.conv(1, activation: :tanh, kernel_size: 3, padding: :same)
end
```

This implementation is slightly different from your decoder implementation in the VAE example. Your generator makes use of a single dense layer to transform the input latent representation into a representation that matches the size of your input image. The generator then uses strided convolutional blocks to downsample the input representation, and it upsamples the representation using a combination of convolutional layers and resize layers. Resize layers in Axon do exactly what they say they do—resize inputs. Specifically, Axon's resize layers are for upsampling or downsampling the spatial dimensions of image data. In this instance, you use them to resize the downsampled spatial dimensions to the correct output size.

Now, run the following to create two new models with your functions:

```
discriminator = GAN.discriminator(Axon.input("image"))
generator = GAN.generator(Axon.input("latent"))
```

With your models implemented, you need to write the training loop. You'll need to implement a custom training loop—just as in the VAE example. Fortunately, most of the same concepts you learned while writing your VAE training loop also apply here. You need to make them work with the GAN training framework. Remember, for a custom training loop you need to implement an initialization function and a step function. It's easiest to start with the step function. When training a GAN, the basic workflow is:

1. Compute the gradient of the discriminator on its objective
2. Scale the gradients by the discriminator's optimizer
3. Update the discriminator
4. Compute the gradient of the generator on its objective
5. Scale the gradients by the generator's optimizer
6. Update the generator

Again, you'll also want some basic loss monitoring so you can keep track of training progress. You can implement your train step inside the GAN module like this:

```
defn train_step(
      discriminator_fn,
      generator_fn,
      discriminator_optimizer,
      generator_optimizer,
      batch,
      state
    ) do
  d_params = state[:model_state]["discriminator"]
  g_params = state[:model_state]["generator"]
```

```elixir
d_optimizer_state = state[:optimizer_state]["discriminator"]
g_optimizer_state = state[:optimizer_state]["generator"]

# Update discriminator
{d_loss, d_grads} = value_and_grad(d_params, fn d_params ->
  d_objective(
    d_params, g_params, discriminator_fn, generator_fn, batch
  )
end)

{d_updates, new_d_optimizer_state} = discriminator_optimizer.(
  d_grads, d_optimizer_state, d_params
)
new_d_params = Axon.Updates.apply_updates(d_params, d_updates)

# Update generator
{g_loss, g_grads} = value_and_grad(g_params, fn g_params ->
  g_objective(
    d_params, g_params, discriminator_fn, generator_fn, batch
  )
end)

{g_updates, new_g_optimizer_state} = generator_optimizer.(
  g_grads, g_optimizer_state, g_params
)
new_g_params = Axon.Updates.apply_updates(g_params, g_updates)

# Update Losses
new_d_loss =
  state[:loss]["discriminator"]
  |> Nx.multiply(state[:i])
  |> Nx.add(d_loss)
  |> Nx.divide(Nx.add(state[:i], 1))

new_g_loss =
  state[:loss]["generator"]
  |> Nx.multiply(state[:i])
  |> Nx.add(g_loss)
  |> Nx.divide(Nx.add(state[:i], 1))

new_loss = %{
  "discriminator" => new_d_loss,
  "generator" => new_g_loss
}
new_model_state = %{
  "discriminator" => new_d_params,
  "generator" => new_g_params
}
new_optimizer_state = %{
  "discriminator" => new_d_optimizer_state,
  "generator" => new_g_optimizer_state
}
```

```
  %{
    model_state: new_model_state,
    optimizer_state: new_optimizer_state,
    loss: new_loss,
    i: Nx.add(state[:i], 1)
  }
end
```

This implementation might seem like a lot, but it's relatively straightforward once you break it down. First, for convenience, you access the individual model and optimizer state for the discriminator and generator with the following code:

```
d_params = state[:model_state]["discriminator"]
g_params = state[:model_state]["generator"]
d_optimizer_state = state[:optimizer_state]["discriminator"]
g_optimizer_state = state[:optimizer_state]["generator"]
```

Next, you update the discriminator by computing the gradient of its objective function with respect to its parameters before scaling the gradients with its optimizer and applying them to obtain new parameters with the following code:

```
{d_loss, d_grads} = value_and_grad(d_params, fn d_params ->
  d_objective(
    d_params, g_params, discriminator_fn, generator_fn, batch
  )
end)

{d_updates, new_d_optimizer_state} = discriminator_optimizer.(
  d_grads, d_optimizer_state, d_params
)
new_d_params = Axon.Updates.apply_updates(d_params, d_updates)
```

You repeat the same process to update the generator with its own objective function and optimizer:

```
{g_loss, g_grads} = value_and_grad(g_params, fn g_params ->
  g_objective(
    d_params, g_params, discriminator_fn, generator_fn, batch
  )
end)

{g_updates, new_g_optimizer_state} = generator_optimizer.(
  g_grads, g_optimizer_state, g_params
)
new_g_params = Axon.Updates.apply_updates(g_params, g_updates)
```

Next, you update a running average loss for both the generator and discriminator:

```
new_d_loss =
  state[:loss]["discriminator"]
  |> Nx.multiply(state[:i])
```

```
  |> Nx.add(d_loss)
  |> Nx.divide(Nx.add(state[:i], 1))

new_g_loss =
  state[:loss]["generator"]
  |> Nx.multiply(state[:i])
  |> Nx.add(g_loss)
  |> Nx.divide(Nx.add(state[:i], 1))
```

Finally, you construct an updated return state:

```
new_loss = %{
  "discriminator" => new_d_loss,
  "generator" => new_g_loss
}
new_model_state = %{
  "discriminator" => new_d_params,
  "generator" => new_g_params
}
new_optimizer_state = %{
  "discriminator" => new_d_optimizer_state,
  "generator" => new_g_optimizer_state
}

%{
  model_state: new_model_state,
  optimizer_state: new_optimizer_state,
  loss: new_loss,
  i: Nx.add(state[:i], 1)
}
```

If you compare this training step with your VAE training step, you'll notice the common structure. In fact, if you routinely write custom training steps, you'll notice they all have similar structures and implementations, with some minor tweaks. In general, the process of writing a custom training loop is only as difficult as writing a custom objective function. Objective functions are the meat and potatoes of the training process because they implicitly control the performance of your model.

That being said, you still need to implement your objective functions for both the discriminator and generator. You can start by copying the following code to implement the discriminator's objective:

```
defn d_objective(
  d_params,
  g_params,
  discriminator_fn,
  generator_fn,
  real_batch
) do
  batch_size = Nx.axis_size(real_batch, 0)
```

```
  real_targets = Nx.broadcast(1, {batch_size, 1})
  fake_targets = Nx.broadcast(0, {batch_size, 1})
  latent = Nx.random_normal({batch_size, 128})
  %{prediction: fake_batch} = generator_fn.(g_params, latent)

  %{prediction: real_labels} = discriminator_fn.(d_params, real_batch)
  %{prediction: fake_labels} = discriminator_fn.(d_params, fake_batch)

  real_loss = Axon.Losses.binary_cross_entropy(
    real_targets, real_labels, reduction: :mean
  )
  fake_loss = Axon.Losses.binary_cross_entropy(
    fake_targets, fake_labels, reduction: :mean
  )

  0.5 * real_loss + 0.5 * fake_loss
end
```

There isn't any magic going on here either. You generate fake images by obtaining predictions from your generator on a random latent representation. You finally compute labels for both real training images and fake images using your discriminator. Then you compute the discriminator's loss on both real and fake targets. Because this is a binary classification problem, you use the binary cross-entropy loss function. Additionally, you average the discriminator's loss on both real and fake images.

The most important takeaway here is that the discriminator's objective is to classify real images as real (positive labels) and fake images as fake (negative labels).

Now, you can implement your generator's objective function by adding the following code to your module:

```
defn g_objective(
  d_params,
  g_params,
  discriminator_fn,
  generator_fn,
  real_batch
) do
  batch_size = Nx.axis_size(real_batch, 0)
  real_targets = Nx.broadcast(1, {batch_size, 1})
  latent = Nx.random_normal({batch_size, 128})

  %{prediction: fake_batch} = generator_fn.(g_params, latent)
  %{prediction: fake_labels} = discriminator_fn.(d_params, fake_batch)

  Axon.Losses.binary_cross_entropy(
    real_targets, fake_labels, reduction: :mean
  )
end
```

This implementation is similar to the objective function for your discriminator. You generate a fake batch using the generator and then generate a set of labels for that batch using the discriminator. But you should notice the subtle difference in the loss computation. Rather than trying to assign fake labels to fake images, the objective is to trick the discriminator into applying real labels to fake images. The generator implicitly learns to generate data similar to the training data by learning to fool the discriminator.

Now you need to implement an initialization function for your training loop. Given your training step, your state needs to contain :model_state, :optimizer_state, and :loss for both "generator" and "discriminator", as well as a counter to track the current iteration:

```
defn init_state(
      discriminator_init_fn,
      generator_init_fn,
      discriminator_optimizer_init,
      generator_optimizer_init,
      batch,
      init_state
    ) do
  d_params = discriminator_init_fn.(batch, init_state)
  g_params = generator_init_fn.(Nx.random_normal({64, 128}), init_state)
  d_optimizer_state = discriminator_optimizer_init.(d_params)
  g_optimizer_state = generator_optimizer_init.(g_params)

  model_state = %{
    "discriminator" => d_params,
    "generator" => g_params
  }
  optimizer_state = %{
    "discriminator" => d_optimizer_state,
    "generator" => g_optimizer_state
  }
  loss = %{
    "discriminator" => Nx.tensor(0.0),
    "generator" => Nx.tensor(0.0)
  }

  %{
    model_state: model_state,
    optimizer_state: optimizer_state,
    loss: loss,
    i: Nx.tensor(0)
  }
end
```

There's nothing new here. You initialize both of your models and their respective optimizers and then construct maps for each item you want to track.

As with the VAE, you'll probably want to also track how well your generator learns to generate images between epochs. You can achieve this by converting your display_sample/2 function from the previous section to this example here:

```
def display_sample(
  %Axon.Loop.State{step_state: state} = out_state,
  generator_fn
) do
  latent = Nx.random_normal({3, 128})
  %{prediction: out} = generator_fn.(state[:model_state]["decoder"], latent)
  out_image = Nx.multiply(out, 255) |> Nx.as_type(:u8)
  upsample = Axon.Layers.resize(
    out_image,
    size: {512, 512},
    channels: :first
  )
  for i <- 0..2 do
    Kino.Image.new(Nx.reshape(upsample[i], {512, 512, 1})) |> Kino.render()
  end
  {:continue, out_state}
end
```

The final step is to implement your custom training loop. Overall, the process is similar to your VAE example. Start by building both of your models' initialization and prediction functions with the following code:

```
{discriminator_init_fn, discriminator_fn} =
  Axon.build(discriminator, mode: :train)
{generator_init_fn, generator_fn} =
  Axon.build(generator, mode: :train)
```

Next, you need to build optimizers for each model:

```
{d_optimizer_init, d_optimizer} = Axon.Optimizers.adam(1.0e-4)
{g_optimizer_init, g_optimizer} = Axon.Optimizers.adam(1.0e-3)
```

Notice that you're using slightly different optimizers for each model. To prevent the discriminator from dominating the generator before it can get its bearings during training, you need to lower the learning rate of the discriminator. GAN training is really fickle—feel free to mess with different hyperparameters and optimizers to see if you can find a better configuration.

Now you can implement parameterized forms of your initialization and step functions:

```
init_fn = &GAN.init_state(
  discriminator_init_fn,
  generator_init_fn,
  d_optimizer_init,
  g_optimizer_init,
```

```
  &1,
  &2
)
step_fn = &GAN.train_step(
  discriminator_fn,
  generator_fn,
  d_optimizer,
  g_optimizer,
  &1,
  &2
)
```

Finally, you're ready to run your training loop:

```
step_fn
|> Axon.Loop.loop(init_fn)
|> Axon.Loop.handle(
  :epoch_completed,
  &GAN.display_sample(&1, generator_fn)
)
|> Axon.Loop.log(fn
  %Axon.Loop.State{epoch: epoch, iteration: iter, step_state: state} ->
    d_loss = state[:loss]["discriminator"]
    g_loss = state[:loss]["generator"]
    "\rEpoch: #{epoch}, batch: #{iter},"
      <> " d_loss: #{Nx.to_number(d_loss)},"
      <> " g_loss: #{Nx.to_number(g_loss)}"
end, event: :iteration_completed, device: :stdio)
|> Axon.Loop.run(train_data, %{}, compiler: EXLA, epochs: 10)
```

During training, you'll see this:

```
Epoch: 2, batch: 827, d_loss: 0.722309589, g_loss: 0.9743837
```

You'll also see some images that look like this:

It's difficult to demonstrate the power of GANs on low-resolution handwritten digits, but you might find these generations are a bit better than your VAE. You might also find that your model collapses during training and starts to converge to bad generations. Training GANs is fun but can be difficult in practice. You should explore more complex GAN implementations and training techniques to learn how to take your low-resolution digit generations and turn them into high-resolution, photo-realistic imagery.

Learning Without Supervision in Practice

So far in this chapter, you've learned a bit about deep unsupervised learning mostly from the perspective of deep generative modeling. You progressed from compressing data with autoencoders to generating data with VAEs and finally to generating data with GANs. You were able to train some models to generate decent-looking, low-resolution, handwritten digits—which you might think is exciting. But at the same time, you might still be wondering about the secrets of power models like DALL-E and why learning about GANs, VAEs, and Autoencoders is even useful. In this section, you'll dive a bit deeper into modern unsupervised learning in practice.

Unsupervised Learning in Theory

Yann Lecun, one of the godfathers of deep learning, once called unsupervised learning—specifically self-supervised learning—the "cake" when compared to supervised learning and reinforcement learning. In other words, Lecun believes unsupervised learning is the most important research area in machine learning. More recently, Lecun wrote about self-supervised learning being the Dark Matter of Intelligence.[2]

Self-supervised learning can be considered a subset of unsupervised learning in the sense that no labels are provided. The most common self-supervised models you see in practice are transformers. Transformer models learn to model language from raw text without labels—the tokens in the text act as labels during the pre-training process. This eliminates the need to carefully hand-label datasets and exponentially increases the size of available training data.

In a philosophical sense, generative modeling can be considered the purest form of unsupervised learning and might even possibly be at the core of intelligence. Learning to *generate* data that matches some distribution is far more powerful than learning to model some specific relationship between input data and labels. This is part of the reason pre-trained, self-supervised

---

2.   https://ai.facebook.com/blog/self-supervised-learning-the-dark-matter-of-intelligence/

models like transformers are so powerful in practice. They learn to capture relationships in semantics and syntax in language—not whether the presence of certain words maps to certain labels.

What Is the State of the Art?

After learning a bit about generative modeling, you might be left wondering what other types of generative models are out there and which ones you should use.

Perhaps the most famous generative model today is stable diffusion. Stable diffusion is a text-to-image model which makes use of *latent diffusion*. Diffusion is the process of progressively denoising images starting from random noise over a fixed number of timesteps.

The forward diffusion process progressively adds noise to an input image, until the image essentially becomes random noise. The reverse diffusion process learns to map the random noise back to the input image.

Diffusion models have picked up in popularity in recent years thanks to the success of generative models like stable diffusion. Before diffusion models, GANs were the preferred architecture for generative modeling. In many ways, GANs are still the most popular generative model used in practice.

Applications of Autoencoders, VAEs, and GANs

So what practical applications do unsupervised models like autoencoders, VAEs, and GANs actually have? Actually, quite a few, but in this section, you'll learn about only a handful. I highly recommend you research additional applications on your own. You'll find that these and other unsupervised models are incredibly useful in practice.

Image Denoising

One practical application of autoencoders is in *Image Denoising [Gon16]*. Image denoising is the process of taking a noisy image and mapping it to a clean image. By applying a variety of noise to input images, you can train an autoencoder to defeat intentional and unintentional defects in imagery.

Super-resolution

Super-resolution is a class of image techniques to enhance the resolution of an input image. GANs have been applied with great success to *Super-resolution. [LTHC17]* Super-resolution itself has a number of applications in medical imaging, microscopic imaging, and more.

Anomaly Detection

One unique application of generative models such as VAEs and GANs is in anomaly detection. *Anomaly detection* is the process of detecting anomalous data points. One such example of GANs applied to anomaly detection uses GANs to identify anomalies in *images of the retina [SSWS17]*. Because generative models like GANs are capable of modeling what real data is supposed to look like, they're also capable of modeling what anomalous data looks like.

Wrapping Up

In this chapter, you implemented three types of deep unsupervised learning and deep generative modeling algorithms in Axon: an autoencoder, a variational autoencoder, and a generative adversarial network. You implemented custom event handlers in Axon and wrote your first custom training loop. You also used some new Axon layers such as Axon.conv_transpose/3 and Axon.resize/3.

Finally, you learned a bit about unsupervised learning and generative modeling in theory and practice. You also learned about the state of the art in generative modeling and about some applications of generative models in the real world.

At this point, you've learned essentially everything you need to know about deep learning and Axon. You're more than ready to learn how to put machine learning into practice at any scale with Elixir. In the next chapter, you'll dive into a practical machine learning problem and put a solution into production with Nx, Axon, and Phoenix.

Part III

Machine Learning in Practice

## CHAPTER 13

Put Machine Learning into Practice

At this point in the book, you have experience applying machine learning to many different input modalities. You've worked with structured data, text, images, time-series data, and more. You've created and applied both supervised and unsupervised machine learning algorithms. You know how to use Nx, Axon, and Livebook to train and validate models. You're well on your way to becoming a proficient Elixir machine learning engineer. There's one more question you need to answer: how do I go from Livebook to running machine learning in production?

In this chapter, you'll learn how to operationalize your machine learning models with Nx.Serving and Elixir's web framework Phoenix.[1] You'll create a machine-learning-powered web application and see firsthand some of the considerations you must have in a production deployment. This chapter is designed to serve as an introduction to *machine learning operations (MLOps)*. Machine learning operations is a blanket term for the set of practices used to deploy and monitor machine learning models in production. This chapter covers some of the basics, but if you're looking for a more comprehensive book, I suggest looking at *Designing Machine Learning Systems [Huy22]* by Chip Huyen.

Deciding to Use Machine Learning

Imagine you've been tasked with improving the book search experience for local readers. Rather than requiring readers to search based on specific authors or genres they like, or memorize the Dewey decimal system, the library wants readers to have the power to search with natural language.

---

1. https://phoenixframework.org

Before attacking this problem with machine learning, you need to decide if it's actually worth using machine learning over a more traditional approach. Machine learning is a powerful tool, but if you apply it to every problem without thought, you risk building applications that use hammers for screws and screwdrivers for nails.

Machine learning comes with a number of costs that might not be worth it when compared to the benefits of a naive solution. When making the decision of whether or not to use machine learning, there are no one-size-fits-all metrics or decision criteria to use. You need to make the decision in the context of your specific application and business goals.

To add to the challenge of deciding between machine learning or naive solutions, requirements are often vague. If you break down the problem statement above, you end up with a single requirement: "improve the book search experience for local readers." That's not a good requirement. What counts as an improvement?

Without concrete metrics, it's difficult to make a sound decision. At this time, you'd probably want to go back to the drawing board and hash out what success looks like, with concrete metrics and milestones. Part of hashing out requirements for machine learning applications is knowing what questions to ask. You should consider some common things for every application you create, such as the following:

- How do machine learning and naive solutions compare in terms of the application's KPIs?

- What are the compute and storage constraints of the application?

- What are the development and maintenance requirements/constraints of the application?

- Is it ethical to solve this problem with machine learning?

To understand the decision-making process, you'll consider each of these questions in the context of the book search service. But, before you can do that, you need to understand the possible approaches you can use to solve this problem with and without machine learning: *full-text search* and *semantic search*.

Full-Text Search vs. Semantic Search

If you're familiar with search applications, your first inclination might be to reach for full-text search capabilities, which are built into Postgres and Elasticsearch.

Full-text search is a search technique for retrieving documents that contain some text from a given keyword query. While full-text search works well for some applications, it pushes some additional burden on users to know the correct keywords to search for to find what they're looking for. Full-text search doesn't capture the nuance or meaning of a document, and thus it can fall short when trying to make good recommendations to users attempting to describe what they want.

An alternative approach is to use a semantic search. Semantic search is a search technique for retrieving documents based on semantic meaning. Rather than literal keyword matching, semantic search retrieves results that are most similar to the meaning conveyed in a user's query. Semantic search is a powerful alternative to full-text search because it allows users to convey what they're looking for with natural language, rather than depending on keyword hacking. Semantic search depends on having access to a model that can accurately represent the meaning and semantics of documents and queries. In practice, semantic search often depends on a combination of machine learning and *vector databases*.

Vector databases are optimized for storing, retrieving, and searching dense vector representations. But why are vector databases applicable to semantic search? Where are the vectors coming from?

Recall from Tokenizing and Vectorizing in Elixir, on page 198, that word embeddings give mathematical meaning to words in a sentence. To perform machine learning on text, you need a way to turn text into a vector representation. Word embeddings do this transformation at the word level. More powerful models based on transformers are capable of doing this transformation at the *sentence level*. That means you can create embeddings that capture the meaning of entire sentences, rather than the meaning of individual words in a sentence. Semantic search makes it possible to express what you want more naturally than keyword search. For example, rather than searching for carefully selected keywords like "horror," "murder mystery," and "historical," you could express your query as a sentence: "A horror story based on a murder in a colonial town."

This is where vector databases come into play. Your vector database stores vectors that represent the meaning of books captured by some machine learning model. You can query your database with another vector, and a vector database will return the books *closest* to your query vector. In a vector search, the word "closest" can take on a variety of meanings as you can measure the distance between two vectors in a number of different ways. To simplify this concept, consider that your vector database contains vectors for each book in your dataset in a two-dimensional space. If you plot this two-dimensional space, it might look something like this:

Horror Books

Mystery Books

Romance Books

Drama Books

Biographies

Cook Books

PragProg Books

Notice that in the two-dimensional space, horror books are closer to mystery books, biographies are closer to PragProg technical books, and so on. Books that are generally more similar will be grouped together visually in space. Now, say you make a query for the "best book on genetic algorithms in elixir" and run that through the same model you used to embed the meaning of each of your books. If you were to plot the query in the same embedding space, it might look something like this:

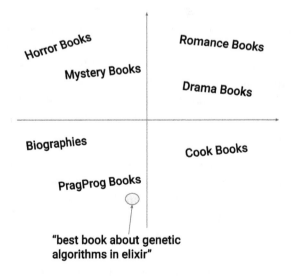

Horror Books

Mystery Books

Romance Books

Drama Books

Biographies

Cook Books

PragProg Books

"best book about genetic algorithms in elixir"

The query falls very close to PragProg books because the PragProg collection contains *Genetic Algorithms in Elixir [Mor21]*. If you were to measure the straight-line distance between every book in the collection in your query, you could then return the books that most closely match the query in semantic meaning by returning the ones that are closest in the embedding space. This is essentially what vector databases do, but with fancy tricks to allow them to scale to quickly search through *billions* of embeddings at once.

How Do Machine Learning and Naive Solutions Compare?

Now that you understand your two options for designing the library search application, you need to know what questions to ask in order to fairly compare solutions. First, you need to look at *key performance indicators (KPIs)*. They are metrics that evaluate the success of an application. Determining KPIs in the context of applications is often a difficult task. For example, in your book search service, how do you measure user satisfaction?

Often, you need to choose auxiliary metrics that align with your overall goal. Note that it's important to think carefully about these auxiliary metrics—you don't want to end up optimizing for the wrong thing. For example, imagine you designed a fraud detection application. You might think it's best to maximize for number of fraudulent transactions declined, but you'd quickly be surprised at the angry complaints from legitimate customers getting their transactions declined. In reality, to provide a good user experience, you need to balance the ratio of legitimate transactions accepted to fraudulent transactions rejected.

Choosing a metric for recommender systems like your book search service is notoriously difficult. Some examples of metrics you might consider:

- Number of queries to find a book
- Aggregate time browsing to find a book
- Rate of top N results being taken

None of these are necessarily better than the others. All of them have potentially problematic confounding variables. For now, imagine the library has chosen the number of queries needed to find a book as it's top metric.

What Are the Compute and Storage Constraints of the Application?

Certain approaches to machine learning come with significant compute and storage requirements. Semantic search depends on transformers—the deep learning models you used in Chapter 11, Model Everything with Transformers, on page 237.

Transformer models are often computationally expensive. Depending on the strength of the model, you may need to rely on GPU compute to provide a good enough experience in production. Otherwise, your application will end up being relatively high-latency due to the inference overhead of a large model like a transformer.

You should always consider the compute and storage constraints of your application, especially with respect to latency. If you're not able to scale up the resources necessary to provide low-latency inference in production, then your users will have a bad experience even with the most powerful machine learning model in the world.

Additionally, for certain applications of machine learning like semantic search, you need to consider the storage constraints of your application. Remember, you need to store a dense vector for each book in the library, which will come with a storage cost. But when compared to a full-text search, this storage cost might actually be better. Vector search tools often support compressed indices which allow them to scale efficiently in size. Additionally, the vector representing a book is itself a compressed representation of the text in the book. With a semantic search, you get some storage benefit when compared to storing full documents in a full-text search.

For this example, you can assume that no significant compute and storage constraints exist that would prevent you from using either semantic or full-text search.

What Are the Development and Maintenance Constraints of the Application?

When compared to alternative solutions, machine-learning-based solutions often introduce significant developer and maintenance costs. Machine learning in production is still a relatively new concept, and the tools and best practices are still evolving. Unlike traditional software, machine learning models atrophy in production—a phenomenon known as *model drift*.

If you leave a model in production without retraining on new data, it will slowly deteriorate overtime and deliver a worse experience for your users. Model drift often occurs because the distribution of data the model is exposed to in production slowly drifts from the distribution of data the model was trained on.

Additionally, while with traditional software you can write tests to help ensure the correctness of your software, the same doesn't go for machine learning. Models in production require constant monitoring to verify predictions remain good. Even with constant monitoring, it can be difficult to tell when models are starting to deteriorate.

Finally, the unique combination of data, code, and models involved in building machine learning systems makes developing them extremely difficult. It's common for machine learning projects to devolve into nightmares of unmaintainable code, unversioned data, and barely working models. When deciding to use machine learning in production, it's important to remain disciplined, start with a simple MLOps solution, and scale in complexity as needed.

In the context of the book-search application, some of the development and maintenance costs for the machine learning approach are dissipated because you can take advantage of pre-trained models. That being said, there's still some development overhead in deploying any machine learning in production—despite how easy Elixir may make it.

Choosing a Solution

Given the requirement to build a book search tool capable of helping users find books in fewer search queries, you need to decide between a machine-learning-based solution (semantic search) or a naive solution (full-text search). In terms of compute and storage costs, machine learning will likely have additional computational overhead. Both solutions will have comparable storage overhead. In terms of development and maintenance costs, the machine learning solution will have more overhead. However, that's mitigated with the use of a pre-trained model. The decision mainly comes down to your KPI—the number of queries to find a book.

In the context of your KPI, semantic search typically provides better results, as it doesn't depend on users knowing exactly what keywords or partial keywords to search for. Semantic search allows users to express what they want naturally and finds the closest representation. Semantic search also opens up the possibility of iteration in the future by training better models based on user preferences in the library.

So, it seems you'll need machine learning after all. By now, you should be pretty familiar with all of the tools you'll need for this application. You have Nx for general data manipulation, Axon and Bumblebee for neural network tasks, and EXLA for hardware acceleration. But what about vector search?

Fortunately, there's a Postgres extension for performing vector search called pgvector,[2] which allows you to build vector search tools directly on top of your

---

2. https://github.com/pgvector/pgvector

existing database. This makes it easy to keep your vector store in sync with your database, as the data lies right next to one another. Best of all, there's an Ecto implementation of pgvector. That means you can embed vector search directly into your existing Ecto queries.

With a plan of attack, it's time to create your application.

Setting Up the Application

To start your book search application, create a new Phoenix project with mix phx.new:

```
mix phx.new book_search
```

Now, run the following command to change to the root directory of your project and list its contents:

```
cd book_search && ls
```

The output of this command will look like this:

```
assets  _build  config  deps  lib  mix.exs  mix.lock  priv  README.md  test
```

Next, you'll need to install pgvector. Start by adding pgvector as a dependency in your mix.exs:

```
{:pgvector, "~> 0.2.0"}
```

Then run mix deps.get. Next, create a new file lib/postgrex_types.ex and add the following code:

```
Postgrex.Types.define(
      BookSearch.PostgrexTypes,
      [Pgvector.Extensions.Vector] ++ Ecto.Adapters.Postgres.extensions(),
      []
)
```

Next, add the following to config/config.exs:

```
config :book_search, BookSearch.Repo, types: BookSearch.PostgrexTypes
```

Then, create a migration with mix ecto.gen.migration create_vector_extension and add the following:

```
defmodule BookSearch.Repo.Migrations.CreateVectorExtension do
  use Ecto.Migration

  def up do
    execute "CREATE EXTENSION IF NOT EXISTS vector"
  end
```

```
  def down do
    execute "DROP EXTENSION vector"
  end
end
```

Finally, you can run the migration with mix ecto.migrate. If it ran without a hitch, pgvector should be installed correctly. Note that you may need to also follow the pgvector installation notes[3] if you run into any issues during this installation process.

With pgvector installed, it's time to start creating your application resources. To simplify things, your book search application will revolve around a single resource: books. You can generate everything you need for the book resource by running the following code:

```
mix phx.gen.html Library Book books \
  author:string title:string description:text embedding:binary
```

mix phx.gen.html is a generator that creates a new HTML resource with views, controllers, and more for your book resource. The generator also creates a Library context, a Book schema, and a books database table. The book schema consists of an author, a title, a description of the book, and a binary embedding. The embedding is a byte array that represents the dense vector representation of a book. You'll use the embedding to perform a vector search in your application. After running this command, you'll see the following output:

```
* creating lib/book_search_web/controllers/book_controller.ex
* creating lib/book_search_web/controllers/book_html/edit.html.heex
* creating lib/book_search_web/controllers/book_html/index.html.heex
* creating lib/book_search_web/controllers/book_html/new.html.heex
* creating lib/book_search_web/controllers/book_html/show.html.heex
* creating lib/book_search_web/controllers/book_html/book_form.html.heex
* creating lib/book_search_web/controllers/book_html.ex
* creating test/book_search_web/controllers/book_controller_test.exs
* creating lib/book_search/library/book.ex
* creating priv/repo/migrations/20230517143726_create_books.exs
* creating lib/book_search/library.ex
* injecting lib/book_search/library.ex
* creating test/book_search/library_test.exs
* injecting test/book_search/library_test.exs
* creating test/support/fixtures/library_fixtures.ex
* injecting test/support/fixtures/library_fixtures.ex

Add the resource to your browser scope in lib/book_search_web/router.ex:

    resources "/books", BookController
```

---

3.   https://github.com/pgvector/pgvector#installation-notes

Remember to update your repository by running migrations:

```
$ mix ecto.migrate
```

Now, you want to edit the embedding type in the migration such that it uses the pgvector vector type. Edit the generated migration so it looks like this:

```
defmodule BookSearch.Repo.Migrations.CreateBooks do
  use Ecto.Migration

  def change do
    create table(:books) do
      add :author, :string
      add :title, :string
      add :description, :text
      add :embedding, :vector, size: 384

      timestamps()
    end
  end
end
```

Notice that we specify :vector with size: 384 in place of :binary. This tells Postgres that we're creating a vector column which we expect to have a dimensionality of 384. You'll also want to edit the book schema to reflect the usage of the vector type:

```
schema "books" do
  field :author, :string
  field :description, :string
  field :embedding, Pgvector.Ecto.Vector
  field :title, :string

  timestamps()
end
```

Next, you need to set up your database. You can combine database creation, migrations, and seeding into a single step using mix ecto.setup, like this:

```
mix ecto.setup
```

This code creates your database, runs your migrations (there should only be one), and runs the seed file in priv/repo/seeds.exs to seed your database.

After setting up your database, add a new resource route to book_search_web/router.ex, like this:

```
get "/", PageController, :index

resources "/books", BookController
```

This code creates CRUD routes for your book resource. You can inspect the routes with mix phx.routes:

```
mix phx.routes
```

And you'll see the following output:

```
GET      /                          BookSearchWeb.PageController :home
GET      /books                     BookSearchWeb.BookController :index
GET      /books/:id/edit            BookSearchWeb.BookController :edit
GET      /books/new                 BookSearchWeb.BookController :new
GET      /books/:id                 BookSearchWeb.BookController :show
POST     /books                     BookSearchWeb.BookController :create
PATCH    /books/:id                 BookSearchWeb.BookController :update
PUT      /books/:id                 BookSearchWeb.BookController :update
DELETE   /books/:id                 BookSearchWeb.BookController :delete
GET      /dev/dashboard             Phoenix.LiveDashboard.PageLive :home
GET      /dev/dashboard/:page       Phoenix.LiveDashboard.PageLive :page
GET      /dev/dashboard/:node/:page Phoenix.LiveDashboard.PageLive :page
*        /dev/mailbox               Plug.Swoosh.MailboxPreview []
WS       /live/websocket            Phoenix.LiveView.Socket
GET      /live/longpoll             Phoenix.LiveView.Socket
POST     /live/longpoll             Phoenix.LiveView.Socket
```

You can now start your application by running mix phx.server:

```
mix phx.server
```

You can navigate to http://localhost:4000 in the browser to verify your server started successfully. If all went well, you'll see the following welcome page.

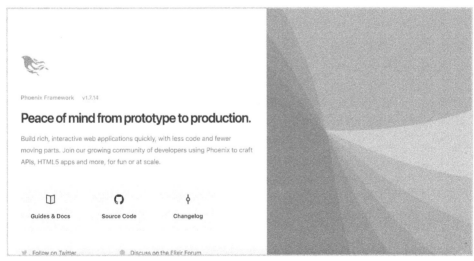

Success! With your Phoenix application set up, you're ready to add a model to the mix.

Integrating Nx with Phoenix

Now that you have a running Phoenix application, you can start working toward integrating your semantic search machine learning model.

First, add the following dependencies to your mix.exs file:

```
{:bumblebee, "~> 0.5"},
{:nx, "~> 0.7"},
{:exla, ">= 0.0.0"},
{:explorer, "~> 0.5"}
```

For your application, you'll need Bumblebee for loading pre-trained models, Nx for manipulating tensors and model serving, and EXLA for providing accelerated inference. You'll also use Explorer for working with some CSV data to seed your database.

Next, run mix deps.get:

```
mix deps.get
```

Then, create a new file book_search/model.ex. This file will contain the logic for loading, serving, and performing inference with your semantic search model. While the Nx ecosystem is still developing best practices around managing and deploying models, here are some emerging best practices:

1. Serialize model state as data, for example, using Nx.serialize/2 or another serialization format, and serialize model code as code. This means if you implement your own model using Axon's model creation API, you should keep the model creation code around, and not rely on serializing the entire model data structure to use the model later on.

2. Keep your creation, loading, serving, and inference logic for a single model in one place. The relationships between model creation, loading, serving, and inference are tightly coupled. If any of these processes change, the others are likely to change as well.

Like all best practices, these rules aren't one-size-fits-all. The *best* best practice is to do whatever works best for your application.

In book_search/model.ex, create a module named BookSearch.Model:

```
defmodule BookSearch.Model do
  @moduledoc """
  Manages the BookSearch model for similarity search.
  """

  @hf_model_repo "intfloat/e5-small-v2"
end
```

Next, create a function load/0, like so:

```
defp load() do
  {:ok, model_info} = Bumblebee.load_model({:hf, @hf_model_repo})
  {:ok, tokenizer} = Bumblebee.load_tokenizer({:hf, @hf_model_repo})

  {model_info, tokenizer}
end
```

This function uses Elixir's Bumblebee library to load a model from Hugging-Face. You should be familiar with Bumblebee from Chapter 11, Model Everything with Transformers, on page 237.

Bumblebee is a library for using pre-trained models and tasks for common applications like image classification, text generation, and more. It's also capable of importing pre-trained models designed for similarity search. For example, the model you're using here is from HuggingFace[4] and is designed specifically for sentence similarity. That means it was trained specifically with tasks like searching and clustering in mind.

The load/0 function will return a tuple of model and tokenizer. The model consists of a model tuple with {model, params}, and the tokenizer is just a Bumblebee tokenizer struct. You'll use both of these for creating an inference pipeline later on.

Next, create a function named serving/1:

```
def serving(opts \\ []) do
  opts = Keyword.validate!(opts, [
    :defn_options, sequence_length: 64, batch_size: 16
  ])

  {model_info, tokenizer} = load()

  Bumblebee.Text.TextEmbedding.text_embedding(model_info, tokenizer, [
    defn_options: opts[:defn_options],
    compile: [
        sequence_length: opts[:sequence_length],
        batch_size: opts[:batch_size]
    ]
  ])
end
```

This function uses the pre-built serving pipeline provided by Bumblebee to perform text embedding.

You'll hear the word "serving" in the context of machine learning quite a bit. In Nx, a serving is a simple abstraction for building inference pipelines. It

---

4. https://huggingface.co/intfloat/e5-small-v2

consists of preprocessing, inference, and postprocessing. If you were writing this serving from scratch, it would look something like this:

```
def serving(opts \\ []) do
        opts = Keyword.validate!(opts, [
    :defn_options, sequence_length: 64, batch_size: 16
  ])

  {%{model: model, params: params}, tokenizer} = load()
  {_, predict_fn} = Axon.build(model)

        Nx.Serving.jit(fn input ->
                pad_size = opts[:sequence_length] - Nx.axis_size(input, 1)
                predict_fn.(params, Nx.Batch.pad(input, pad_size))
        end)
        |> Nx.Serving.client_preprocessing(fn text ->
                tokenized = Bumblebee.apply_tokenizer(tokenizer, text)
                {Nx.Batch.stack(tokenized), :meta}
        end)
        |> Nx.Serving.client_postprocessing(& elem(&1, 0))
end
```

This function is known as serving/1 because it returns your Nx.Serving pipeline. The Nx.Serving module contains functions for building servings, like the ones you can see here, such as Nx.Serving.jit/1 and Nx.Serving.client_preprocessing/1. But why do you need a special-purpose serving pipeline? Why can't you just call a model's predict_fn?

There are a few good reasons, but the most important reason is that servings allow you to maximize research usage by taking advantage of *dynamic batching*. Deep learning models are expensive. However, they're also designed to take advantage of batch inference. Neural network inference latency doesn't scale linearly with batch size for accelerators. In fact, some accelerators, such as TPUs, *require* inputs to have a batch size of at least 128 and will even pad inputs to that batch size before executing inference. Every inference you don't execute with the maximum possible batch size is a waste of resources.

Dynamic batching is a way to take advantage of the resources available to you. When you start an Nx.Serving process, behind the scenes it spins up a queue. As you make calls to the serving process to perform inference, Nx.Serving will automatically batch overlapping requests for you behind the scenes and then dispatch them back out to the calling process. That means if you make an inference request at the same time as another person, both of your inference requests will be executed within the same batch, and then returned to you as if executed standalone. Dynamic batching is critical to effectively scaling machine learning inference in production.

As you can see in serving/1, every Nx.Serving starts with a call to Nx.Serving.jit/1 or Nx.Serving.new/1. Nx.Serving.jit/1 accepts an arity-1 creation function that returns a just-in-time compiled inference inference function. In this example, your Nx.Serving.jit/1 function creates a compiled encoding function. Your actual inference function accepts serving inputs and returns the encoded outputs. Before calling encoding_fun/2, you need to call Nx.Batch.pad/2. Nx.Batch.pad/2 is a helper function that pads your inputs to the required batch size specified by your compiled encoding function. If your dynamic batch queue doesn't feel up to the required batch size, Nx.Batch.pad/2 will pad the inputs to the required size.

In addition to an inference function specified in Nx.Serving.jit/1, you can specify client preprocessing and postprocessing functions using Nx.Serving functions. In this simple example, you can just call out to Bumblebee.apply_tokenizer/2.

Preprocessing is any work you want done before an input reaches the inference step. Typically, it converts raw data into a cleaned-up tensor. Preprocessing, like inference, is also performed in batches under the hood. While it's common to perform preprocessing on the server, for some applications it makes sense to perform it on the client to avoid saturating the server with work. For example, you can use the Javascript canvas API to resize images to save resources on the server.

Every client preprocessing function accepts raw inputs and returns a tuple of {processed, meta}. The additional metadata is forwarded to postprocessing, as it's common in some tasks to need access to the raw inputs in order to perform postprocessing.

Bumblebee implements a number of common machine learning pipelines out of the box for you, so it saves you the complexity of worrying about what's going on under the hood. For certain applications, you may want or need to implement your own custom-serving pipeline, so it's important to understand how it works.

With your serving implemented, you can add the following code to your application's supervision tree:

```
{Nx.Serving,
 serving: BookSearch.Model.serving(defn_options: [compiler: EXLA]),
 batch_size: 16,
 batch_timeout: 100,
 name: BookSearchModel}
```

This code will start a new Nx.Serving process using the serving you defined in BookSearch.Model.serving/1. The serving process will be named BookSearchModel, so you can reference by name when performing inference later on. The other two options, batch_size and batch_timeout, control the batch queue used in Nx.Serving.

batch_size refers to the maximum batch size the queue will accept before dispatching to predict. The batch_timeout refers to the amount of time the queue will wait to fill up to the maximum batch size before dispatching to predict. In this example, your model will run inference either when it reaches a batch size of 16 or after it has waited 100ms since it received the first inference request, whichever comes first. Depending on your application, model, and resources, you might need to play with these configuration options to maximize your performance.

Now that you have an Nx.Serving process running in your application, you can use it to conduct inference. To do so, add the following predict/1 method to your BookSearch.Model module:

```
def predict(text) do
  Nx.Serving.batched_run(BookSearchModel, text)
end
```

This function just wraps the Nx.Serving.batched_run/2 method. Nx.Serving.batched_run/2 performs dynamic batch inference with the given process and inputs. In this case, calls to BookSearch.Model.predict/1 will return an embedded representation of the input text provided in text. To verify your model is up and running, restart your Phoenix server:

```
iex -S mix phx.server
```

You may notice a slight delay on application start-up—that's EXLA actually compiling and loading your model under the hood.

Next, run the following code in IEx:

```
iex(1)> BookSearch.Model.predict("a good book on machine learning")
```

Almost instantly you'll see the following output:

```
%{embedding: #Nx.Tensor<
  f32[1][384]
  EXLA.Backend<host:0, 0.2486389031.1855586325.245579>
  [
    [-0.01250604260712862, 0.027123818174004555, ...]
  ]
>}
```

Success! You have a working machine learning model running inside a Phoenix application. You can now embed documents and queries, but you still can't perform any search. Before you can search though, you need some seed data.

Seeding Your Databases

With your model up and running, it's time to seed your database with the library's books. Before that happens, you need to make some slight modifications to the generated book resource code.

First, modify BookSearch.Book.changeset/2 to match the following:

```
@doc false
def changeset(book, attrs) do
  book
  |> cast(attrs, [:author, :title, :description, :embedding])
  |> validate_required([:author, :title, :description])
end
```

Notice that you removed :embedding as a required argument in attrs. Because you compute the embedding from book attributes, you don't want to have to pass it up front.

Next, add the following put_embedding/1 function to BookSearch.Book:

```
@doc false
def put_embedding(%{changes: %{description: desc}} = book_changeset) do
  %{embedding: embedding} = BookSearch.Model.predict(desc)
  put_change(book_changeset, :embedding, embedding)
end
```

This code embeds the given book based on its description and adds the embedding to the book changeset. Notice that you can use an Nx tensor directly as a type within the changeset. The Elixir pgvector extension supports marshaling directly from Nx tensors to the pgvector postgres type.

Next, in BookSearch.Library, modify the create_book/1 method to match the following:

```
def create_book(attrs \\ %{}) do
  book =
    %Book{}
    |> Book.changeset(attrs)
    |> Book.put_embedding()

  Repo.insert(book)
end
```

This method creates a changeset from the given book attributes, embeds the book, and then inserts the book into your database.

As a final housekeeping measure before seeding your library, you'll want to update your HTML views to remove references to embeddings. Because embeddings are internally represented as raw binaries, they don't render well on a webpage. Additionally, they aren't intended to be edited by the user, so it doesn't make sense to include them in a form. Remove the references to the following code in each of the following files:

```
# book_form.html.heex
<.input field={{f, :embedding}} type="text" label="Embedding" />

# show.html.heex
<:item title="Embedding"><%= @book.embedding %></:item>

# index.html.heex
<:col :let={book} label="Embedding"><%= book.embedding %></:col>
```

You're ready to work with real data. The dataset you'll use to represent your library comes from a book summaries database from David Bamman.[5] Run the following commands to download and extract the database:

```
cd priv/repo
wget https://www.cs.cmu.edu/~dbamman/data/booksummaries.tar.gz
tar -xvf booksummaries.tar.gz
rm booksummaries.tar.gz
```

The database consists of a file of book information, where each book is on a tab-delimited line. To parse this information into something you can use to seed your database, you can use Explorer. Particularly, you want to use Explorer to parse the input file, parse out the author, title, and description, and then add each book to your database. To do this, add the following code to your priv/repo/seeds.exs file:

```
path = "priv/repo/booksummaries/booksummaries.txt"

df = Explorer.DataFrame.from_csv!(path, delimiter: "\t", header: false)
df = df[["column_3", "column_4", "column_7"]]
df = Explorer.DataFrame.rename(df, ["author", "title", "description"])

df
|> Explorer.DataFrame.to_rows()
|> Enum.each(&BookSearch.Library.create_book/1)
```

This script parses the book summary file and extracts the author, title, and description from each book. It then converts the DataFrame to a list of maps and uses BookSearch.Library.create_book/1 to create an entry for each book. Now you can run the following:

```
mix run priv/repo/seeds.exs
```

After a while, your script will finish running, and you've successfully seeded your database with a library of books. Now you need to implement the search functionality.

---

5.   https://people.ischool.berkeley.edu/~dbamman/

For a production application, this process of seeding your database is something you might have to run periodically as new books are added. One way to handle this might be to use Oban[6] in conjunction with FLAME[7] to periodically execute expensive machine learning pipelines on a separate machine. With FLAME, you can spin up a GPU-enabled machine to run a long-running machine learning job such as this one without impacting your production servers.

Building the Search LiveView

At this point, you have a seeded database and a machine learning model ready to embed books. The final requirement is to implement the front-end search application.

In this example, you'll implement the search functionality as a LiveView. Start by creating a new file book_search_web/live/search_live/index.ex and add the following code:

```
defmodule BookSearchWeb.SearchLive.Index do
  use BookSearchWeb, :live_view

  alias BookSearch.Library

  @impl true
  def mount(_params, _session, socket) do
    {:ok, socket}
  end

  @impl true
  def render(assigns) do
    ~H"""
    <h1>Welcome to search</h1>
    """
  end
end
```

This code creates the scaffold of a basic LiveView that renders the welcome header and does nothing else.

Next, add a live route to your LiveView in your router:

```
live "/search", SearchLive.Index, :index
```

Next, start your Phoenix application:

```
iex -S mix phx.server
```

---

6. https://hexdocs.pm/oban/Oban.html
7. https://fly.io/blog/rethinking-serverless-with-flame/

If everything succeeded, when you navigate to https://localhost:4000/search, you'll see the default Phoenix welcome page.

Your search application consists of a simple search form and search results. Edit render/1 to match the following:

```
@impl true
def render(assigns) do
  ~H"""
  <div class="w-full flex flex-col space-y-2">
    <.search_form query={@query} />
    <div :if={@query}>
      <h2 class="text-md">
        <span class="font-semibold">Searching For:</span>
        <span class="italic"><%= @query %></span>
      </h2>
    </div>
    <div>
      <.search_results results={@results} />
    </div>
  </div>
  """
end
```

This code renders the components search_form and search_results. search_results requires an assign @results, which represents book search results. You need to edit the mount/3 method to assign results to an empty list up front so that everything renders properly:

```
@impl true
def mount(_params, _session, socket) do
  {:ok, assign(socket, :results, [])}
end
```

Next, you need to implement components for the search form and results. For now, you can implement them as function components:

```
defp search_form(assigns) do
  ~H"""
  <div class="w-full">
    <form
      id="search"
      phx-change="validate_search"
      phx-submit="search_for_books"
      class="w-full flex space-x-2"
    >
      <input
        placeholder="search for a book"
        type="text"
        name="search"
```

```
          value={@query}
          id="search"
          class={["block w-full rounded-md border-gray-300 pr-12",
          "shadow-sm focus:border-indigo-500 focus:ring-indigo-500",
          "sm:text-sm"]} />
      <button
        type="submit"
        class={["inline-flex items-center rounded-md border",
        "border-transparent shadow-sm text-white",
        "bg-indigo-600 px-3 py-2 text-sm font-medium leading-4",
        "hover:bg-indigo-700 focus:outline-none focus:ring-2",
        "focus:ring-offset-2"]}>
          Search
      </button>
    </form>
  </div>
  """

end

defp search_results(assigns) do
  ~H"""
  <div class="w-full">
    <ul role="list" class="-my-5 divide-y divide-gray-200">
      <%= for result <- @results do %>
        <li class="py-5">
          <div
              class="relative focus-within:ring-2
                focus-within:ring-indigo-500"
            >
            <h3 class="text-sm font-semibold text-gray-800">
              <a
                href={~p"/books/#{result.id}"}
                class="hover:underline
                focus:outline-none"
              >
                <span class="absolute inset-0" aria-hidden="true"></span>
                <%= result.title %>
              </a>
            </h3>
            <p class="mt-1 text-sm text-gray-600 line-clamp-2">
              <%= result.author %>
            </p>
          </div>
        </li>
      <% end %>
    </ul>
  </div>
  """

end
```

search_form is a relatively basic form with a single input and submit button. On submission, it fires the search_for_books event. The search_for_books event will push a patch to the URL, which you can handle in handle_params to actually search for books based on the input query. search_results is a list that renders list entries for each of the elements in the results assign. As you can imagine search_for_books will update the results assign, and search_results will rerender with new results on every query.

Next, add the following event handlers to your LiveView to handle your form events:

```elixir
@impl true
def handle_event("validate_search", %{"search" => _query}, socket) do
  {:noreply, socket}
end

def handle_event("search_for_books", %{"search" => query}, socket) do
  {:noreply, push_patch(socket, to: ~p"/search?q=#{query}")}
end
```

For simplicity, validate_search is a no-op. But you can implement any validation logic you'd like. search_for_books pushes a query to the URL parameters.

Now, implement handle_params/3, like so:

```elixir
@impl true
def handle_params(%{"q" => query}, _uri, socket) do
  results = Library.search(query)

  socket =
    socket
    |> assign(:results, results)
    |> assign(:query, query)

  {:noreply, socket}
end
```

You also need a clause for when no parameters are present:

```elixir
def handle_params(_params, _uri, socket) do
  {:noreply, assign(socket, :query, nil)}
end
```

handle_params/3 conducts a search and assigns the results to :results and the query to :query, which will both be rendered in the LiveView. handle_params/3 dispatches to Library.search, which you still need to implement. To do so, open up book_search/library.ex and add the following search/1 method:

```elixir
@doc """
Searches for books.
"""
```

```
def search(query) do
  %{embedding: embedding} = BookSearch.Model.predict(query)

      Book
      |> order_by([b], l2_distance(b.embedding, ^embedding))
      |> limit(5)
      |> Repo.all()
end
```

You'll also need to add the following import to book_search/library.ex:

```
import Pgvector.Ecto.Query
```

This function uses your model to embed the query and then searches for the five closest vectors in the search index to your query. Notice that you can embed pgvector query functions such as l2_distance directly in your Ecto queries. The l2_distance function will compute the distance between your query embedding and every embedding in your database and order the results by ascending distance. The lower the distance, the more similar the query and book embedding are. You limit your results to only five books and return those to your application front-end.

And that's it. You can now navigate to http://localhost:4000/search and look for a specific book. After running a search, you'll see the following page:

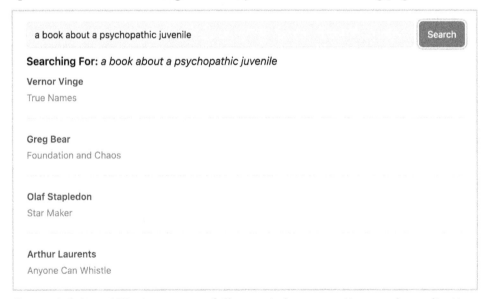

Congratulations! You've successfully created a semantic search application with Phoenix, Bumblebee, and pgvector.

Wrapping Up

In this chapter, you implemented a semantic search application from scratch using Phoenix, Bumblebee, and Elixir. You went through the process of deciding when to use and not use machine learning in an application. You learned a bit about some of the important questions to ask when designing machine learning applications. You used Nx.Serving to wrap machine learning pipelines into a performant, fault-tolerant inference pipeline. You learned about the significance of dynamic batching to machine learning performance, and you saw how Nx.Serving can help you achieve dynamic batching.

In addition, you implemented your own vector index and search functionality using pgvector. In doing so, you learned a bit about vector search.

Finally, you integrated all of your machine learning components into a regular Phoenix application. As you might have seen, integrating machine learning into Phoenix applications doesn't require any special dependencies or tricks. All you need to do is add Elixir's machine learning libraries to your application, and it *just works*.

With this chapter, you've come full circle as an Elixir machine learning engineer. You now know how to use many of the libraries in Elixir's machine learning ecosystem to solve challenging problems on various data modalities, and you know how to deploy your models to a production application with Phoenix.

In the next chapter, you'll conclude your journey and discover some of the next steps to take in your machine learning journey.

## CHAPTER 14

That's a Wrap

Throughout this book, you've implemented a number of different machine learning models in Nx, Axon, Bumblebee, and Scholar. You learned how to manipulate data with Nx, train models with Axon, and integrate them into your Phoenix applications. You discovered how to take advantage of the vast ecosystem of pre-trained models with Bumblebee. You know everything you need to know to create your own models on your own data and integrate them into your own applications. You're ready to take on the challenges of machine learning in the real world.

While this book covered a breadth of topics, it's by no means comprehensive. Machine learning is a vast field. You can't possibly learn everything about machine learning from a single book. In this chapter, you'll get up to speed with the current trends in machine learning and discover some of the interesting machine learning topics this book wasn't able to cover.

Learning from Experience

One of the largest subfields in machine learning this book didn't cover is *reinforcement learning*. Reinforcement learning is concerned with creating agents capable of making intelligent actions and learning from reward signals in an environment. Reinforcement learning is fundamentally different from both supervised and unsupervised learning. In a reinforcement learning problem, there's no concept of labeled or unlabeled data. Instead, the learning process is entirely online as an agent interacts with its environment.

The most common training ground for reinforcement learning agents is video games. For example, the Arcade Learning Environment[1] is an environment designed to allow researchers and hobbyists to create AI agents capable of

---

1.　https://github.com/mgbellemare/Arcade-Learning-Environment

interacting with Atari 2600 games. Reinforcement learning can be credited with some of the superhuman demonstrations of artificial intelligence in the last decade. For example, AlphaGo, the model from Deep Mind which is capable of playing Go at superhuman levels, was trained with reinforcement learning.

In addition to video games, reinforcement learning has proven to be a fruitful paradigm in robotics. As it's difficult to collect data and train robots on performing proper locomotion in a supervised manner, researchers often train locomotion via reinforcement learning. The success of reinforcement learning has dramatically increased with a turn toward methods that combine reinforcement learning with deep learning. Most state-of-the-art reinforcement learning algorithms today rely on deep models.

Reinforcement learning is a rich field of research. If you're interested in exploring reinforcement learning more, I recommend reading *Reinforcement Learning [SB92]* by Richard S. Sutton and Andrew G. Barto.

At the time of this writing, the hottest model in machine learning is ChatGPT.[2] ChatGPT is a large language model from OpenAI optimized for chat dialogue. ChatGPT is part of a growing trend of large language models trained with *reinforcement learning on human feedback (RLHF)*. RLHF combines reinforcement learning with human ratings to optimize the parameters of the model. With lots of human feedback, you end up with a model capable of outputting text that aligns with what humans prefer.

Large language models are already great at modeling text. As you learned in Chapter 11, Model Everything with Transformers, on page 237, large language models pre-trained on a causal language modeling task are great at predicting the next word in a sequence. Some *research [HBDF19]* has shown that as large language models approach the optimal likelihood for a text generation task, they tend to devolve into repetition. What that means is that large language models are great at probabilistically modeling language. But being good at modeling language doesn't mean you're convincing to humans. ChatGPT and related RLHF models are fine-tuned for human preference.

The promise of RLHF is that we can collect enough human feedback so that these models are perfectly aligned with our preferences and capable of performing a wide range of tasks at the human level. Another promise of RLHF is that large language models eventually become powerful enough to give feedback to themselves. This trend is already emerging out of research labs

---

2. https://chat.openai.com/chat

such as Anthropic. Recent works from Anthropic on *Constitutional AI [BKKA19]* have shown that large language models are capable of criticizing and correcting themselves to align with a set of dictated preferences. The trend towards reinforcement learning on artificial intelligence feedback (RLAIF) could eliminate much of the intensive work of collecting human annotations and rapidly accelerate AI research.

Diffusing Innovation

Another recent innovation this book hasn't completely covered is the success of diffusion models in generative applications. As you briefly learned in What Is the State of the Art?, on page 289, latent diffusion is the process of progressively denoising over long time series. This process can be used to start from an image of random noise to generate incredibly realistic images.

At their core, diffusion models are based on a process of iterative refinement. Initially, they start with a pattern of random noise. Over successive iterations, this noise is gradually shaped into a coherent output, whether that be an image, text, or another form of data. While their most popular application is in generative art, diffusion models have been used with great success in video and speech generation. Recent work also shows it's possible to use diffusion models in text generation tasks, such as machine translation and code generation.

For a more comprehensive introduction to the world of diffusion models, check out Introduction to Diffusion Models for Machine Learning[3] by AssemblyAI.

Talking to Large Language Models

As large language models have become increasingly popular, an emerging field in machine learning and artificial intelligence is one that attempts to improve the performance of large language models at inference time through *prompt engineering*. Prompt engineering is the process of strategically formulating input prompts to effectively guide a large language model to generate the output you want. Large language models are great at understanding text, but they need specific instructions to carry out a task.

One of the most popular prompt engineering techniques is *chain-of-thought prompting*. Chain-of-thought prompting involves prompting a large language model to break a problem into subtasks and chain them together into an output. In other words, you're guiding a large language model to show its

---

3.   https://www.assemblyai.com/blog/diffusion-models-for-machine-learning-introduction/

chain of thought before producing the output. It's been shown that chain-of-thought prompting increases the reasoning ability of large language models as measured on some specific benchmarks.

In-context learning via *retrieval augmented generation* is another popular methodology for guiding large language models to provide correct responses to certain questions. Retrieval augmented generation, or RAG as it's often referred to, is the process of retrieving appropriate facts and context for a large language model to then use in its response. The retrieval process typically involves some sort of semantic search to take a question and retrieve appropriate facts related to that question. RAG is effective, but it requires a robust retrieval pipeline. For certain applications, it can be difficult to create a robust retrieval pipeline to provide sufficient context to large language models.

A standing challenge with large language models is reliably deploying them and using them within traditional software applications. The most popular applications of large language models deploy them through chat interfaces. However, they can be useful in many other applications as well.

Getting large language models to reliably interact with traditional, deterministic software is difficult. Recent work in *structured prompting* attempts to address this issue. Structured prompting relies on some large language model's ability to generate outputs according to a JSON Schema specification. OpenAI, for example, released a function-calling API that allows you to specify a structured schema that their large language models would follow during generation. Open-source libraries implement similar functionality through the use of constrained generation. This functionality ensures a large language model will output valid JSON that can then be used in your application.

Structured prompting relies on the ability of large language models to generate structured outputs. Basically, you define a schema you'd like your large language model to follow, prompt the model, and receive a data structure that your application understands back from the model's generation. Libraries such as instructor_ex[4] allow you to define Ecto Schemas, prompt a large language model on some task, and receive a valid data structure following your defined schema as a result. This library is based on the original Instructor[5] library from the Python ecosystem.

---

4. https://github.com/thmsmlr/instructor_ex
5. https://github.com/jxnl/instructor

Structured prompting presents a potential bridge between Software 1.0 and Software 2.0. It's a way to reliably interact with large language models within the context of your application. Rather than attempting to parse the unstructured result of a large language model into something useful, you receive something useful directly from the large language model.

Compressing Knowledge

As a result of the large language model boom, there has been significant innovation in techniques for model compression at training and inference time. The two most prominent examples of this are *quantization* and *low-rank adaptation (LoRA)*.

Quantization is the process of converting a continuous range of values to a finite range of values. Quantization has been around for a *very* long time. It's fundamental to the fields of digital signal processing. In the context of machine learning, quantization refers to the quantization of machine learning model weights. Models are typically trained in 32-bit, 16-bit (half), or mixed (both) precision. *Post-training quantization* is the process of taking these 32-bit or 16-bit model weights and converting them to 8-bit or even 4-bit integers. Quantization significantly reduces the storage and memory requirements of large language models such that they can run efficiently on consumer hardware. Prior to large language models, quantization was still a common technique for reducing the storage and memory requirements of neural networks on embedded hardware.

Recent innovations have also made it possible to train quantized representations of models. Training large language models is a memory-hungry process. Quantization reduces the memory requirements of training such that you can fine-tune large models on specific tasks on consumer hardware.

Low-rank adaptation is a technique for reducing the memory requirements of fine-tuning pre-trained large language models. It works by reducing the number of parameters required to fine-tune a pre-trained large language model. Rather than updating a model's full weights, you initialize and train a small number of adapters on specific layers. This significantly reduces memory requirements and facilitates fine-tuning large language models on consumer hardware.

Moving Forward

As you move forward into the wonderful world of machine learning, you might find it's difficult to keep up with the intense pace of advancement. It seems that every week there's a new research paper or mind-blowing demo. It can be hard to determine what's worth exploring and what's worth ignoring. Fortunately, there are resources out there for keeping up.

If you're interested in keeping up with the state of the art in machine learning research, arxiv-sanity[6] is an excellent tool for filtering through trending papers in machine learning. As you get your start in machine learning, I recommend spending some time trying to dissect research papers. It can be a difficult task, but you'll learn a ton in the process.

In order to stay up-to-date with trending models and advancements in implementations, HuggingFace[7] does an excellent job documenting trending models and staying at the cutting edge of machine learning that works. If you don't want to dive into the academic details of a research paper, I recommend at least following along with the open-source work coming out of HuggingFace and available on the HuggingFace hub.

Finally, no matter what machine learning work you choose to do in the future, I hope you consider doing it in Elixir. As you've seen throughout this book, Elixir is an excellent language for building idiomatic, concurrent, and performant machine learning applications. And because you've read this book, you're well on your way to becoming an expert on machine learning in Elixir.

The Elixir machine learning ecosystem has made great strides in the past three years. The ecosystem now includes the following:

- Data Processing and Exploration (Explorer)
- Data Visualization (Vega, Tucan)
- Numerical Computation (Nx)
- Traditional Machine Learning (Scholar)
- Decision Trees (EXGBoost)
- Neural Networks (Axon)
- Pre-trained models and machine learning tasks (Bumblebee)
- Code Notebooks (Livebook)

Combined with the incredible foundation of libraries and capabilities Elixir offers out of the box, machine learning on the BEAM is incredibly promising. With the emergence of libraries such as FLAME and the continual growth of the machine learning ecosystem, Elixir will continue to grow in popularity as a choice for production machine learning applications.

---

6. https://arxiv-sanity-lite.com/
7. https://huggingface.co

While Python certainly has a first-mover advantage, and a large ecosystem of researchers and innovators to support it, the promise of Elixir is enticing for small teams looking to build and scale on proven technology. Additionally, the ability to interop and take advantage of pre-trained models from Python makes the decision to switch from Python to Elixir much easier.

The future of machine learning is bright—and so is your future in machine learning. Don't stop here.

Bibliography

[Bis06]   Christopher M. Bishop. *Pattern Recognition and Machine Learning*. Springer, New York, NY, 1, 2006.

[BKKA19]   Yuntao Bai, Saurav Kadavath, Sandipan Kundu, Amanda Askell, Jackson Kernion, Andy Jones, Anna Chen, Anna Goldie, Azalia Mirhoseini, Cameron McKinnon, Carol Chen, Catherine Olsson, Christopher Olah, Danny Hernandez, Dawn Drain, Deep Ganguli, Dustin Li, Eli Tran-Johnson, Ethan Perez, Jamie Kerr, Jared Mueller, Jeffrey Ladish, Joshua Landau, Kamal Ndousse, Kamil Lukosuite, Liane Lovitt, Michael Sellitto, Nelson Elhage, Nicholas Schiefer, Noemi Mercado, Nova DasSarma, Robert Lasenby, Robin Larson, Sam Ringer, Scott Johnston, Shauna Kravec, Sheer El Showk, Stanislav Fort, Tamera Lanham, Timothy Tellen-Lawton, Tom Conerly, Tom Henighan, Tristan Hume, Samuel R. Bowman, Zac Hatfield-Dobbs, Ben Mann, Dario Amodei, Nicholas Joseph, Sam McCandlish, Tom Brown, and Jared Kaplan. The Curious Case of Neural Text Degeneration. *International Conference on Learning Representations, 2020*. 2019.

[CMFg20]   Beidi Chen, Tharun Medini, James Farwell, sameh gabriel, Charlie Tai, and Anshumali Shrivastava. SLIDE : In Defense of Smart Algorithms over Hardware Acceleration for Large-Scale Deep Learning Systems. *Proceedings of Machine Learning and Systems 2*. 2020.

[DFO20]   Marc Peter Deisenroth, A. Aldo Faisal, and Cheng Soon Ong. *Mathematics For Machine Learning*. Cambridge University Press, Cambridge, United Kingdom, 1, 2020.

[GBC16]   Ian Goodfellow, Yoshua Bengio, and Aaron Courville. *Deep Learning*. MIT Press, Cambridge, MA, 1, 2016.

[Gon16]   Lovedeep Gondara. Medical image denoising using convolutional denoising autoencoders. *Fourth Workshop on Data Mining in Biomedical Informatics and Healthcare at ICDM*. 2016.

[Gos21]   Svilen Gospodinov. *Concurrent Data Processing in Elixir*. The Pragmatic Bookshelf, Dallas, TX, 2021.

[GW08]   Andreas Griewank and Andrea Walther. *Evalauting Derivatives: Principles and Techniques of Algorithmic Differentiation*. Society for Industrial and Applied Mathematics, University City, Philadelpha, PA, 2, 2008.

[HBDF19] Ari Holtzman, Jan Buys, Li Du, Maxwell Forbes, and Yejin Choi. The Curious Case of Neural Text Degeneration. *International Conference on Learning Representations, 2020.* 2019.

[Hoo21]   Sara Hooker. The Hardware Lottery. *Communications of the ACM.* 64[12]:58–65, 2021.

[Huy22]   Chip Huyen. *Designing Machine Learning Systems*. O'Reilly & Associates, Inc., Sebastopol, CA, 1, 2022.

[KSH12]   Alex Krizhevsky, Ilya Sutskever, and Geoffrey Hinton. ImageNet Classification with Deep Convolutional Neural Networks. *Conference on Neural Information Processing Systems.* 2012.

[Lef19]   Melanie Lefkowitz. Professor's perceptron paved the way for AI – 60 years too soon. *Cornell Chronicle.* 2019.

[LTHC17] Christian Ledig, Lucas Theis, Ferenc Huszar, Jose Caballero, Andrew Cunningham, Alejandro Acosta, Andrew Aitken, Alykhan Tejani, Johannes Totz, Zehan Wang, and Wenzhe Shi. Photo-Realistic Single Image Super-Resolution Using a Generative Adversarial Network. *IEEE Conference on Computer Vision and Pattern Recognition.* 2017.

[Mac16]   Dougal Maclaurin. Modeling, Inference, and Optimization with Composable Differentiable Procedures. *Harvard Library.* 2016.

[Met21]   Cade Metz. *Genius Makers: The Mavericks Who Brought AI to Google, Facebook, and the World*. Dutton, New York, NY, 1, 2021.

[Mit97]   Tom M. Mitchell. *Machine Learning*. McGraw-Hill, Emeryville, CA, 1, 1997.

[Mor21]   Sean Moriarity. *Genetic Algorithms in Elixir*. The Pragmatic Bookshelf, Dallas, TX, 1, 2021.

[Mur22]   Kevin P. Murphy. *Probabilistic Machine Learning*. MIT Press, Cambridge, MA, 1, 2022.

[PP08]   K.B. Petersen and M.S. Pedersen. The Matrix Cookbook. *Technical University of Denmark.* 2008.

[RDGF16] Joseph Redmon, Santosh Divvala, Ross Girschick, and Ali Farhadi. You Only Look Once: Unified, Real-Time Object Detection. *IEEE Conference on Computer Vision and Pattern Recognition.* 2016.

[RFB15]   Olaf Ronneberger, Philipp Fischer, and Thomas Brox. U-Net: Convolutional Networks for Biomedical Image Segmentation. *Medical Image Computing and Computer-Assisted Intervention.* 2015.

[SB92]   Richard S. Sutton and Andrew Barto. *Reinforcement Learning: An Introduction.* MIT Press, Cambridge, MA, 1, 1992.

[SFF19]   Edirlei Soares de Lima, Bruno Feijó, and Antonio L. Furtado. Procedural Generation of Quests for Games Using Genetic Algorithms and Automated Planning. *XVIII Brazilian Symposium on Computer Games and Digital Entertainment.* 2019.

[Sha48]   Claude Shannon. A mathematical theory of communication. *The Bell system technical journal.* 1948.

[SHKS14]   Nitish Srivastava, Geoffrey Hinton, Alex Krizhevsky, Ilya Sutskever, and Ruslan Salakhutdinov. A Simple Way to Prevent Neural Networks from Overfitting. *Journal of Machine Learning Research.* 2014.

[SSWS17]   Thomas Schlegl, Philipp Seeböck, Sebastian M. Waldstein, Ursula Schmidt-Erfurth, and Georg Langs. Unsupervised Anomaly Detection with Generative Adversarial Networks to Guide Marker Discovery. *Information Processing in Medical Imaging (IPMI).* 2017.

[Str16]   Gilbert Strang. *Introduction to Linear Algebra.* Wellesley Cambridge Press, 7 Southgate Rd, Wellesley, MA 02482, 5, 2016.

[VSPU17]   Ashish Vaswani, Noam Shazeer, Niki Parmar, Jakob Uszkoreit, Llion Jones, Aidan N. Gomez, Lukasz Kaiser, and Illia Polosukhin. Attention is All You Need. *Conference on Neural Information Processing Systems.* 2017.

[WR74]   J.H. Wilkinson and C. Reinsch. *Handbook for Automatic Computation: Linear Algebra.* Springer, New York, NY, 1, 1974.

Index

Thank you!

We hope you enjoyed this book and that you're already thinking about what you want to learn next. To help make that decision easier, we're offering you this gift.

Head on over to https://pragprog.com right now, and use the coupon code BUYANOTHER2024 to save 30% on your next ebook. Offer is void where prohibited or restricted. This offer does not apply to any edition of *The Pragmatic Programmer* ebook.

And if you'd like to share your own expertise with the world, why not propose a writing idea to us? After all, many of our best authors started off as our readers, just like you. With up to a 50% royalty, world-class editorial services, and a name you trust, there's nothing to lose. Visit https://pragprog.com/become-an-author/ today to learn more and to get started.

We thank you for your continued support, and we hope to hear from you again soon!

The Pragmatic Bookshelf

SAVE 30%!
Use coupon code
BUYANOTHER2024

Genetic Algorithms in Elixir

From finance to artificial intelligence, genetic algorithms are a powerful tool with a wide array of applications. But you don't need an exotic new language or framework to get started; you can learn about genetic algorithms in a language you're already familiar with. Join us for an in-depth look at the algorithms, techniques, and methods that go into writing a genetic algorithm. From introductory problems to real-world applications, you'll learn the underlying principles of problem solving using genetic algorithms.

Sean Moriarity
(242 pages) ISBN: 9781680507942. $39.95
https://pragprog.com/book/smgaelixir

Genetic Algorithms and Machine Learning for Programmers

Self-driving cars, natural language recognition, and online recommendation engines are all possible thanks to Machine Learning. Now you can create your own genetic algorithms, nature-inspired swarms, Monte Carlo simulations, cellular automata, and clusters. Learn how to test your ML code and dive into even more advanced topics. If you are a beginner-to-intermediate programmer keen to understand machine learning, this book is for you.

Frances Buontempo
(234 pages) ISBN: 9781680506204. $45.95
https://pragprog.com/book/fbmach

Programming Machine Learning

You've decided to tackle machine learning — because you're job hunting, embarking on a new project, or just think self-driving cars are cool. But where to start? It's easy to be intimidated, even as a software developer. The good news is that it doesn't have to be that hard. Conquer machine learning by writing code one line at a time, from simple learning programs all the way to a true deep learning system. Tackle the hard topics by breaking them down so they're easier to understand, and build your confidence by getting your hands dirty.

Paolo Perrotta
(340 pages) ISBN: 9781680506600. $47.95
https://pragprog.com/book/pplearn

Craft GraphQL APIs in Elixir with Absinthe

Your domain is rich and interconnected, and your API should be too. Upgrade your web API to GraphQL, leveraging its flexible queries to empower your users, and its declarative structure to simplify your code. Absinthe is the GraphQL toolkit for Elixir, a functional programming language designed to enable massive concurrency atop robust application architectures. Written by the creators of Absinthe, this book will help you take full advantage of these two groundbreaking technologies. Build your own flexible, high-performance APIs using step-by-step guidance and expert advice you won't find anywhere else.

Bruce Williams and Ben Wilson
(302 pages) ISBN: 9781680502558. $47.95
https://pragprog.com/book/wwgraphql

Functional Web Development with Elixir, OTP, and Phoenix

Elixir and Phoenix are generating tremendous excitement as an unbeatable platform for building modern web applications. For decades OTP has helped developers create incredibly robust, scalable applications with unparalleled uptime. Make the most of them as you build a stateful web app with Elixir, OTP, and Phoenix. Model domain entities without an ORM or a database. Manage server state and keep your code clean with OTP Behaviours. Layer on a Phoenix web interface without coupling it to the business logic. Open doors to powerful new techniques that will get you thinking about web development in fundamentally new ways.

Lance Halvorsen
(218 pages) ISBN: 9781680502435. $45.95
https://pragprog.com/book/lhelph

Metaprogramming Elixir

Write code that writes code with Elixir macros. Macros make metaprogramming possible and define the language itself. In this book, you'll learn how to use macros to extend the language with fast, maintainable code and share functionality in ways you never thought possible. You'll discover how to extend Elixir with your own first-class features, optimize performance, and create domain-specific languages.

Chris McCord
(128 pages) ISBN: 9781680500417. $17
https://pragprog.com/book/cmelixir

From Ruby to Elixir

Elixir will change the way you think about programming. Use your Ruby experience to quickly get up to speed so you can see what all of the buzz is about. Go from zero to production applications that are reliable, fast, and scalable. Learn Elixir syntax and pattern matching to conquer the basics. Then move onto Elixir's unique process model that offers a world-class way to go parallel without fear. Finally, use the most common libraries like Ecto, Phoenix, and Oban to build a real-world SMS application. Now's the time. Dive in and learn Elixir.

Stephen Bussey
(222 pages) ISBN: 9798888650318. $48.95
https://pragprog.com/book/sbelixir

Programming Elixir 1.6

This book is *the* introduction to Elixir for experienced programmers, completely updated for Elixir 1.6 and beyond. Explore functional programming without the academic overtones (tell me about monads just one more time). Create concurrent applications, but get them right without all the locking and consistency headaches. Meet Elixir, a modern, functional, concurrent language built on the rock-solid Erlang VM. Elixir's pragmatic syntax and built-in support for metaprogramming will make you productive and keep you interested for the long haul. Maybe the time is right for the Next Big Thing. Maybe it's Elixir.

Dave Thomas
(410 pages) ISBN: 9781680502992. $47.95
https://pragprog.com/book/elixir16

The Pragmatic Bookshelf

The Pragmatic Bookshelf features books written by professional developers for professional developers. The titles continue the well-known Pragmatic Programmer style and continue to garner awards and rave reviews. As development gets more and more difficult, the Pragmatic Programmers will be there with more titles and products to help you stay on top of your game.

Visit Us Online

This Book's Home Page
https://pragprog.com/book/smelixir
Source code from this book, errata, and other resources. Come give us feedback, too!

Keep Up-to-Date
https://pragprog.com
Join our announcement mailing list (low volume) or follow us on Twitter @pragprog for new titles, sales, coupons, hot tips, and more.

New and Noteworthy
https://pragprog.com/news
Check out the latest Pragmatic developments, new titles, and other offerings.

Save on the ebook

Save on the ebook versions of this title. Owning the paper version of this book entitles you to purchase the electronic versions at a terrific discount.

PDFs are great for carrying around on your laptop—they are hyperlinked, have color, and are fully searchable. Most titles are also available for the iPhone and iPod touch, Amazon Kindle, and other popular e-book readers.

Send a copy of your receipt to support@pragprog.com and we'll provide you with a discount coupon.

Contact Us

Online Orders:	*https://pragprog.com/catalog*
Customer Service:	*support@pragprog.com*
International Rights:	*translations@pragprog.com*
Academic Use:	*academic@pragprog.com*
Write for Us:	*http://write-for-us.pragprog.com*